IMAGES
of America

QUINCY VALLEY

I0806468

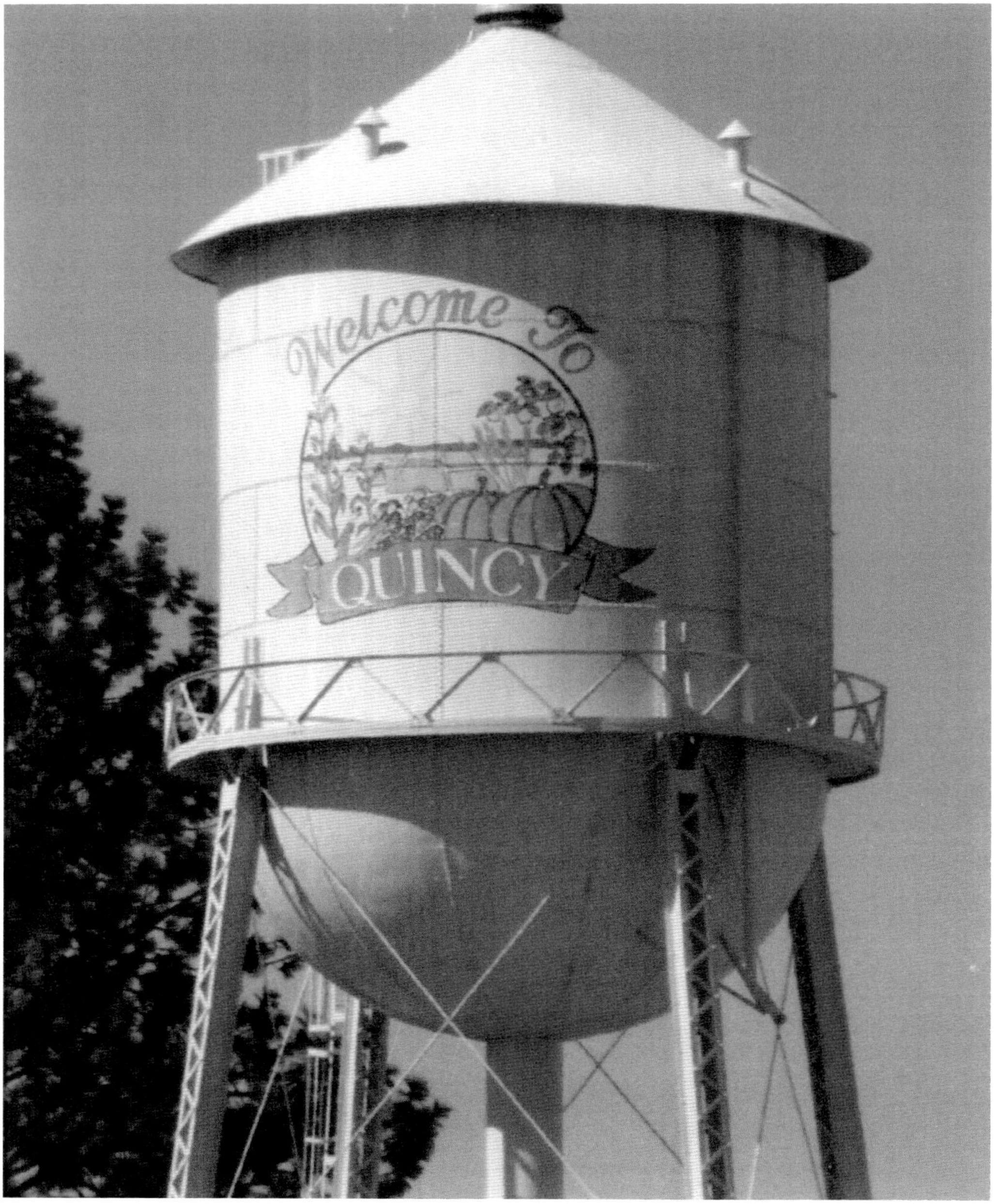

QUINCY WATER TOWER. The Quincy water tower is a landmark for all travelers to Quincy. Not only does it provide an essential service for Quincy residents, it is symbolic of a thriving community. Water is literally the basis of all life; without it, the town would die and the dominance of the sagebrush would return. (Courtesy of the Quincy Valley Historical Society.)

ON THE COVER: PIONEER FAMILY. Many early settlers lived in tents until they could build a more permanent shelter. By 1911, the D. J. and Clara Webb family were comfortably situated in a well-built home with a beautiful horse and a fine buggy. (Otto Henderson photograph; courtesy of the Quincy Valley Historical Society.)

IMAGES
of America

QUINCY VALLEY

Karen Murray

ARCADIA
PUBLISHING

ISBN 978-0-7385-8161-3

Published by Arcadia Publishing
Charleston, South Carolina

Printed in the United States of America

Library of Congress Control Number: 2010928648

For all general information, please contact Arcadia Publishing:
Telephone 843-853-2070
Fax 843-853-0044
E-mail sales@arcadiapublishing.com
For customer service and orders:
Toll-Free 1-888-313-2665

Visit us on the Internet at www.arcadiapublishing.com

To all the families of the Quincy Valley, whose faith in God, family, farm, and hard work made a barren desert blossom as a rose

Contents

Acknowledgments

In 1996, the Reiman-Simmons House was willed to the City of Quincy by Lauren R. Simmons with the provision that it be used for a museum. Four years later, the Quincy Valley Historical Society was born. It has been a labor of love by the dedicated members of the community who have spent countless hours restoring the house and grounds, creating an archives and genealogical research room, and relocating the oldest church in Quincy to the property. It has become a center of community activity by providing agricultural and geological tours of the Quincy Valley and promoting and hosting annual gatherings such as Time Travelers, Harvest Fest, WineFest, Old-Fashioned Christmas, and various themed teas. Weddings, receptions, club meetings, reunions, and other private events are held in the house and on the grounds. The State of Washington recognized their efforts in 2008, when the Quincy Valley Historical Society was awarded the Stewardship Award by the State Department of Historical Preservation during a special ceremony in Olympia. It is also listed on the State Historic Register and the National Register of Historic Places.

This book would not have been possible without the ceaseless and tireless drive of board members Annie Rapp, Gar Pilliar, Harriet Weber, Dave Weber, Marge Koeppe, and archivist Vianna Jensen in their efforts to preserve the history and community of the Quincy Valley.

I would like to thank my editors at Arcadia Publishing—Sarah Higginbotham, Devon Weston, and Donna Libert—first for approaching the Quincy Valley Historical Society with the idea, then patiently providing guidance and support throughout the process. Thanks also to Mina Kyle, Wayne Smith, Lydia Westover, Dorothy Schroeder, the *Quincy Valley Post-Register*, Shirley Bergerud, Scott Lybbert, and all of the many friends and acquaintances who took the time to share their memories with me.

INTRODUCTION

Ten miles north of Interstate 90 in the middle of Washington lies a small community that is mostly unnoticed by the world at large. Yet over 27 different ethnic groups have made their home here throughout the first 100 years of its existence, and its native sons and daughters have extended its influence throughout the nation and the world.

The story of the Quincy Valley is the story of families working together and with their community to make a sagebrush desert blossom as a rose. A rose indeed, since apples are of the genus *Malus*, in the same biological family (*Rosaceae*) as roses and can be grafted to grow and bloom on apple rootstock. Imagine what the valley might look like if all of its apple trees also sprouted roses.

In the beginning, not even the indigenous tribes could survive the waterless expanse of sagebrush desert that covered the Quincy Valley. Jackrabbits and coyotes were the only creatures to thrive, even when the population was diminished by early farmers. Their reputation for tenacity remains today, as evidenced by the Quincy High School Jacks. The valley is a product of the cataclysmic Glacial Lake Missoula floods that swept across eastern Washington several times thousands of years ago, leaving behind rich fertile soils as deep as 50 feet in some places, and the more recent 1980 eruption of Mount St. Helens, when several inches of volcanic ash stranded residents and travelers for several days.

During the 1880s, only cattlemen and sheepherders roamed with their herds and flocks through the area, the animals feasting on abundant cheatgrass while the men sated their hunger with the ever-present jackrabbits. By 1892, the Great Northern Railroad had founded the whistle stop of Quincy, named by the daughter of Great Northern owner, Jim F. Hill, or by a brakeman from Quincy, Illinois. Not even a search of the James F. Hill Reference Library reveals a clue to this puzzle. A hundred years later, the sound of passing trains as they rumble through the night on their never-ceasing task of bringing goods to and from the ports in Seattle still disturbs sleeping Quincyites. Products from Quincy's own industrial and food production plants are among these items being distributed in a global economy.

The first great migration began in 1904, when Samuel F. Reiman built a home, later to become the Reiman-Simmons House Museum. By 1910, nearly 20 nations from South Africa to Wales were represented among the residents of the Quincy Valley, including Austrians, Belgians, Bohemians, French and English Canadians, Danes, English, Germans, Irish, Japanese, Macedonians, Norwegians, Russians, Scots, Swedes, Swiss, and Turks. Americans from 37 states and territories could also be found living here, according to the 1920 U.S Census. One can add Kryzghistanis, Cambodians, Ukranians, Peruvians, Guatemalans, Mexicans, East Indians, Chileans, Pacific Islanders, and many others to the list of people living peaceably in Quincy—a microcosm of the world in small town America.

What has brought the world to Quincy? Three values hold the most prominent places in the hearts of the people of Quincy: faith, family, and farming. Everything about Quincy grows out of these concepts. Early families, many of whom were descendants of the Volga Germans, formed a core around which a town and a community were built. The first church was a nondenominational community church with services in German where all were welcome. This church, now known as the Old Pioneer Church, was moved from its original location to a site adjacent to the Reiman-Simmons House—a fitting place since one of its early pastors, Rev. Simon Reiman, was brother to Samuel Reiman, builder of the house. In this one place, a visitor can see the merging of the three foundations upon which the Quincy Valley was built and continues to thrive.

The one thing the Quincy Valley lacked was water. Rich, fertile soils are unproductive without water. The early settlers hauled water from Willow Springs or from the Columbia River. Dryland wheat was the major cash crop. A major drought in the 1920s forced many families to move to wetter pastures. That all changed in the 1950s with the completion of Grand Coulee Dam and the formation of the Columbia Basin Irrigation Project. Lands once empty and barren could now be abundant and prosperous. And so the second great migration to the Quincy Valley began.

The second great migration to the Quincy Valley was very different than the first. In the 1900s, land was homesteaded or bought and sold in a free market fashion. After the irrigation project began in the 1950s, land was allotted to military veterans by means of a lottery run by the U.S. government. Many of the farmers came from Idaho and Utah, bringing a new religion into the mix, the Latter-day Saints. They joined the Lutherans, Presbyterians, Baptists, Free Methodists, Friends, Seventh-day Adventists, Nazarenes, Catholics, Jehovah's Witnesses, Foursquare Church, Christian Reformed, and others. Many of these churches now conduct their services in both English and Spanish. Not only is the Quincy Valley ethnically diverse, it is also religiously diverse.

The future of Quincy remains to be written. It has a history of successfully withstanding economic financial adversity, weather extremes, and current events. Each struggle has made the community stronger and better able to present a united front against the next challenge to come. With the planting of data server farms by Internet companies, such as Microsoft and Yahoo, it adds yet another piece to its economic portfolio as a hedge against hard times.

A diversity of faith, a diversity of families, and a diversity of farms, from dryland crops to orchards to data server centers, these span the history of American times, all growing together, each in its own time, like a fine wine. The pages of this book will serve as a brief glimpse into the richness and variety that is the Quincy Valley.

One

Jackrabbits and Sagebrush

Two things were certain when early settlers arrived in the Quincy Valley: one, there was a lot of sagebrush, and, two, there were even more jackrabbits. Both had their benefits. Sagebrush provided a fuel source, and though it was not considered clean-burning, it was good for cooking when nothing else was handy. Jackrabbit could taste pretty good roasted on a spit.

Wild horses, cattle, and sheep found good grazing on the bunchgrass growing underneath the sagebrush. Wild horses had been rounded up by local tribes for years. Enterprising cowboys rounded them up from time to time to make a living. The last great roundup was in the spring of 1906, when thousands were herded into train cars and shipped back east by rail.

Cattlemen and sheepherders begin arriving in the 1880s, many working for Lord Thomas S. Blythe, an Englishman with the dream of being a cattle baron. They often objected to settlers in the area and would pull down their cabins by lassoing the boards.

The men with the largest sheep herd in the area were Willard H. Babcock and E. T. Benson, owners of the B and B Ranch in the Trinidad area. In 1904, their men brought 16,000 head of sheep into their Crescent Bar headquarters for shearing. Descendants of many of these sheepherders, such as the Escure family, still reside in the Quincy Valley.

As more settlers began to arrive, putting up fences and planting gardens, conflicts began to arise. The cattlemen objected to sheep and fences, often pulling down fences and cabins. Two sheepherders and two cowboys were shot dead following a dispute over the sale of a haystack in the midst of a harsh winter. The settlers objected to the jackrabbits eating their gardens and crops. Jackrabbits were rounded up and killed by the thousands over the years. In the end, there is still sagebrush, and the jackrabbit has survived as the high school mascot.

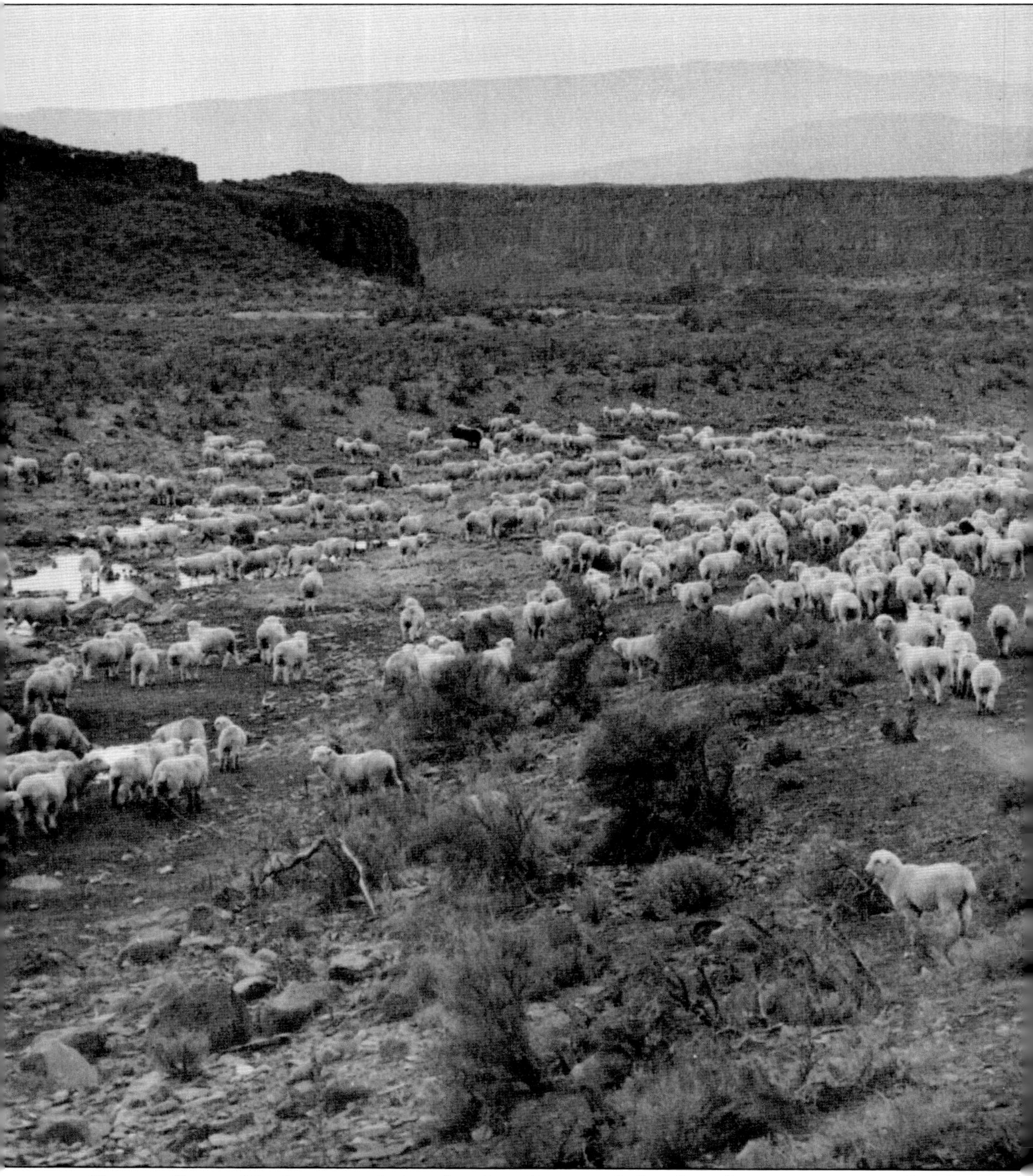

Escure Sheep. Cattlemen and sheepherders discovered that bunchgrass growing under the sagebrush made great winter pasture for livestock. One harsh winter left two cowboys and two sheepherders wounded in a shoot-out over a disputed haystack. Cattle arrived first when Lord Thomas S. Blythe, dreaming of being a cattle baron, bought out another cattleman and moved the stock to what is now western Grant County. Willard H. Babcock set up a sheep operation on

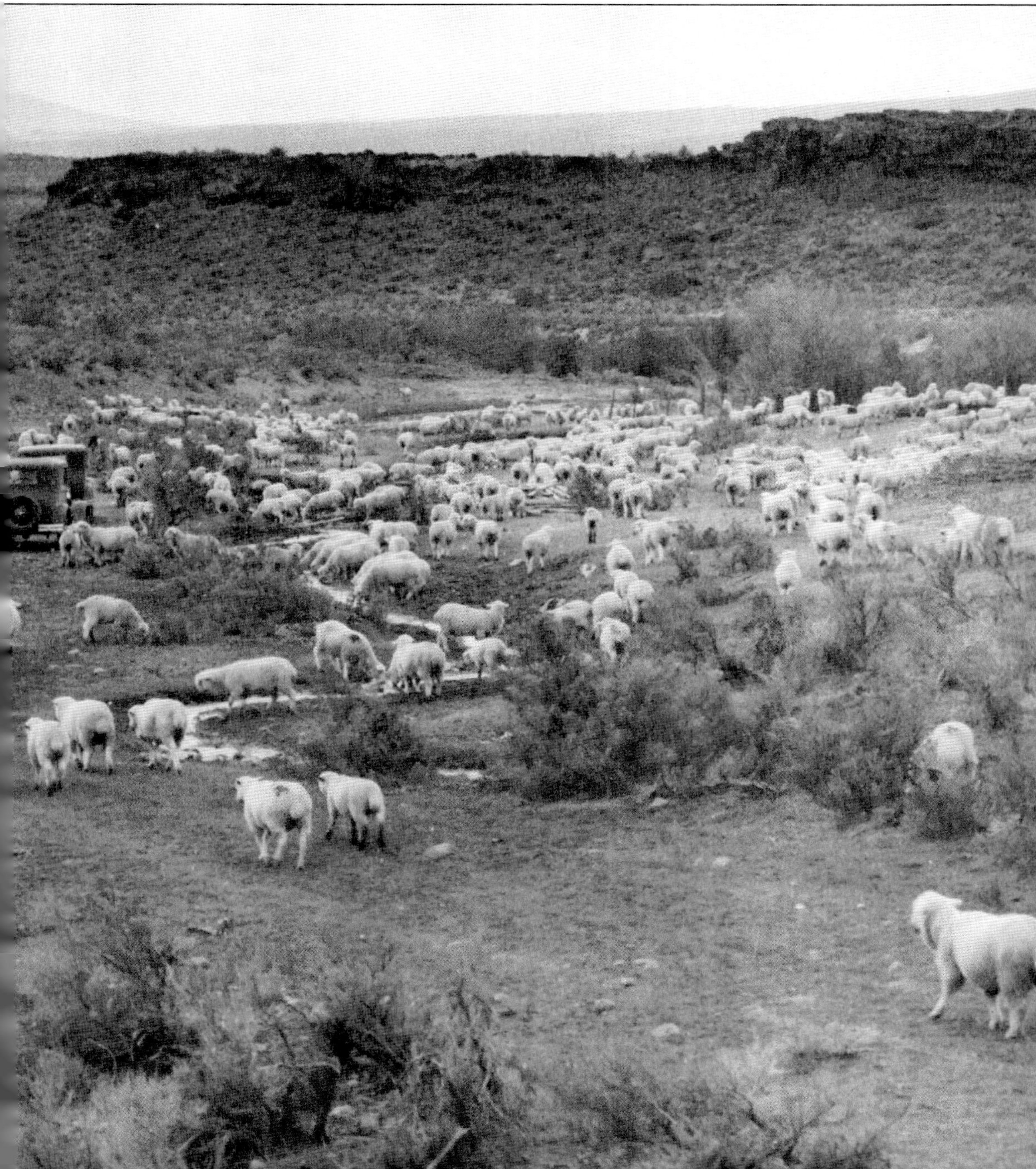

what became known as Babcock Ridge shortly before 1900. Walter Blanchett, whose son would later purchase the Reiman House, worked Babcock's sheep for $1 per day. In 1906, some 100,000 pounds of wool were shipped from the Quincy Valley. These sheep belong to Ramon and Martina Escure, immigrants from Spain who settled in the Burke (now George) area. (Courtesy of the Quincy Valley Historical Society.)

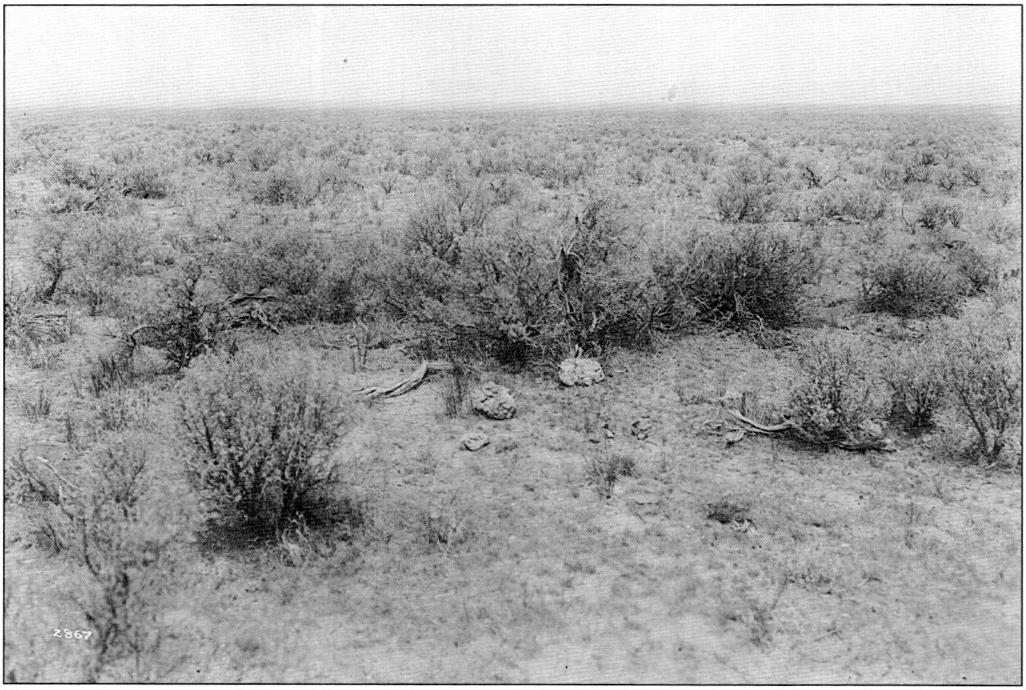

Endless Sagebrush. Quincy Flats, as the area was known in its early days, was a barren sagebrush desert inhabited mainly by jackrabbits, coyotes, rattlesnakes, and an occasional bobcat or cougar. With very little surface water, even the local Native American tribes had no reason to stay. Cowboys and sheepherders roasted their jackrabbit dinners over sagebrush fires, keeping their .22 rifles handy to fend off the coyotes. The empty expanse can be seen in the photograph above. The coming of the railroad broke the solitude and brought settlers who saw potential hiding in the rich soil. All they needed was water. Below, a group of early settlers take time out for a Sunday afternoon picnic amid Quincy dust and sagebrush. (Both images courtesy of the Quincy Valley Historical Society.)

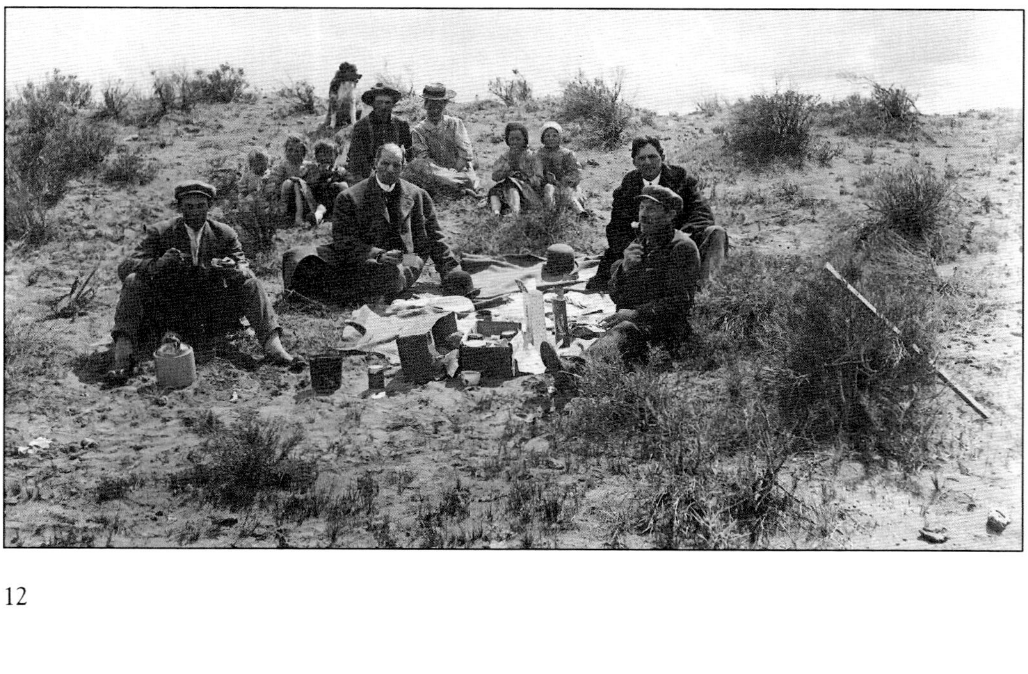

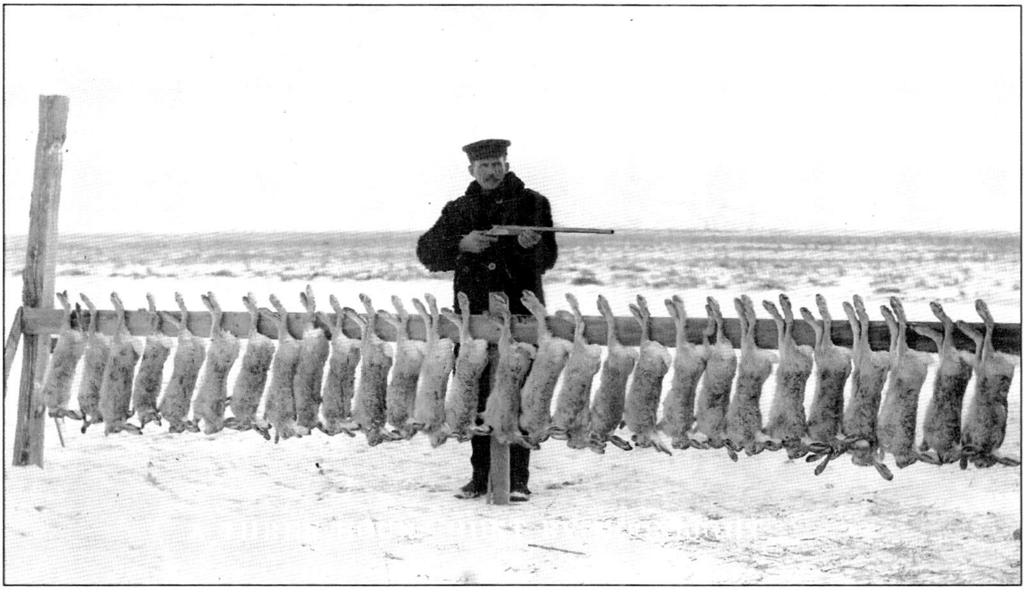

Moonlight Jackrabbit Hunt, 1911. Henry Reiman shows off his catch of the night. Jackrabbits were abundant and devoured young crops. Homesteaders rounded them up into specially constructed corrals and shot them. The meat was shipped to Seattle and then sold as a source of chrome for the tanneries or donated as food to an orphanage. (Courtesy of the Quincy Valley Historical Society.)

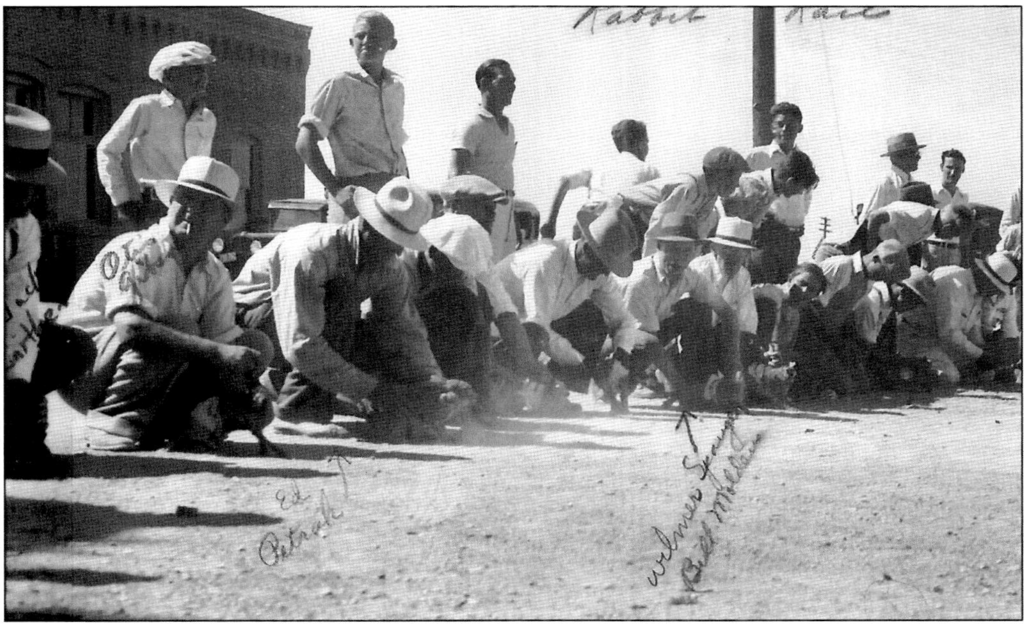

Jackrabbit Races. Since NASCAR did not exist in early Quincy, local men invented the jackrabbit race to satisfy their need for speed. Jack Gaither, Otis Gibson, Ed Petrak, Wilmer Spangle, and Bill Molden can be seen here, getting their own champion jacks ready to run. Racing jackrabbits was a way of showing respect for their agility and tenacity. (Courtesy of the Quincy Valley Historical Society.)

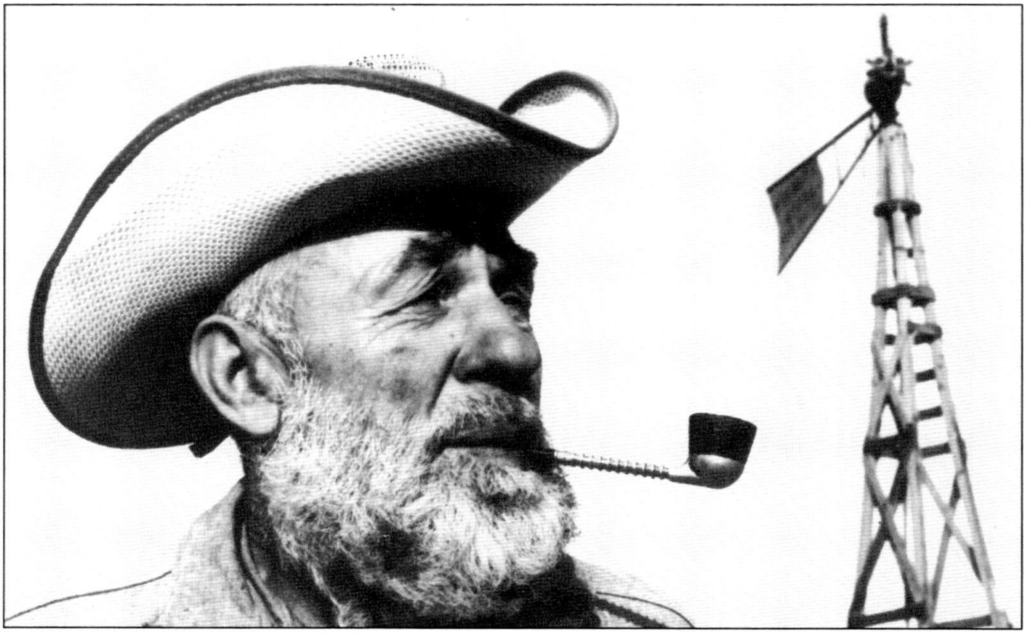

Quincy Valley Man. Though this early settler remains unidentified, he represents the men of his day: grizzled and weatherworn with hard work, he is determined and pleased with his efforts. The windmill in the background completes the symbolism of what can be accomplished with a determined man and a steady water supply. (Courtesy of the Quincy Valley Historical Society.)

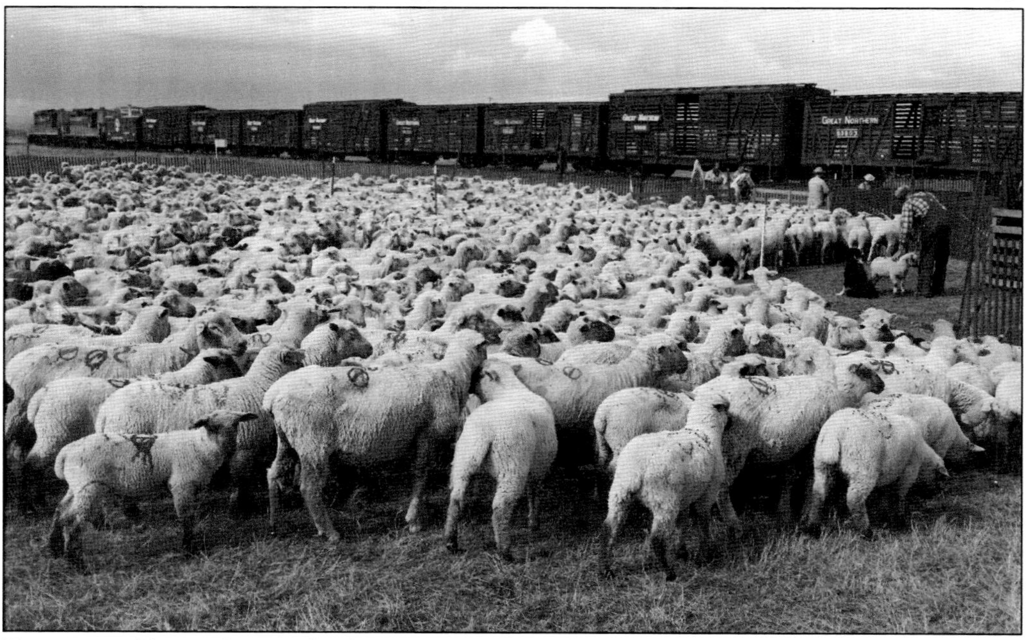

Taking the Train. As more land was put into crops, there was less land available for driving herds to summer pastures in the Okanogan region. Eventually sheepherders began driving their herds to the nearest railhead and taking the train to summer pasture. In the fall, they would return to winter grazing in the Quincy Valley area. (Courtesy of the *Quincy Valley Post-Register.*)

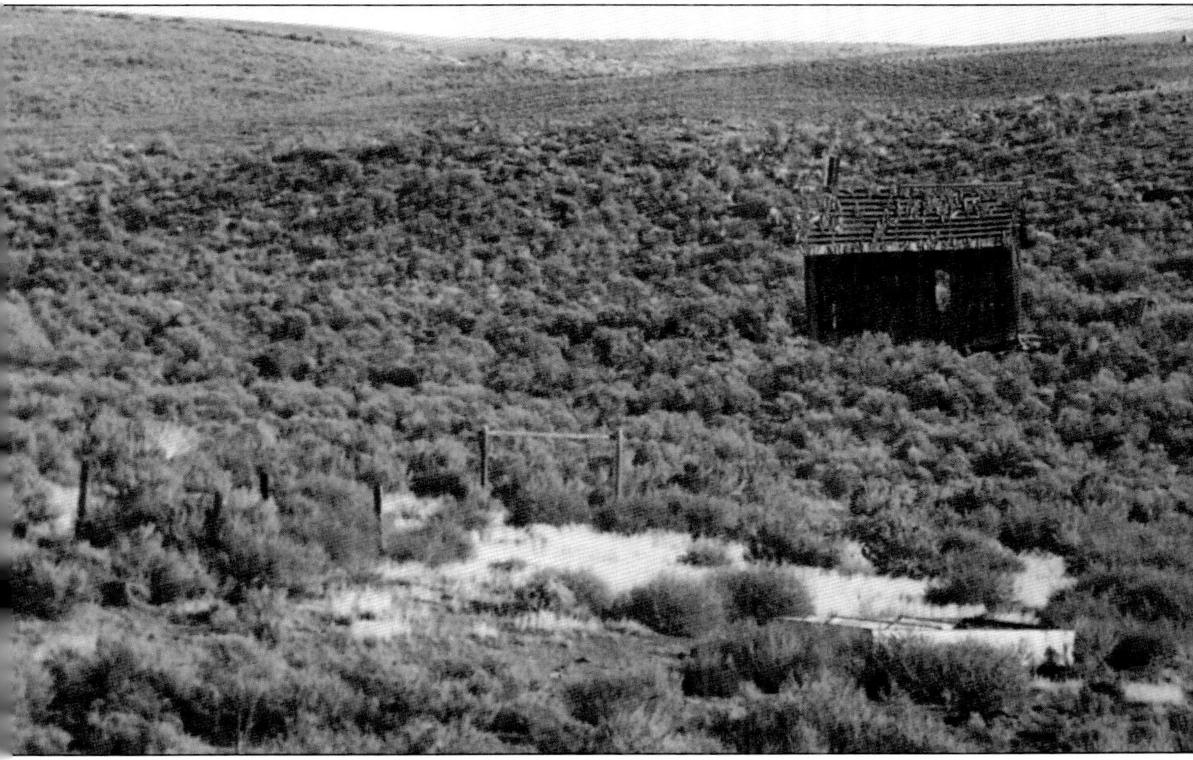

Old Pioneer Cabin. The earliest settlers in 1901 often started their homestead living in a tent or their wagon. As soon as a garden was planted and some ground cleared, a simple cabin was constructed. The daily diet might consist of oatmeal, hot cakes, and beans, supplemented by the family garden and jackrabbits. Water had to be hauled from Willow Springs, usually by an entrepreneur with a wagon and a team for $1 a barrel, until a well could be dug and a windmill erected to raise the water. Families often gathered together to build a cabin or outbuilding for a neighbor. Eventually bigger and better houses were built as finances allowed. Here are the remains of a cabin that once sheltered a family struggling to build a life in this barren land. (Courtesy of the Quincy Valley Historical Society.)

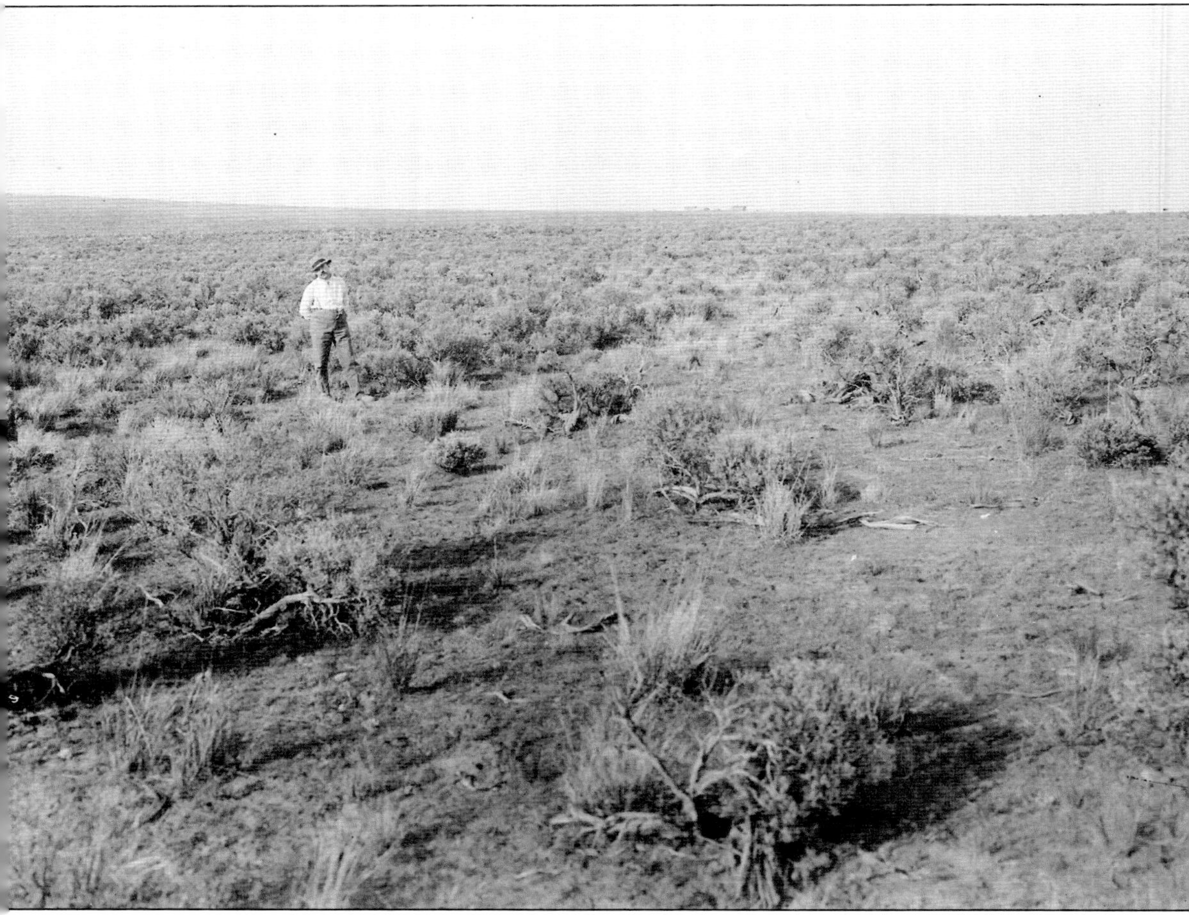

Quincy Rises to the East. Like the morning sun, Quincy rises from the sagebrush plain in the distance. During the droughts of the 1920s, many people left the Quincy Valley. Wells began to go dry, and abandoned wheat fields gave way to mustard and tumbleweeds. The annual winds still experienced in the Quincy Valley kicked up dust storms and drifting sands that covered crops and blew into homes. People wore damp cloths over their faces in order to breathe. Charles Hatfield, a Kansas-born sewing machine salesman who was known as "the Rainmaker," was hired to produce rain, but none appeared. The hardy souls who remained held fast, eventually reaping the benefits of both natural rainfall and the steady water supply brought by the Columbia Basin Irrigation Project, formed by the vote of the affected landowners in 1939. This gentleman in this image remains unidentified. (Courtesy of the Quincy Valley Historical Society.)

Two

WAGONS AND TRAINS

Walking was the first form of travelling through the area. Wild horses came next as the indigenous tribes and later the white man made use of them. William (Wild Goose Bill) Condon supplied miners and surveyors in the region with pack mule trains.

Immigrant wagon trains brought settlers in huge caravans originating in Ritzville or Spokane. The Gibson family, accompanied by Josh Cox, arrived by sleigh in midwinter. Some people coming from the West crossed the Columbia River in ferries.

The train arrived in 1892, but Quincy was just a name. For a few years the nearest stop and mail drop was at Winchester, about 7 miles east of Quincy.

The automobile arrived about 1912. Fred George owned the first Quincy dealership, where he sold Fords for $345. The first gas station was owned by William Conlan, on the same corner where the Short Stop is today.

Airplanes eventually landed in Quincy, with the occasional barnstormer flying through. An accident involving one of these killed two young boys in 1931.

Today nearly every form of transportation known to man—paragliders, hot air balloons, helicopters, military aircraft, semitrailers, tractors, harvesters, motorcycles—can be found in the Quincy Valley.

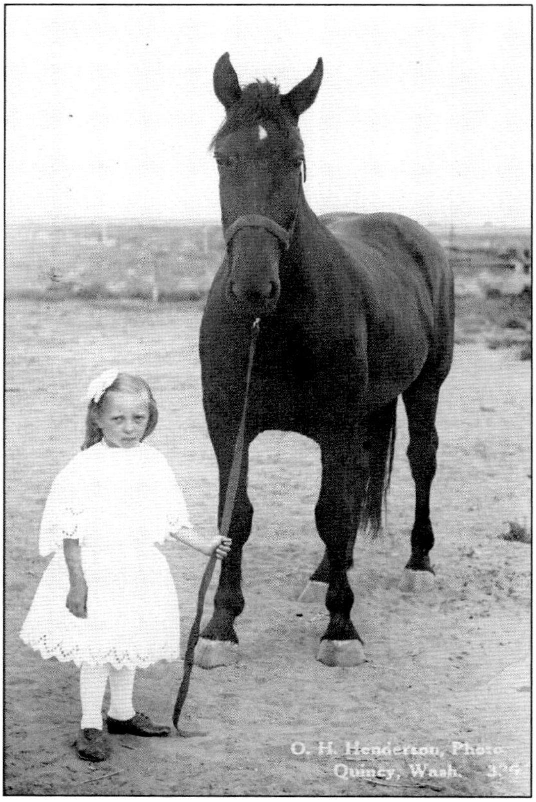

Beautiful Horses. Horses have played an important role in the history of the Quincy Valley. Wild horses roamed the open desert with Lord Thomas S. Blythe's white-faced, long-horned cattle. Native American tribes had long made sport of catching and taming them, the measure of a man's wealth being the number of horses he owned. Over 5,000 wild horses were corralled in what is known as "The Last Great Roundup" and shipped to St. Paul, Minnesota, by train from the nearby town of Ephrata. Even buyers for the Japanese army travelled to the area looking for suitable horses. The young girl at left may be holding one of the black Percherons brought in from Illinois about 1916. Below, a farmer displays a beautiful pair of workhorses. (Otto Henderson photographs; both images courtesy of the Quincy Valley Historical Society.)

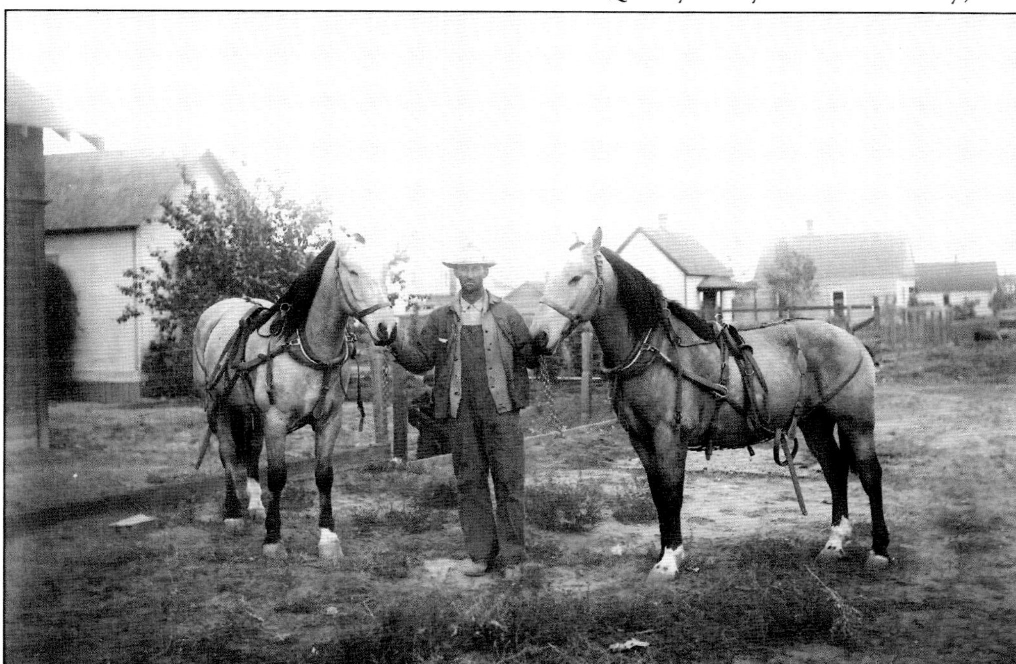

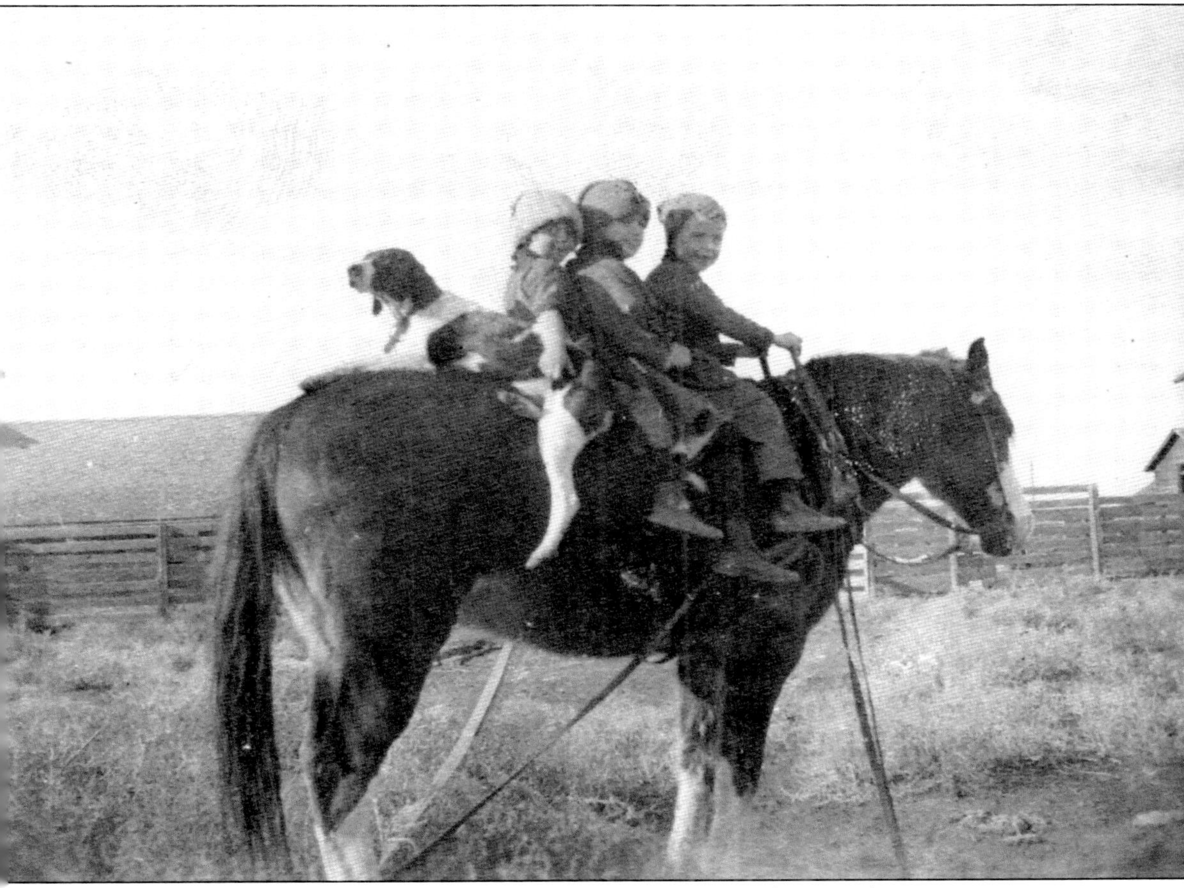

On Top of Old Baldy. Old Baldy, the horse in this picture, patiently carries her young passengers on a ride around the farm. Farm children learned to be comfortable around large animals at an early age, including riding bareback. Horsepower was used to accomplish almost all the tasks of daily life: pulling a buggy to town for church or school, pulling a plow or thresher, hauling a wagon full of wheat to the railroad, bringing supplies from town, herding livestock, and providing rides for entertainment. Many early settlers arrived in caravans of wagons pulled by teams of horses. Chris C. Ledbetter and his son, Hurbert, opened the Quincy Livery Stable in Quincy during 1902. In 1907, fifteen Quincy farmers and businessmen invested $3,750 in a handsome strawberry roan Belgian stallion. Other breeding stock included an Arcadian stallion and three Percheron stallions, including one named Hardi owned by the Schempp brothers. (Courtesy of the Quincy Valley Historical Society.)

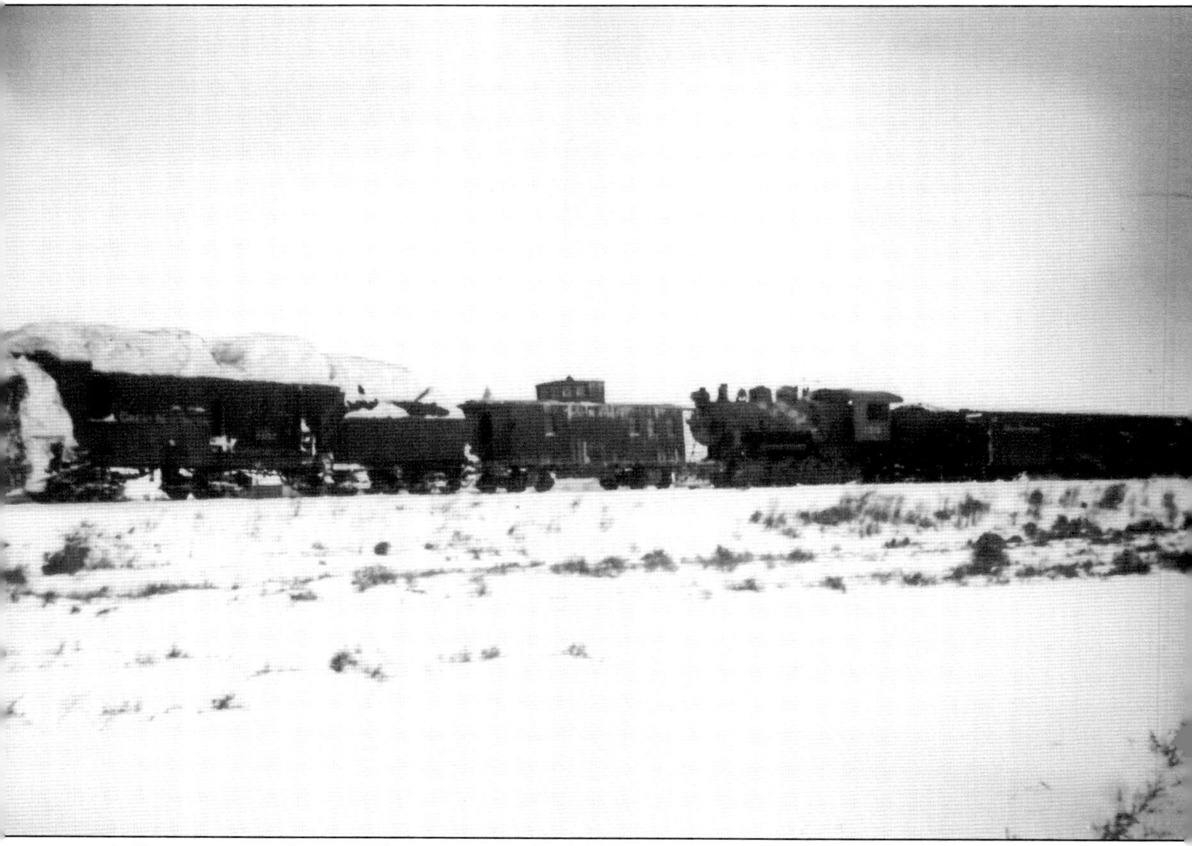

A Spoonful of Snow. The train was the lifeblood of the Quincy Valley, transporting people, supplies, crops to market, livestock to pasture, mail, and the occasional town pet. The station cat certainly used up a few of her nine lives in surviving an unexpected trip in a baggage car, being funneled into a wheat sack at the grain elevator, and losing her tail when it became frozen to the track. Her official job was to walk through the stamp pad and leave her paw prints on telegrams. Mike the dog, self-appointed guardian of the bank, was accidently steam-heated when standing too near the train. He sought revenge by attacking the cowcatcher each time the train passed, eventually resulting in his death by train wheel. *Dinky*, the train serving the area, had a reputation for slow service and misplaced passengers. The editor of the *Quincy Quill* said, "A spoonful of snow in the mountains and no mail either way today." *Dinky* seems to have acquired several spoonfuls in this picture. (Courtesy of the Quincy Valley Historical Society.)

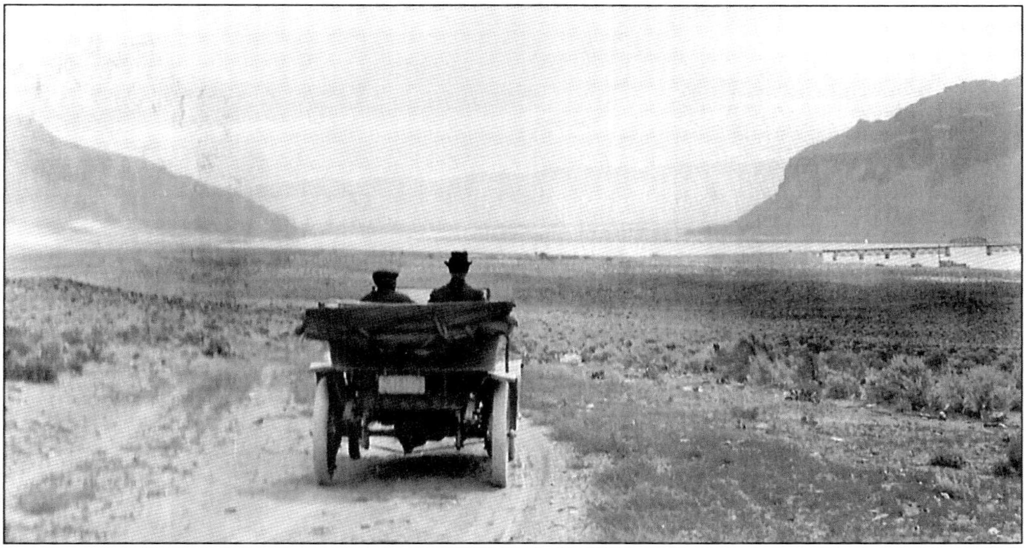

Trip to Mattawa. Traveling south towards Mattawa, these two gentlemen have a great view of the Beverly and Milwaukee Railroad Bridge, which crosses the Columbia River at Beverly, Washington. The automobile appeared in the Quincy Valley as early as 1912. The first dealership was owned by Fred George. (Otto Henderson photograph; courtesy of the Quincy Valley Historical Society.)

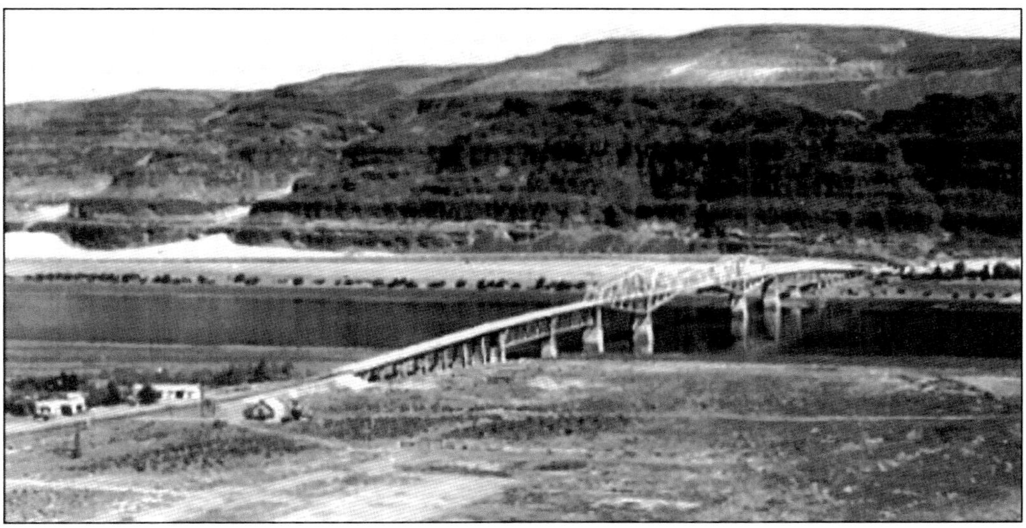

Vantage Bridge. Before construction of the Wanapum Dam, just south of the Vantage Bridge, the Columbia River was much narrower and shallower. This continues to be the main route to Seattle for travelers from eastern Washington. Today a busy four-lane Interstate 90 crosses the river at this same spot. Water covers most of the low-lying land shown in this picture. (Courtesy of Fran Miller.)

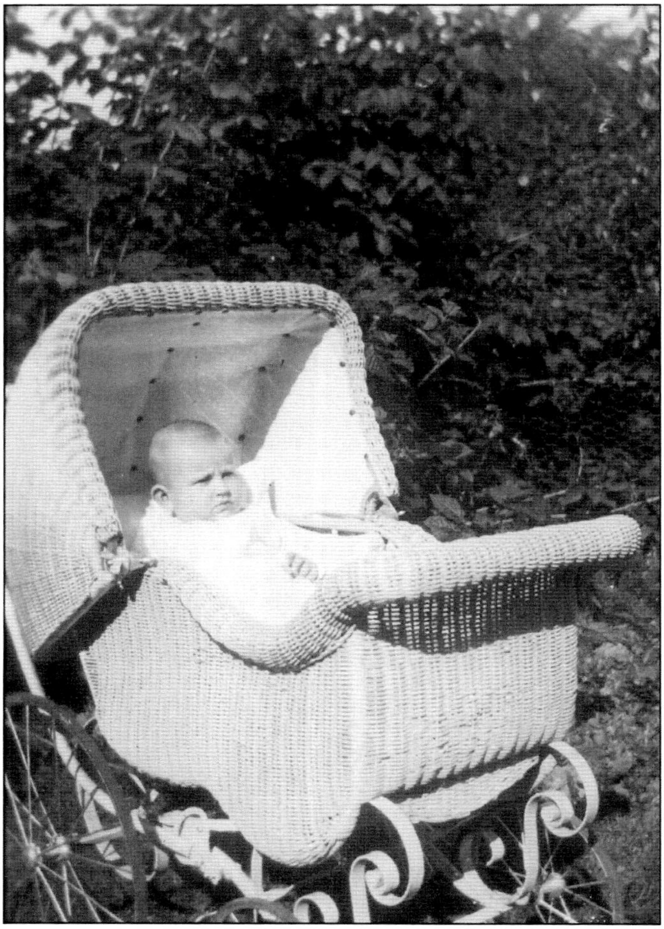

Going for a Buggy Ride. Babies in the Quincy Valley needed transportation too. This might not be a fancy yellow surrey with fringe on the top, but a stylish baby carriage was just the thing to show off a family's pride and joy during a stroll around town. (Courtesy of the Quincy Valley Historical Society.)

Bicycle Built For Two. Courting on a bicycle built for two was considered so romantic it was used as a marriage proposal in the song "Daisy Bell" written in 1892 by Henry Dacre. Here a Quincy couple sets off on an afternoon jaunt. (Courtesy of the Quincy Valley Historical Society.)

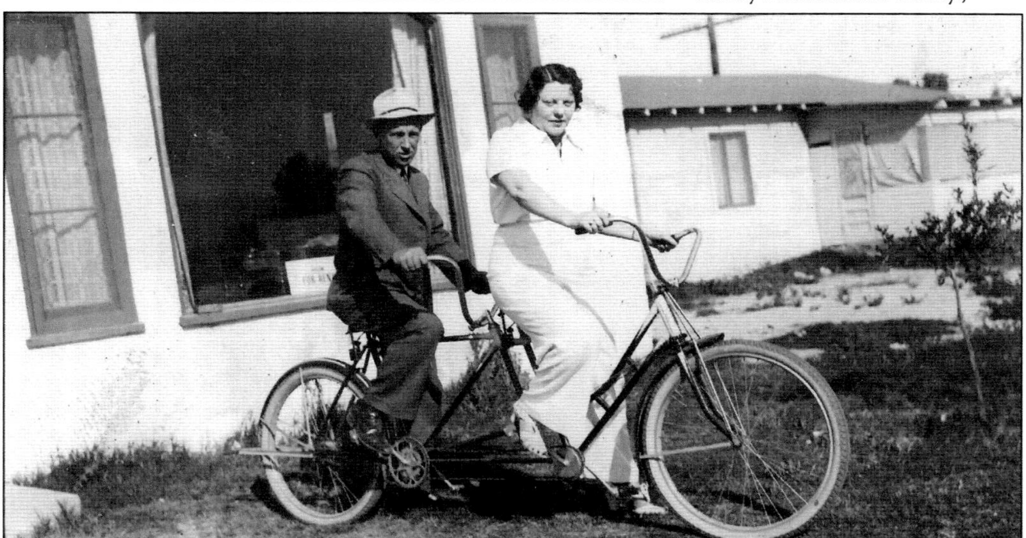

Three

Faith, Family, and Farm

Three things intertwine the lives of the people of the Quincy Valley—faith, family, and farm. Both early settlers and their descendants have a resolute belief in God, a steadfast sense of family values, and a strong work ethic.

Faith sustained them in good times and bad. Faith supported the family by providing the rites of Christendom: weddings, christenings, baptisms and confirmations, funerals, and weekly communion. Faith in God's will and plan saw them through fires, floods, droughts, windstorms, accidents, and the challenges of daily life on a homestead farm in a sagebrush desert.

Families provided each other with loving companionship, helping hands to get the work done, and a social security system that took care of the young and the old, without government assistance.

The cemetery speaks to this generational consideration, with beautiful well-kept headstones and monuments, some in German, some in Spanish, most in English. The first grave was that of Hubert Ledbetter. Hubert and his father, Chris C. Ledbetter, went out rabbit hunting one fall day in 1902. Hubert wanted to try out his new gun. It fell and discharged, accidentally killing the boy. For a time it was private land. In 1949, Arnold Westover and his daughter-in-law Lydia went door to door collecting funds to purchase the cemetery for the city. They were able to purchase the land for $2,000, creating the Quincy Cemetery Association. It is still a center of the community on holidays such as Memorial Day and the Fourth of July, when flags are raised from sunrise to sunset to honor the veterans buried there. Each veteran has his own named flag provided by the American Legion.

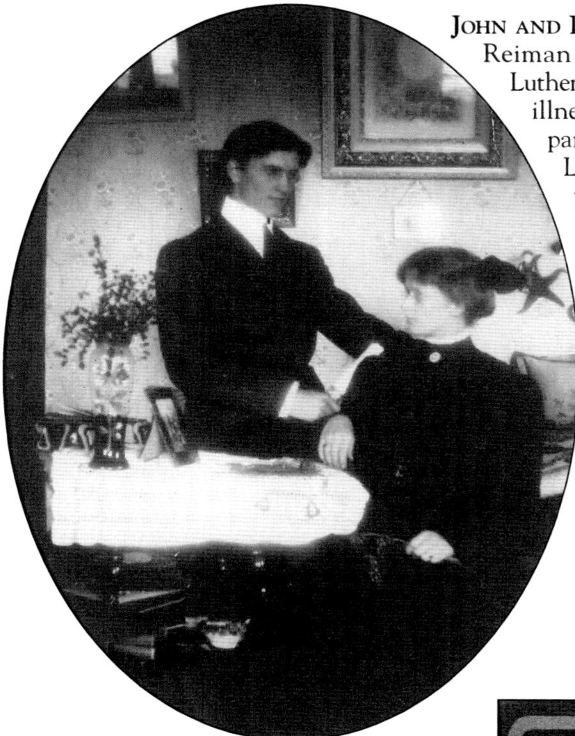

JOHN AND LINA HELEN REIMAN. Rev. John (Johann) Reiman became pastor of the St. Paul German Lutheran Church in 1910, serving full-time until an illness overtook him a year later. He continued part-time until he died in 1916, leaving wife Lina to raise five small children. He was 34 years old. (Courtesy of the Quincy Valley Historical Society.)

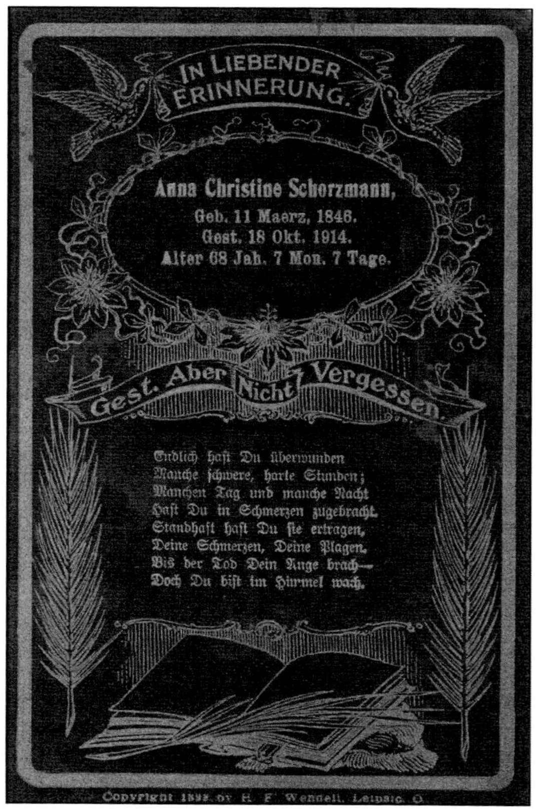

ANNA CHRISTINE SCHORZMAN. Funeral cards and other religious documents were often in German, the native language of many early settlers. This card gives the length of Anna Schorzman's life as 68 years, 7 months, and 7 days. The main banner translates to "Gone, but not forgotten." (Courtesy of the Quincy Valley Historical Society.)

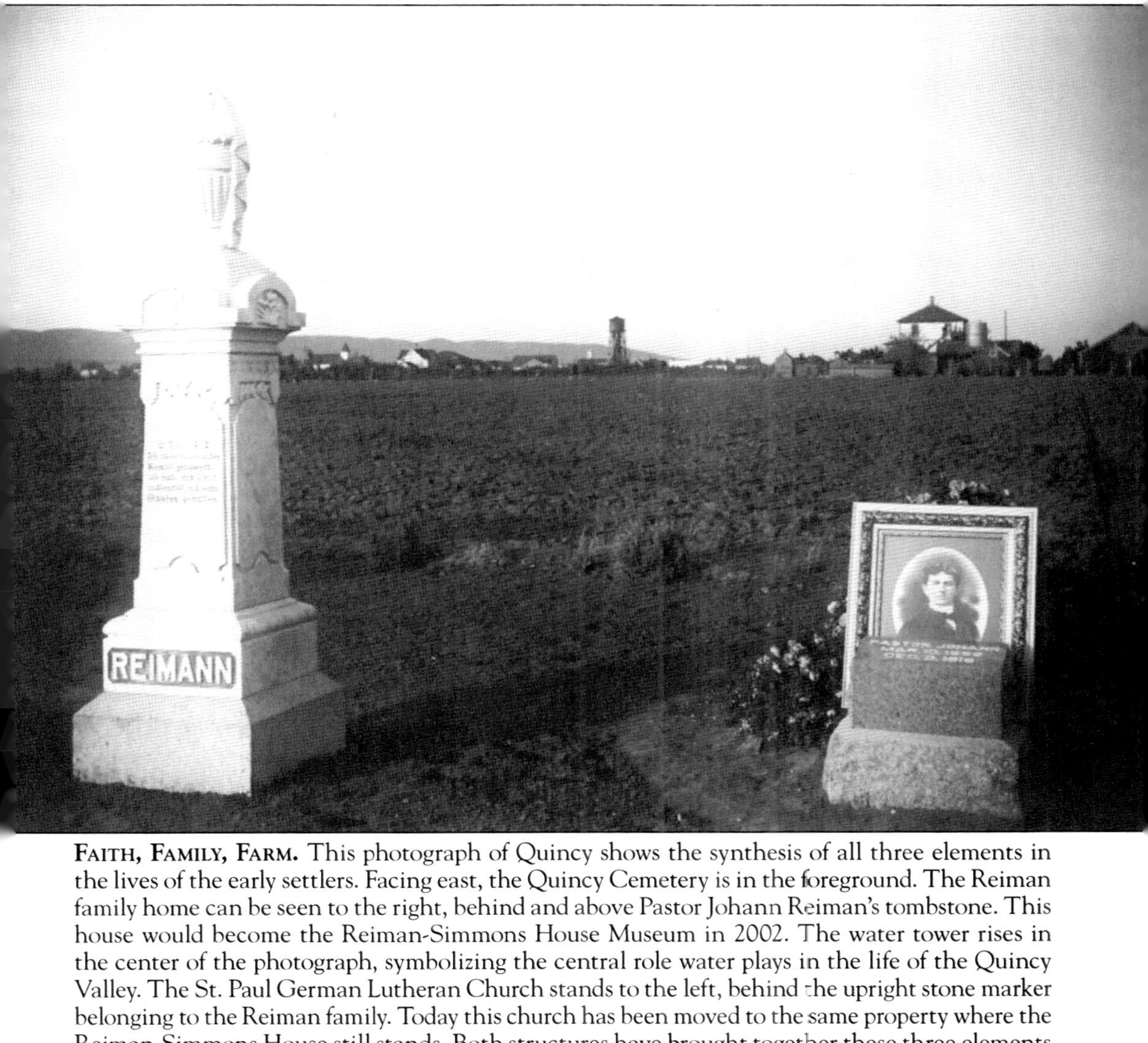

FAITH, FAMILY, FARM. This photograph of Quincy shows the synthesis of all three elements in the lives of the early settlers. Facing east, the Quincy Cemetery is in the foreground. The Reiman family home can be seen to the right, behind and above Pastor Johann Reiman's tombstone. This house would become the Reiman-Simmons House Museum in 2002. The water tower rises in the center of the photograph, symbolizing the central role water plays in the life of the Quincy Valley. The St. Paul German Lutheran Church stands to the left, behind the upright stone marker belonging to the Reiman family. Today this church has been moved to the same property where the Reiman-Simmons House still stands. Both structures have brought together these three elements into one place, with the financial and volunteer support of the entire community. (Courtesy of the Quincy Valley Historical Society.)

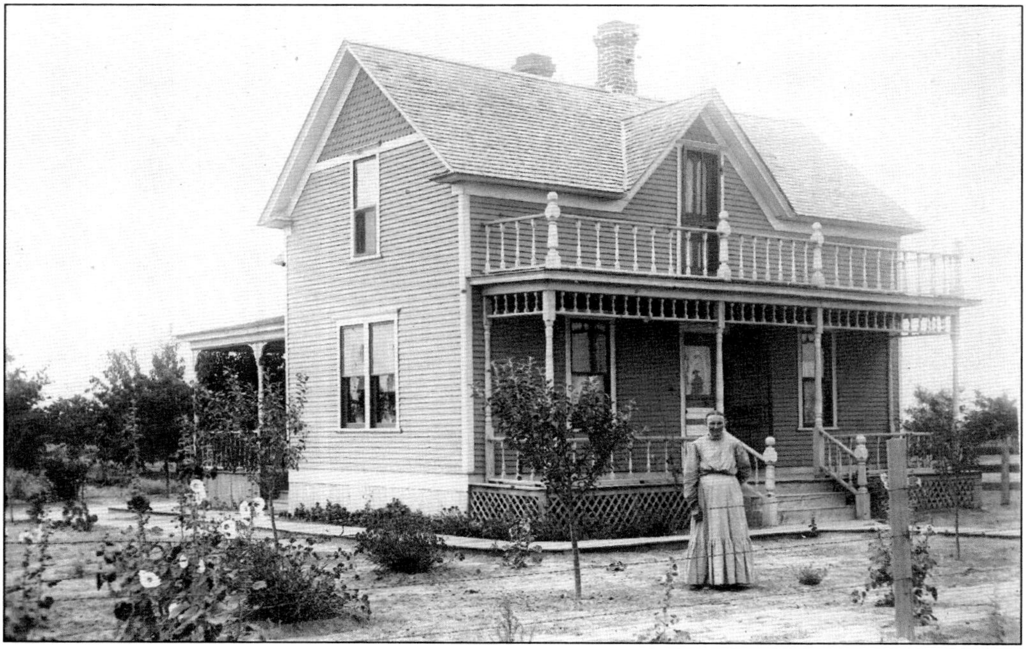

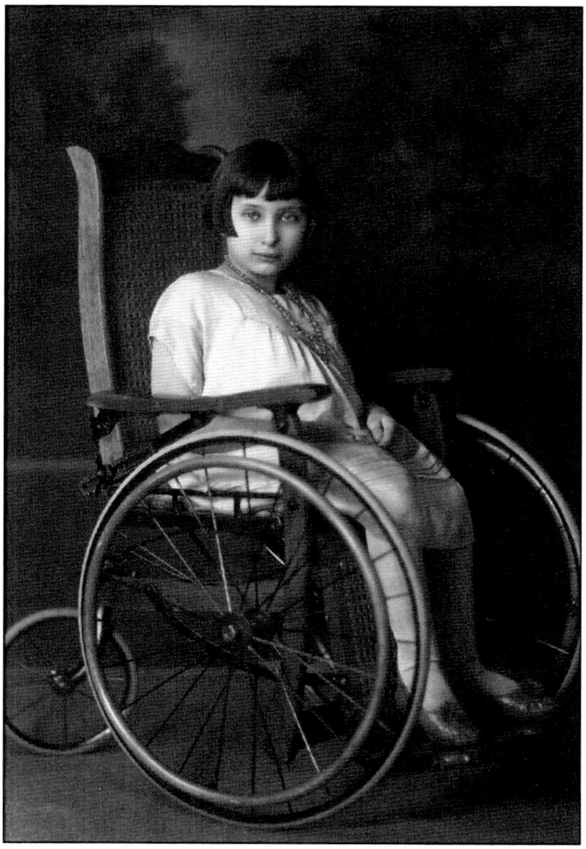

WILLIAM SCHORZMAN HOME. William Schorzman, born in South Dakota, arrived in the Quincy Valley with his parents and siblings about 1902. He married Rebeka Reiman, who was also born in South Dakota. His parents were Russian immigrants. Many of their descendants have remained in the area. The house was located on Road 5. (Courtesy of the Quincy Valley Historical Society.)

VIOLA KATHERINE SCHORZMAN. This lovely girl is Viola Katherine Schorzman, daughter of William and Rebeka Schorzman. She was born in 1918 and spent her life in a wheelchair. This picture was probably taken when she was baptized in 1908. She is buried in the Quincy Cemetery. (Courtesy of the Quincy Valley Historical Society.)

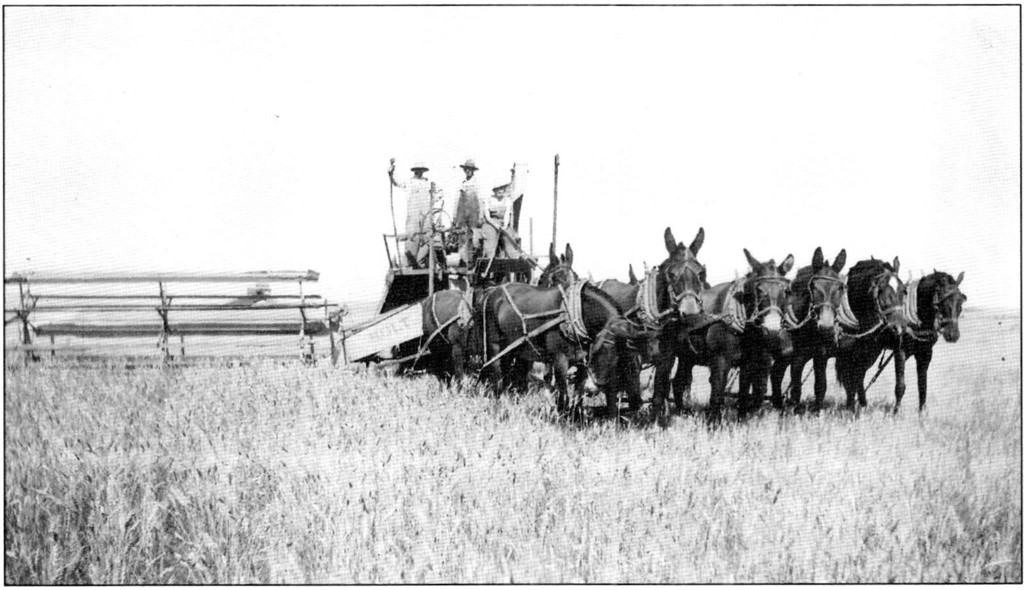

Harvesting the Wheat. On the William Schorzman farm, this machine, called a "header," cuts the wheat and feeds it into a wagon. It is powered by a mule team. The crew seems to be waiting for the wagon to return from delivering its load to the thresher. (Courtesy of the Quincy Valley Historical Society.)

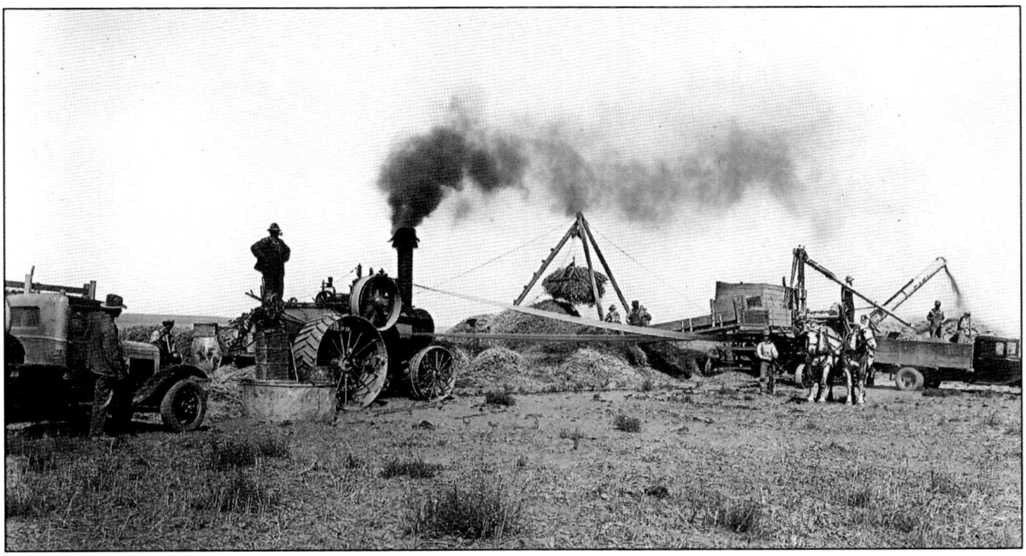

Processing the Wheat, 1935. This thresher is located on the Schorzman farm. Wheat cut with the header is unloaded under the derrick. The block-and-tackle operation moves the wheat to the thresher, which separates the wheat from the straw. George Petrak is one of the laborers. This picture illustrates the transition between horsepower, manpower, and mechanical horsepower. (Courtesy of Fran Miller.)

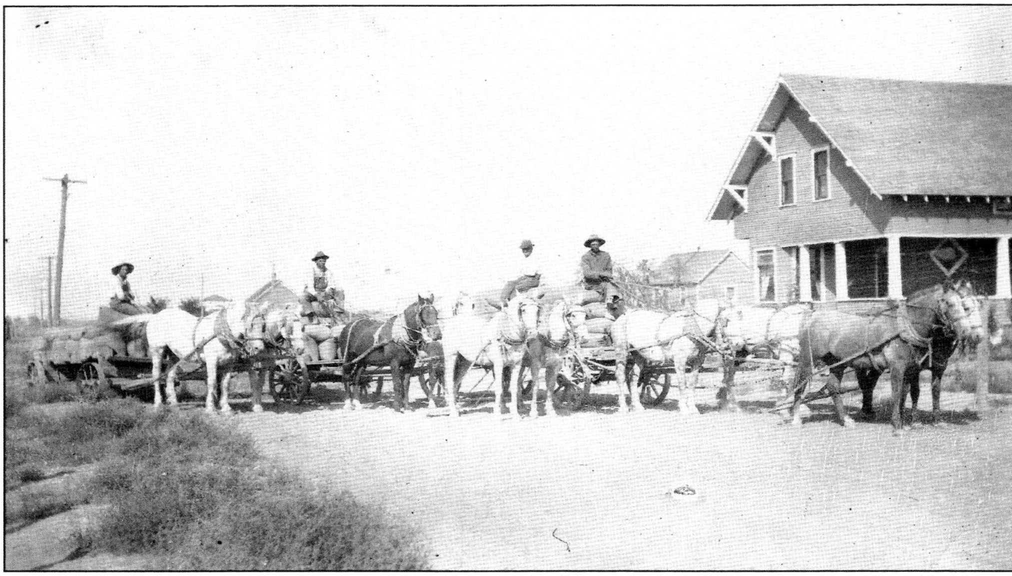

HAULING WHEAT, 1914. Workers from the William Schorzman farm haul wheat to the Quincy Farmer's Elevator, where it would be stored until it could be shipped to market by train. Drivers of horse-and-mule teams were known as teamsters. (Courtesy of the Carl Schulz Collection, Quincy Valley Historical Society.)

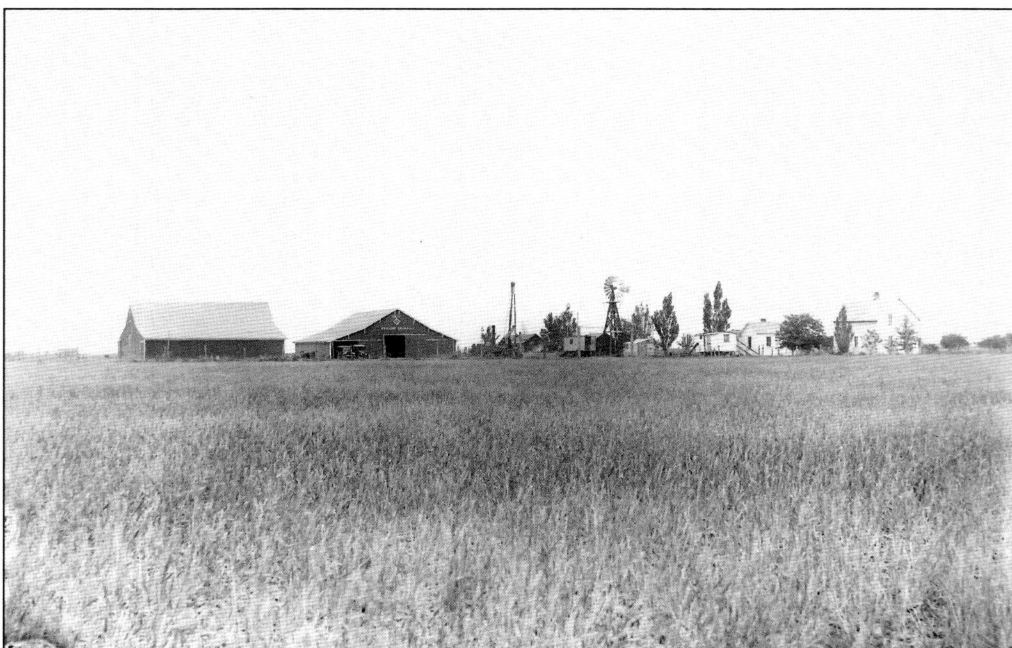

DRYLAND WHEAT FARM. The Phillip Dormaier family arrived from South Dakota in 1904. Phillip and Katarina raised 17 children. The first 10 were girls. These barns and farmhouse are still in use. Johnny Dormaier's general store burned down in the "Great Quincy Fire" on July 13, 1917, started by a grease fire in the butcher's shop. (Otto Henderson photograph; courtesy of the Carl Schulz Collection, Quincy Valley Historical Society.)

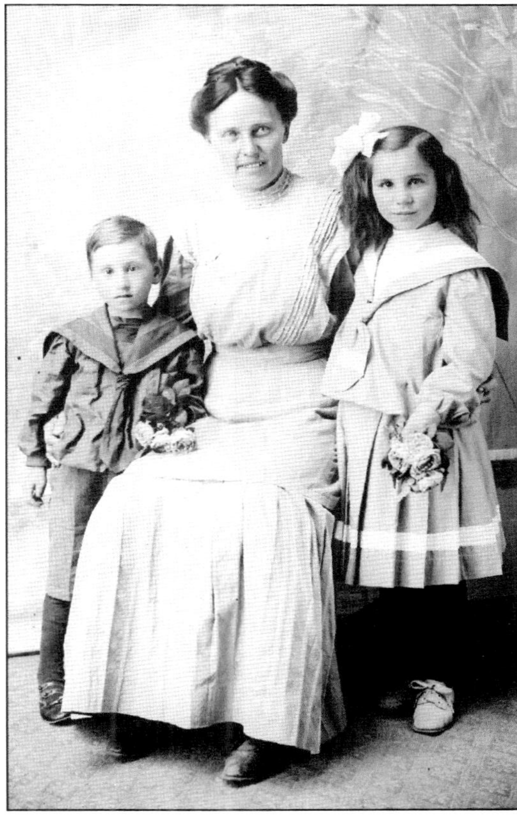

The Schulz Family, 1911. Emanuel and Sophia Schorzman Schulz adopted Carl and Lillian in 1911. Carl was five years old. Emanuel arrived in Quincy in 1904, along with his two brothers. They were the stepsons of Christian Sprecker, who, though not a doctor, was often called upon to provide medical aid to Quincy Valley residents. (Courtesy of the Carl Schulz Collection, Quincy Valley Historical Society.)

Schorzman Family Gathering. Phillip and Christina Schorzman Schatz, John and Regina Schorzman Bauer, and other Schorzman family members can be found in this picture. Reverend Shields is standing in the back, sporting a beard and a bowler hat. John Bauer, Phillip Schatz, and other Schorzman men were among the 13 charter members of the German Reformed Church. (Courtesy of the Quincy Valley Historical Society.)

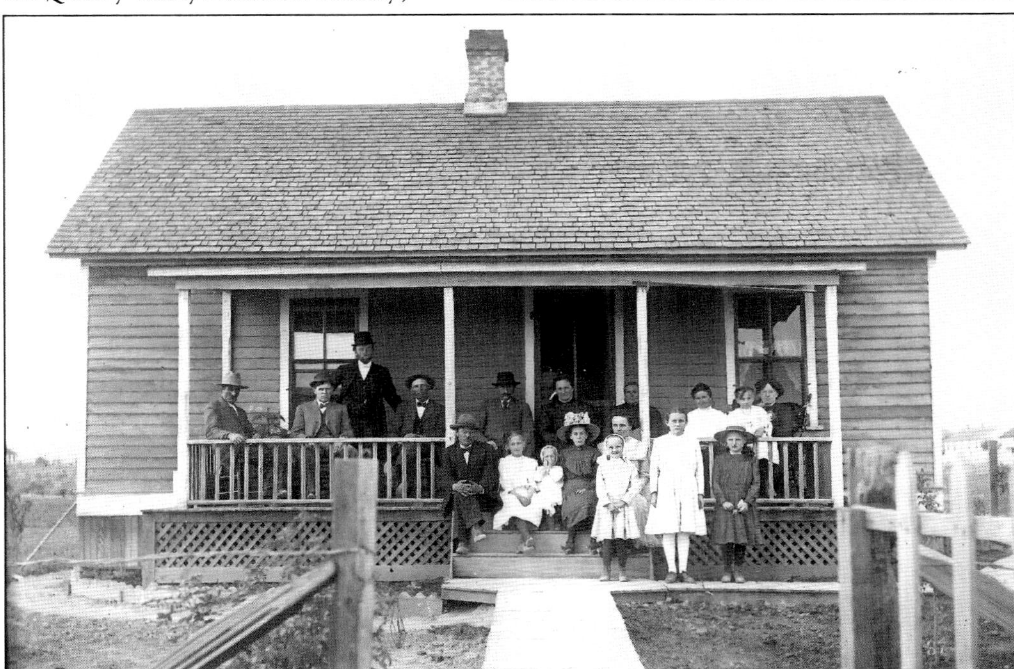

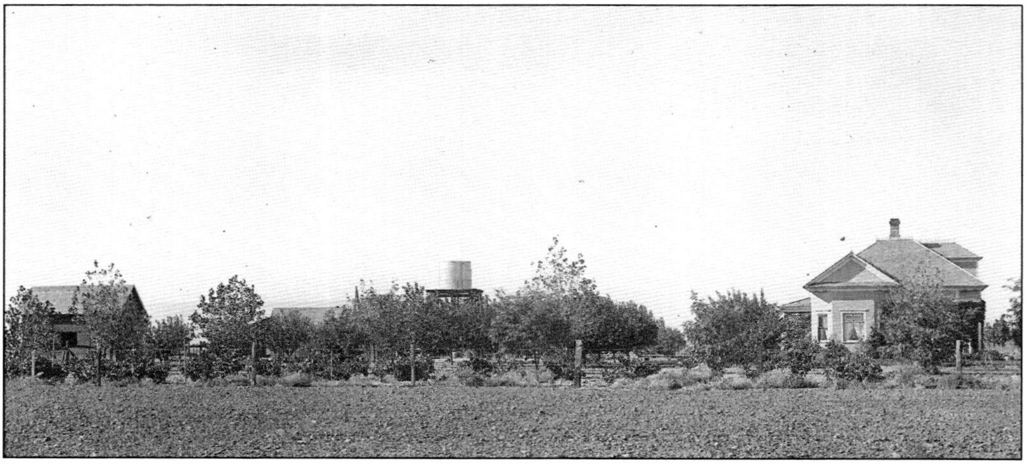

PHILLIP SCHATZ HOME, 1914. Phillip Schatz came to Quincy in 1902, along with his wife, Christina Schorzman Schatz. He opened a general store, which was sold five years later to his brother-in-law, John Bauer. This home was considered one of the nicest in Quincy for many years. (Courtesy of the Carl Schulz Collection, Quincy Valley Historical Society.)

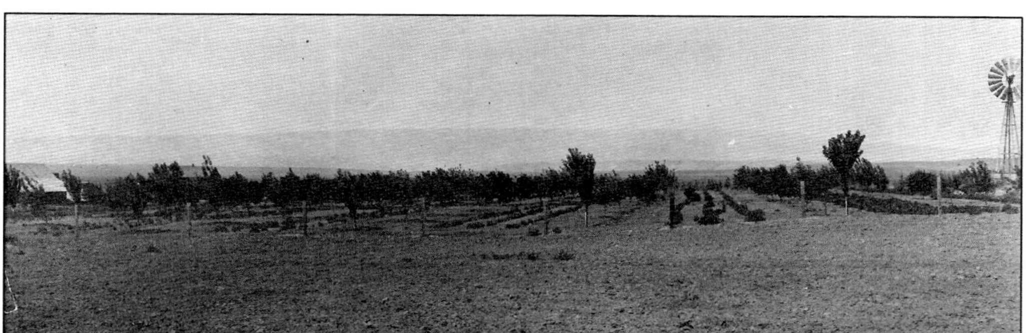

J. FRANK BLACK RANCH. J. Frank Black was one of the first 10 people to file homestead claims in the Quincy Valley. He promptly set up housekeeping in a tent, became a land commissioner, and opened a real estate office. In 1902, he donated his office for the first Quincy schoolroom and served on the first school board. (Courtesy of the Quincy Valley Historical Society.)

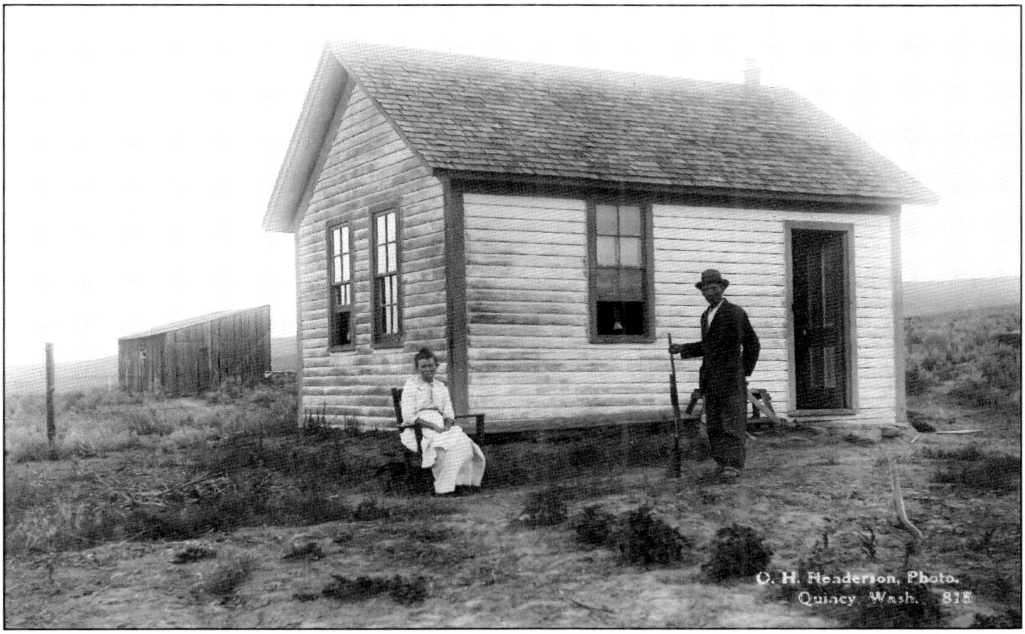

RIDGEWAY CABIN, JULY 13, 1916. The scene presented above is representative of early settler homesteads built in the Quincy Valley. One step above a tent, the cabin provided shelter from the storms and dangers inherent to frontier life. Garden planted and rifle at the ready, Samuel and Rosa Ridgeway are prepared for survival. (Otto Henderson photograph; courtesy of the Quincy Valley Historical Society.)

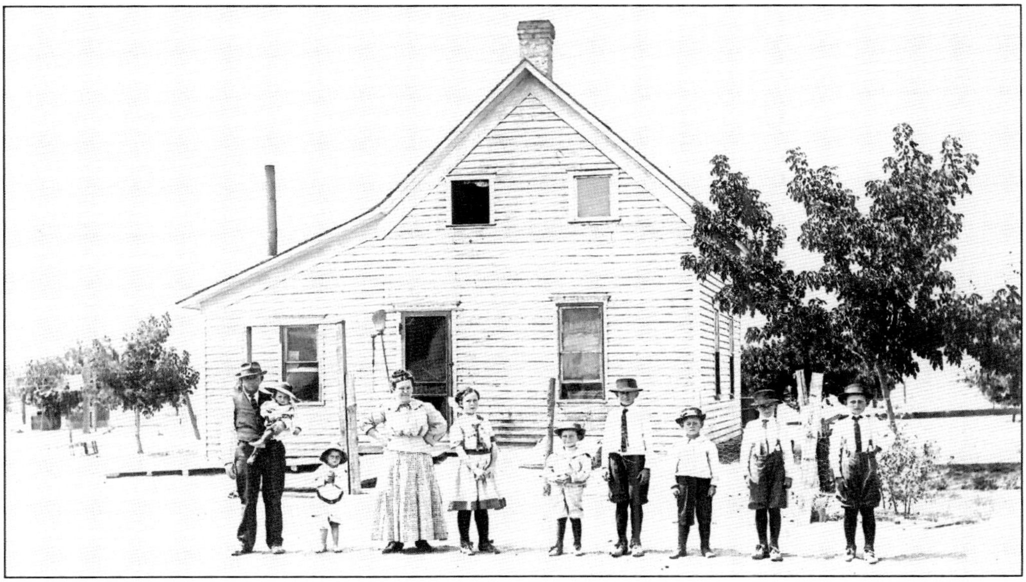

ALL IN THE FAMILY. Father, mother, five sons, and three daughters round out this pioneering family. The house is built, trees have been planted, and everyone is in their Sunday best. Families like this were the foundation of life in the Quincy Valley. Together families traveled in wagon trains, worked the land, celebrated weddings and new babies, and buried their dead. (Courtesy of the Quincy Valley Historical Society.)

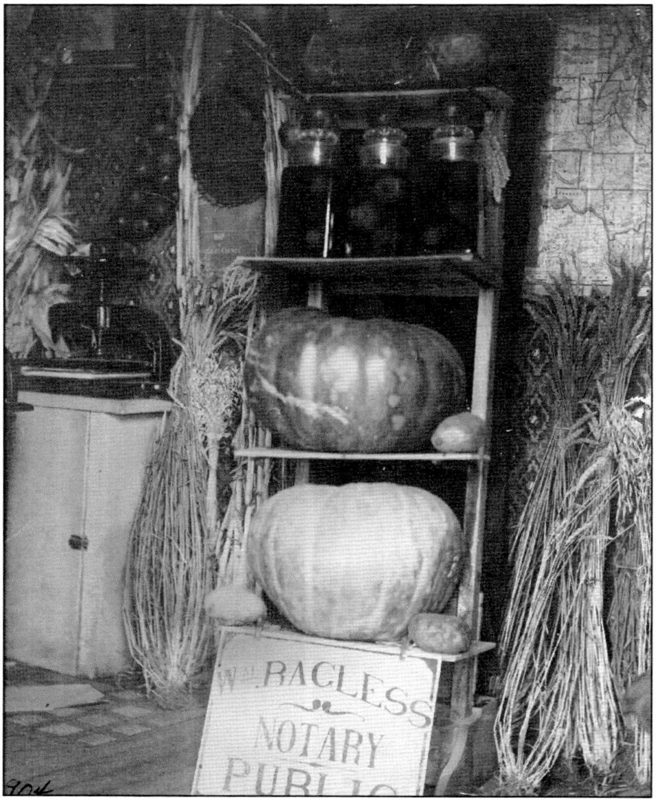

William Ragless Vegetables. William Ragless loved to grow vegetables. He also had an artist's eye, as demonstrated in his famous displays of his homegrown produce. Squash, potatoes, onions, wheat, corn, and canned produce from his garden can be seen in this photograph, a beautiful advertisement for his notary public services. (Courtesy of the Quincy Valley Historical Society.)

Early Quincy Produce, 1910. Here are sugar beets topped with onions—both crops have been staples in Grant County, almost since the first settlers arrived. Sugar beets reached a boom in the 1960s, and the amount of acreage put into this crop has since dwindled, though they are still grown. (Courtesy of the Quincy Valley Historical Society.)

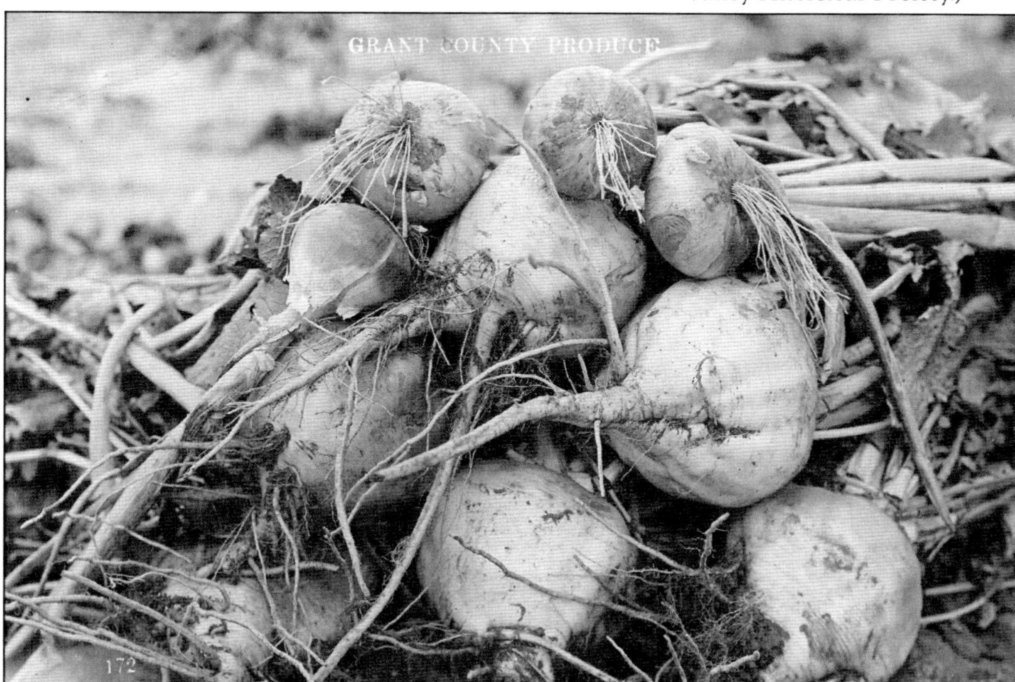

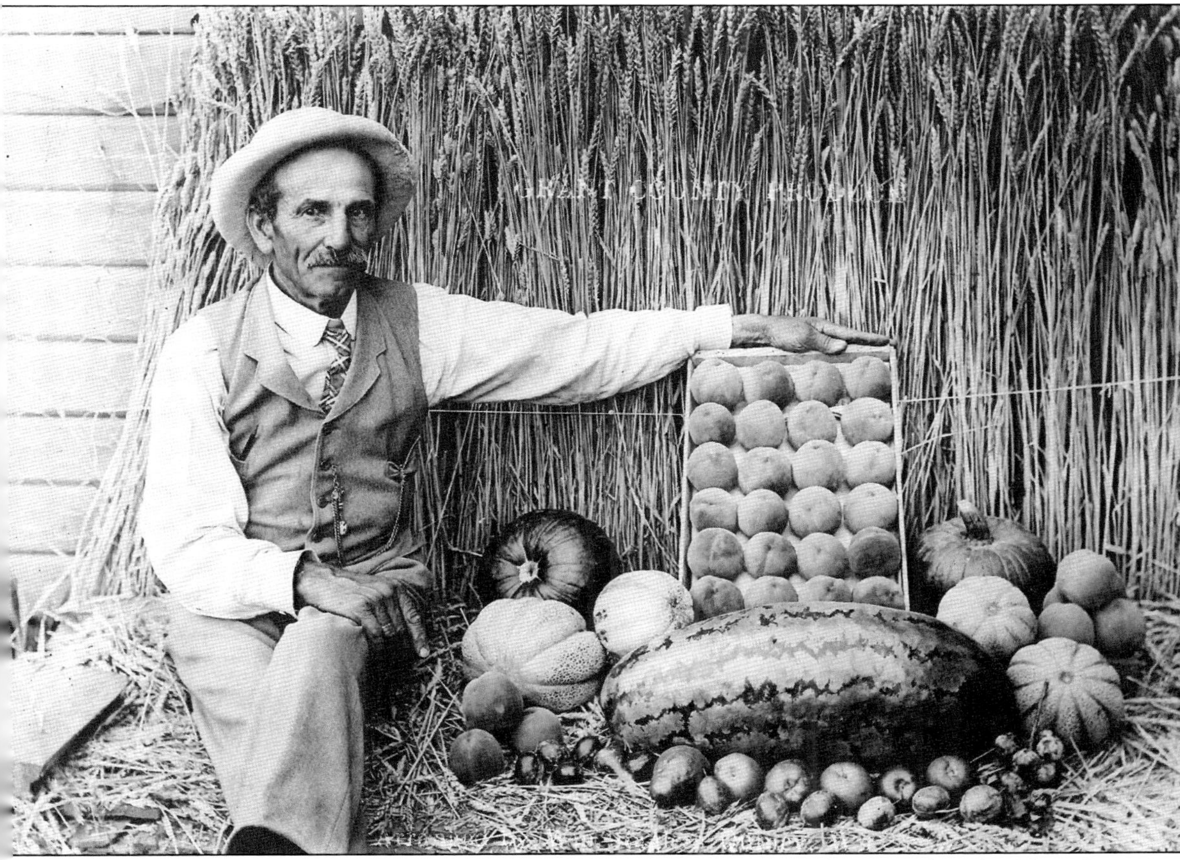

WILLIAM "BILLIE" RAGLESS. William Ragless was born in England and migrated to the United States as a child. He became a resident of Tenino, Washington, where he was one of the founders of the Tenino Masonic Lodge, and he finally settled in Quincy in 1907. He was a real estate agent, a state land appraiser, and gardener extraordinaire. He was also ahead of his time as a promoter of the Rock Island Project, which advocated the use of alternative energy sources, such as extra large windmills, sun engines, treadmills, and the growing of potatoes to produce alcohol for internal combustion engines. He would have been pleased at the sight of the huge windmills that now fill the ridges on the far west reaches of the Quincy Valley region, producing electricity for the city of Seattle. He died in 1941 and is buried in the Quincy Cemetery beside his wife, Mary Jane Symons Ragless. They married in Lincoln Creek, Washington, before moving to Quincy. Mary Jane and her twin brother, Sylas W. Symons, were born in Oregon. (Courtesy of the Quincy Valley Historical Society.)

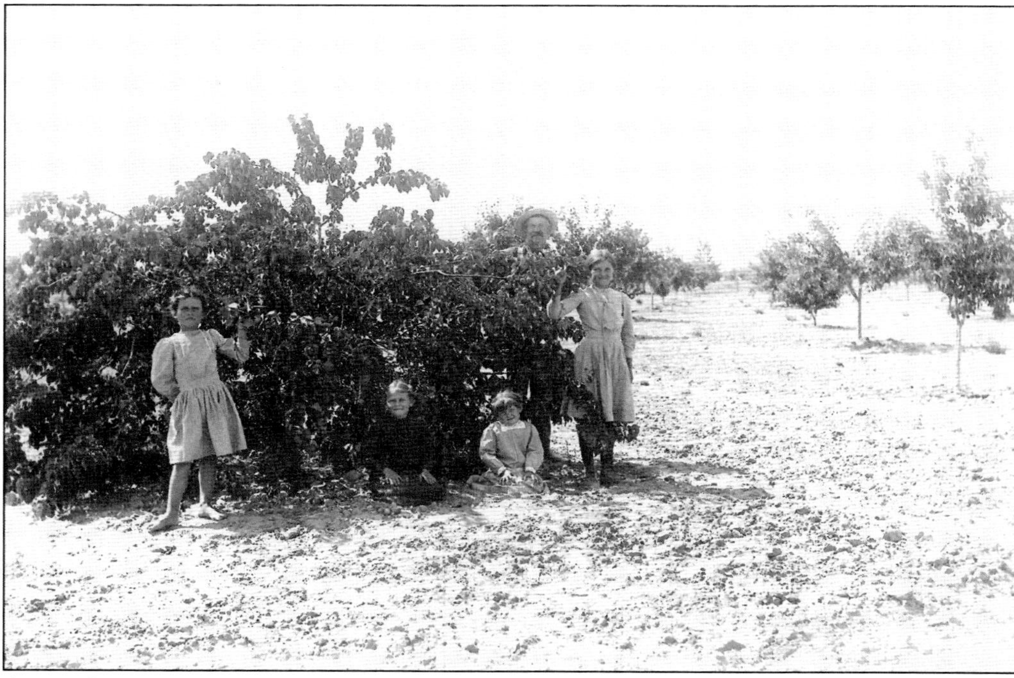

Anton Petrak Orchard. Anton Petrak and his wife, Anna, were both immigrants from Austrian Bohemia. They had 11 children, one of whom died in 1916. Anton can be seen standing behind the trees in this picture of his orchard to the north of town. Four of his daughters are in front, from left to right: Blanche, Helen, Bertha, and Libby. Anton also maintained a blacksmith shop in Quincy. (Otto Henderson photograph; courtesy of the Quincy Valley Historical Society.)

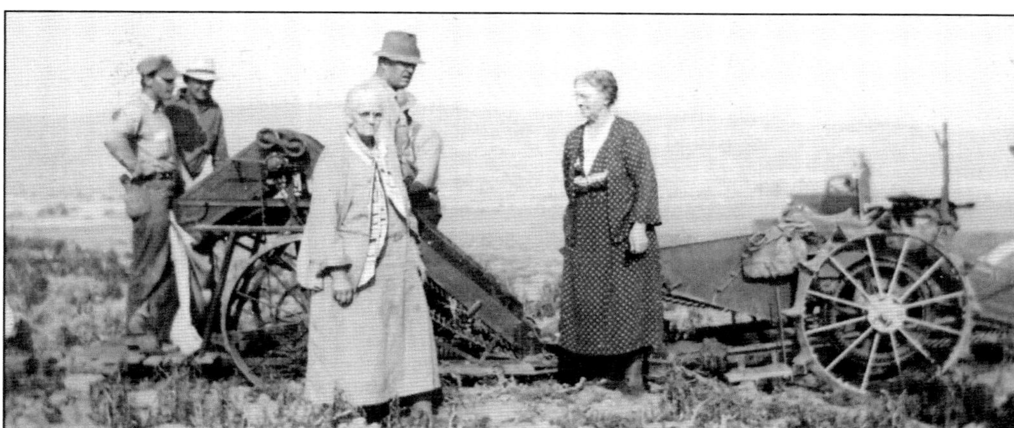

Digging for Potatoes. Potatoes were one of the Quincy Valley's earliest crops. The area continues to be one of the largest potato-growing regions in the nation. This photograph shows an early potato digging and sacking machine. Potatoes are dug in the front, drawn up by a conveyor belt, the dropped into a sack, which is then tied and stacked by the laborers. (Courtesy of the Quincy Valley Historical Society.)

Four

Small Town Life

The Volga Germans were enticed to settle the fertile Volga River region of Russia by Catherine the Great with the promise of land and an assurance that they could retain their ethnic identity. They discovered they were deceived when land titles were withheld and their young men were to be drafted into the Russian army. They then migrated to the Dakotas and other states, eventually coming to the Quincy Valley.

Faith inspired them to organize a church as soon as they arrived in the Quincy Valley. Even with limited resources, they were able to build and support four churches by 1909: St. Paul German Lutheran in 1904 (with services conducted in German), Presbyterian in 1905 (with services conducted in English), St. Anthony's Catholic in 1905 (with services conducted in German, English, and Spanish), and German Reformed in 1909 (with services conducted in German).

Families needed good homes, education, and general stores. The first school began in 1902, and stores to meet every need—clothing, barbershops, butchers, and groceries—opened, as well as doctor's offices.

Farms required hardware stores, livery stables, harness makers, blacksmiths, lumberyards, and feed stores. Hotels, saloons, banks, social gathering places, and the *Quincy Quill* newspaper round out the list of establishments to be found in early Quincy.

World War I and World War II took the young men away for a time. Men had already served in the Spanish-American War and the Civil War. Henry Tidd, a veteran of the Civil War, is buried in the Quincy Cemetery, along with many others who served their country. They did not choose to serve Russia or Germany, for they did not think of themselves as Russian or German. If asked, they would say they were not Russian American or German American, they were just American. These men and their descendants have fought and died in every American conflict since they first immigrated to the United States.

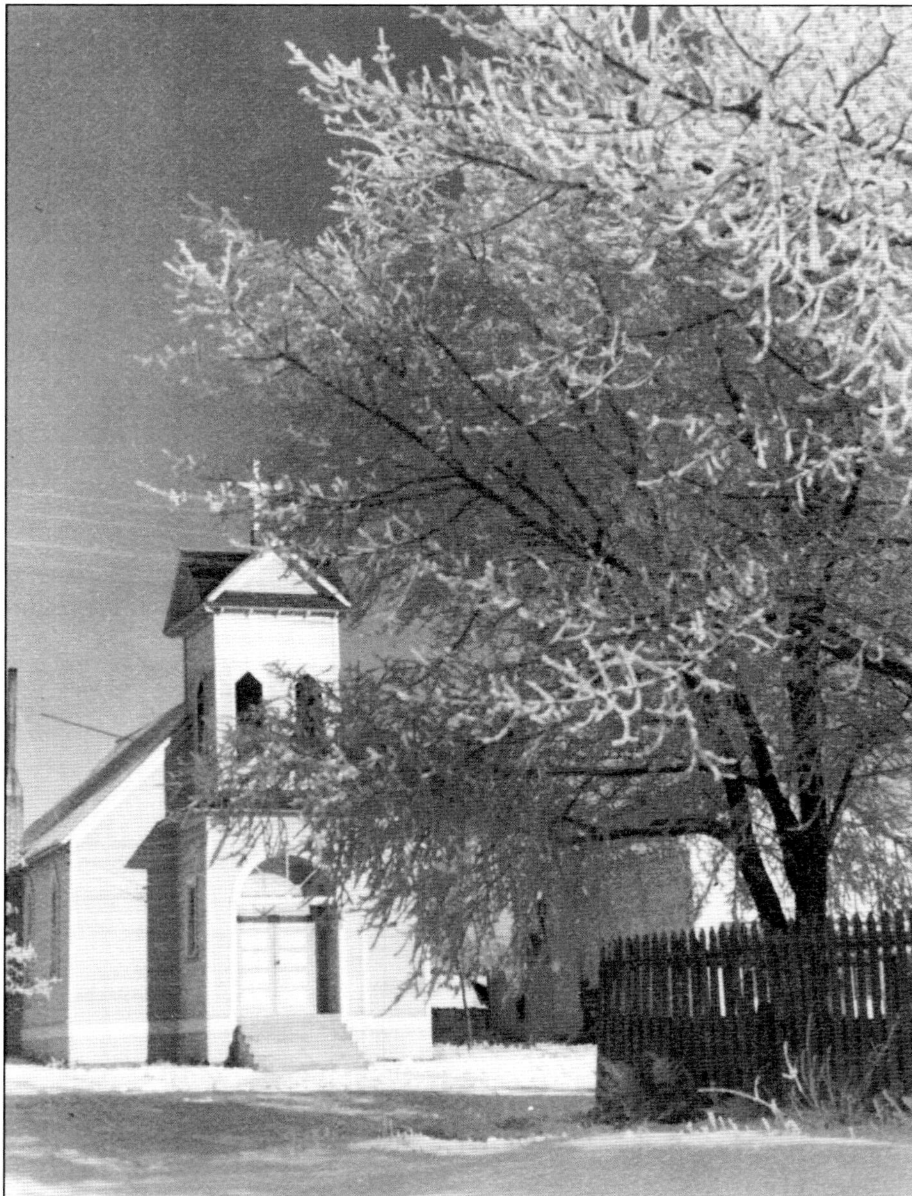

Faith of Their Fathers. Church services in the Quincy Valley began as soon as people started to settle here. Two years before a church was even built, $70 was raised for an organ. St. Paul German Lutheran Church is seen here in a Christmas postcard sent around 1948 by Rev. Charles Weishaupt and his wife. It was built in 1904 as a Congregational church, with services conducted in German. Early pastors included familiar names to the congregation: Pastor Schorzman, Rev. Simon Reiman, and Rev. John Reiman. The first English-speaking church was the Presbyterian church formed in 1905. The German Reformed Church was built in 1909. St. Anthony's Church in nearby Burke (now George) formed in 1905 to serve the Catholic community. It eventually moved to Quincy. Religion undoubtedly played a central role in the lives of the people of the Quincy Valley. (Courtesy of the Quincy Valley Historical Society.)

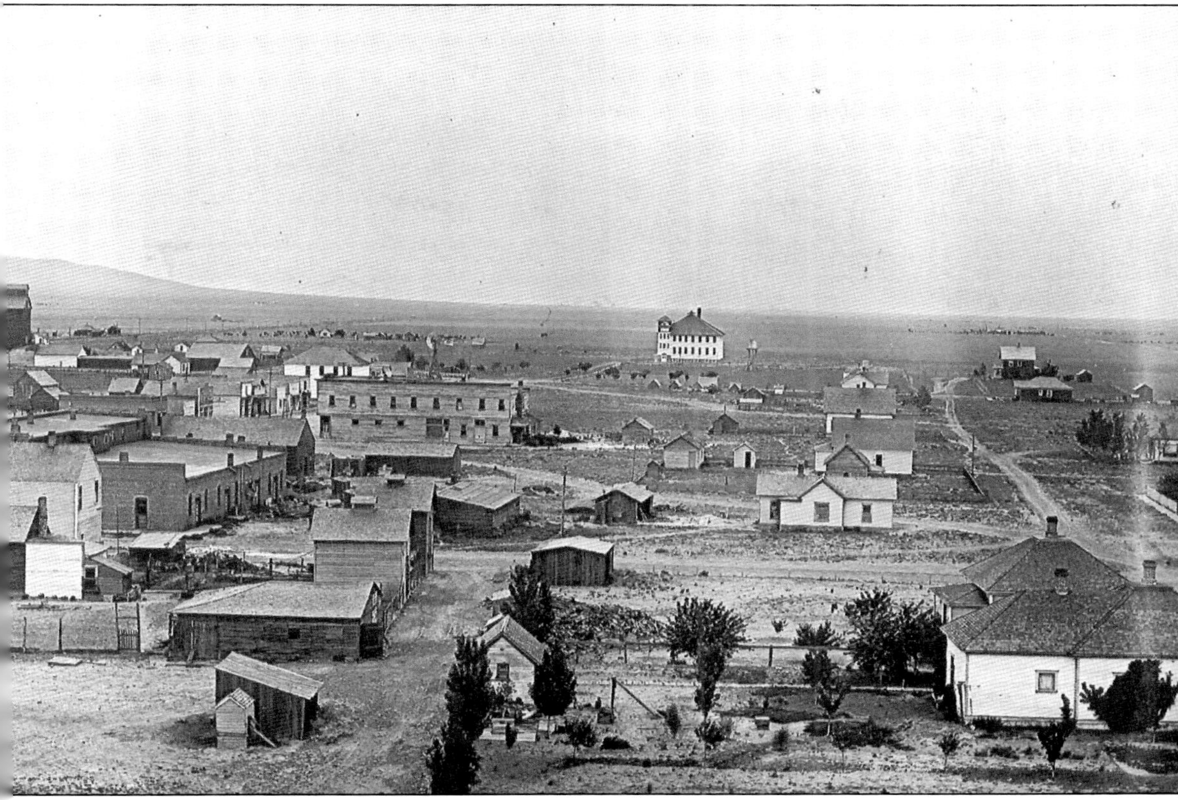

Quincy, c. 1910. The town of Quincy was platted in February 1902. By the end of April, a hotel, general store, hardware store, lumberyard, and a real estate sales office were open. A dispute soon broke out between east-siders and west-siders as to which was the "real Quincy." The east side eventually won. In 1909, a third city center arose when several businesses decided to literally pick up and haul their buildings to a new location south of the railroad tracks. On July 13, 1917, a worker was rendering lard in Warren Platt's butcher shop when the hot grease burst into flames. Fire spread rapidly, destroying six businesses within an hour—the butcher shop, the Dormaier general store, Jonson's Law Office, the post office, the Renz novelty store, and the Little Gem restaurant, which was vacant at the time. Most of the mail was saved, but the losses were so great the businesses never reopened. Others replaced them, though, and the town continued to grow. (Courtesy of Fran Miller.)

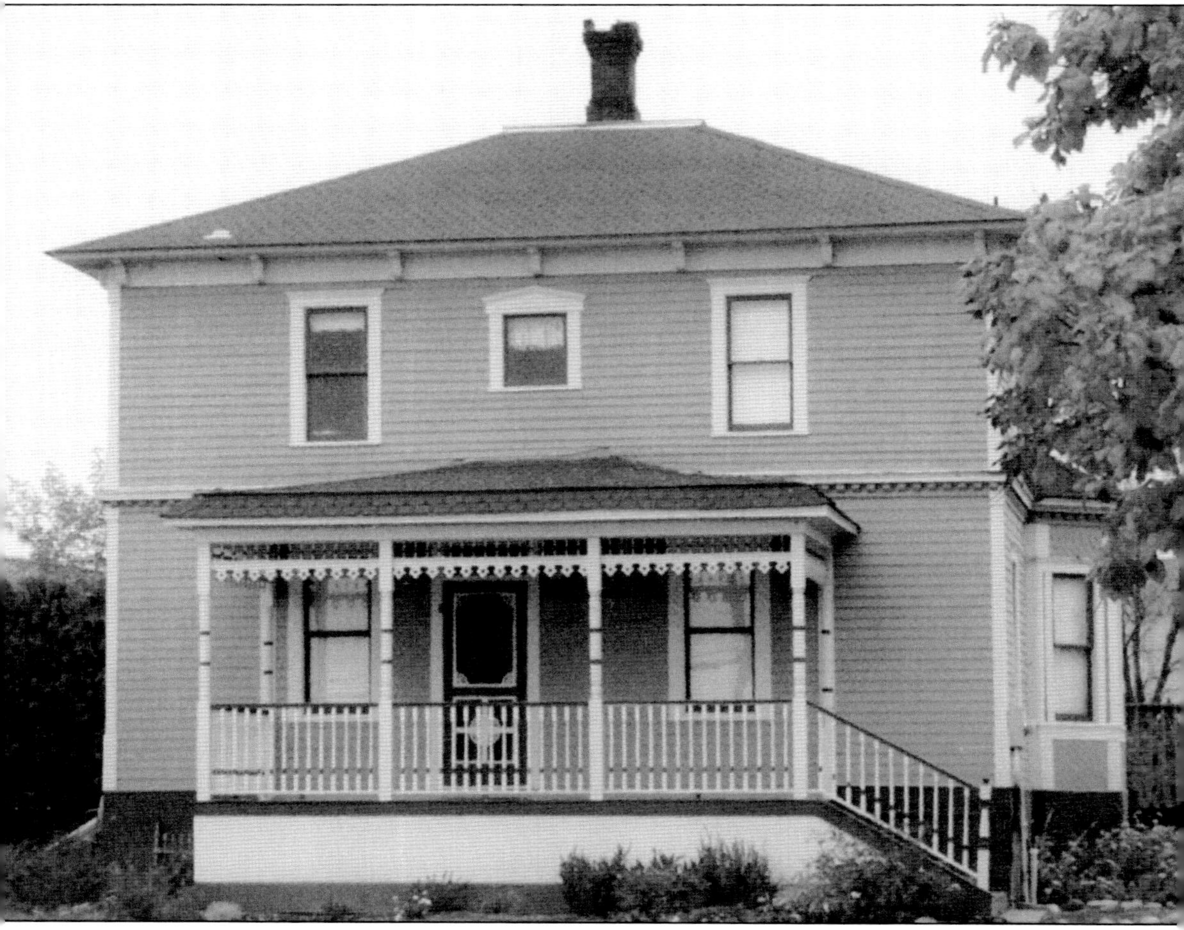

Reiman-Simmons House. This restored farmhouse was built in 1904 by Samuel Reiman. He lived in it until 1920, when he moved to town to live with his brother. Samuel's son Benjamin Reiman lived in the house from 1920 to 1928, when it was sold it to William Calvin Blanchett, another early Quincy Valley homesteader. The Blanchett family lived in the house until Calvin's death in 1955. It then came into possession of Lauren R. Simmons, son-in-law of Calvin Blanchett. Simmons passed away in 1996, bequeathing the house to the City of Quincy for "municipal use, preferable as a museum or park." The Quincy Valley Historical Society was formed in 2000 and took stewardship of the house soon afterward. It is called the Reiman-Simmons House in recognition of both the builder and the final owner. This generous contribution was the impetus for the creation of an educational and social center for residents and visitors to the Quincy Valley. (Courtesy of the Quincy Valley Historical Society.)

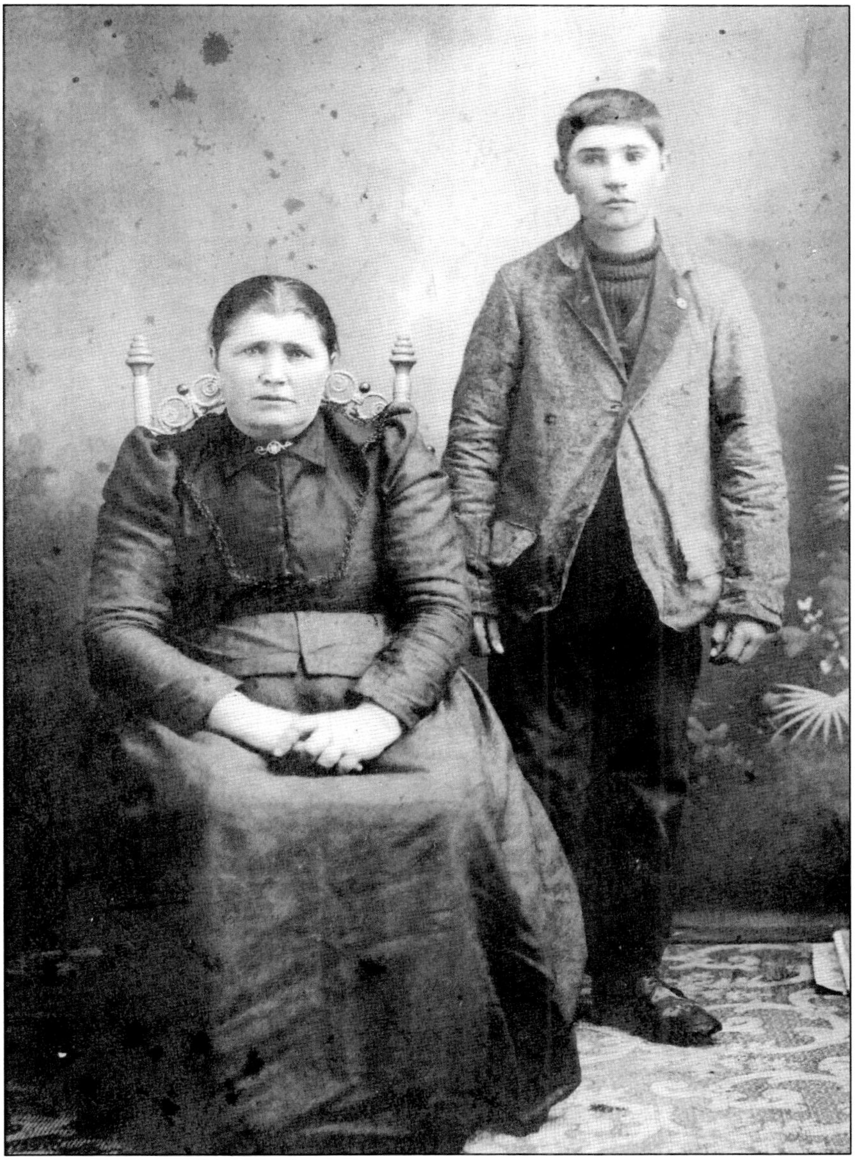

The Reiman Family. Samuel and Katharina Reiman came to the Quincy Valley in the fall of 1903. They were the parents of 14 children whose descendants are still found in the area. Samuel Jr. is pictured here with his mother. The Reiman family arrived from Russia on May 26, 1880, aboard the ship *Lessing* as part of the Volga German migration. Settling first in the Dakotas, then Odessa, Washington, they finally made the Quincy Valley their home. Samuel was a strict, devout patriarch of his home who liked to spend time studying his Bible in the parlor. Two members of the extended Reiman family, Simon and John, were pastors of the St. Paul German Lutheran Church during its formative years. Katharina spent her days doing household chores, including cooking in the summer kitchen, which no longer exists. Katharina passed away in 1928 and Samuel in 1929, almost a year to the day later. They are buried in the Quincy Cemetery, within sight of their home. A beautiful stone monument marks their grave. (Courtesy of the Quincy Valley Historical Society.)

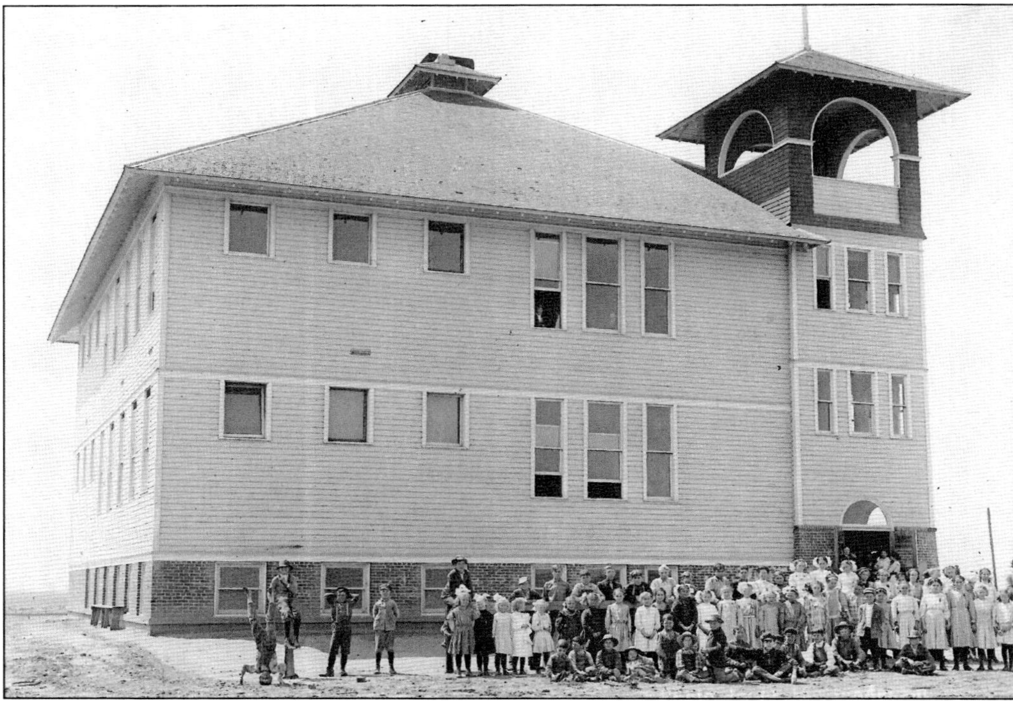

SCHOOL DAYS IN QUINCY. The early settlers of the Quincy Valley struggled to build their farms and a community, but they were also determined that their children would receive a good education. In the fall of 1902, the first school was held in a 16-foot-by-24-foot building donated by Frank Black. A homesteader and Spanish War veteran, Sol Frazier was hired to teach the 19 students for a monthly salary of $50. A year later, in 1903, the first official school building was constructed. By 1907, it became necessary to build the three-story schoolhouse pictured above. It accommodated all 12 grades and about 120 students. The first high school class graduated in 1911. It served the community until 1938, when the brick schoolhouse below was built by the Civilian Conservation Corps, part of Pres. Franklin Delano Roosevelt's New Deal to get America out of the Depression and back to work again. It is still in use today as the Quincy Junior High. (Both images courtesy of the Quincy Valley Historical Society.)

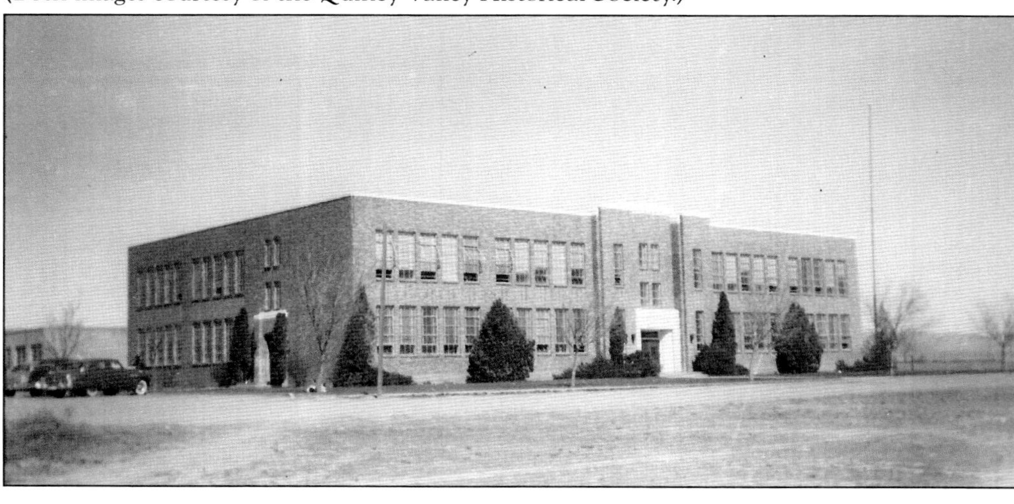

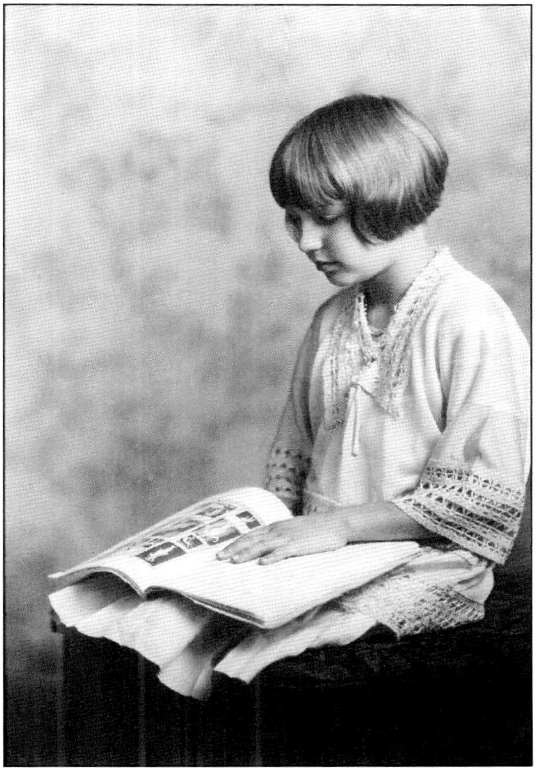

CHILDREN IN QUINCY. Children in Quincy worked hard, but they also found time for playing the games of the era: jump rope, jacks, marbles, and many others. One school outing involved a 10-day camping trip that lasted only four days because there were not enough fish in the stream to feed them. Teenagers branched out into skating, sleigh riding, skiing, sports, music, and other diversions from farmwork and household chores. The girl seen in the photograph at right, identified only as "Harry and Laura's girl," is reading a book. The young boy below had his picture taken in front of a painting of a donkey cart. Sometimes a traveling photographer would set up a backdrop of this type at a fair or other local event. (Both images courtesy of the Quincy Valley Historical Society.)

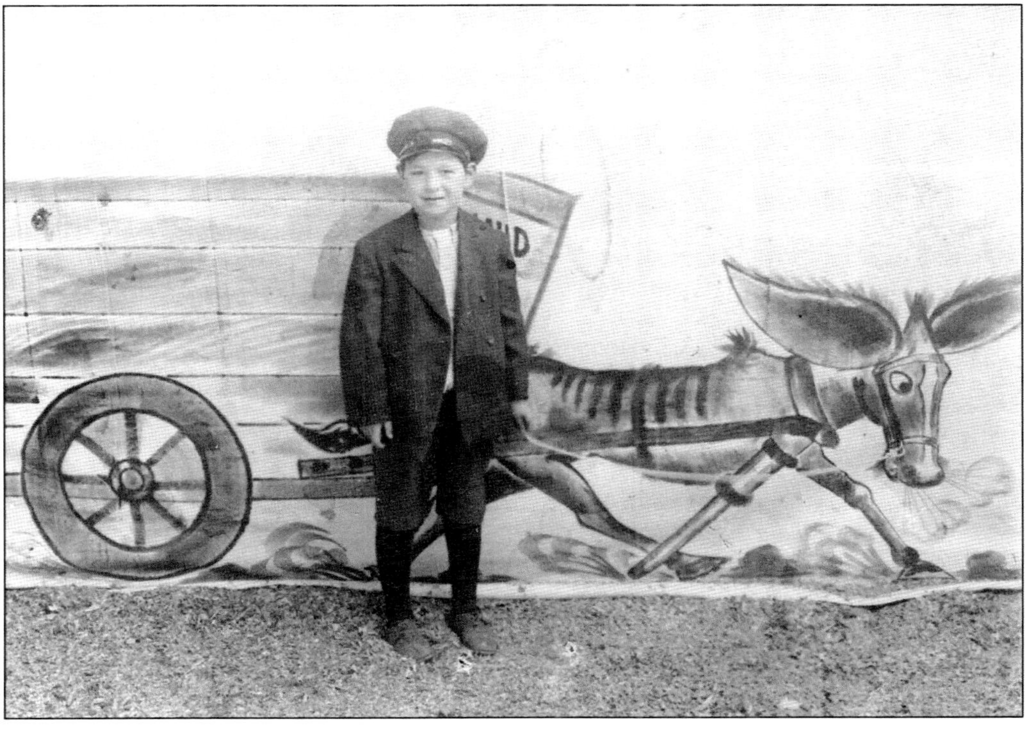

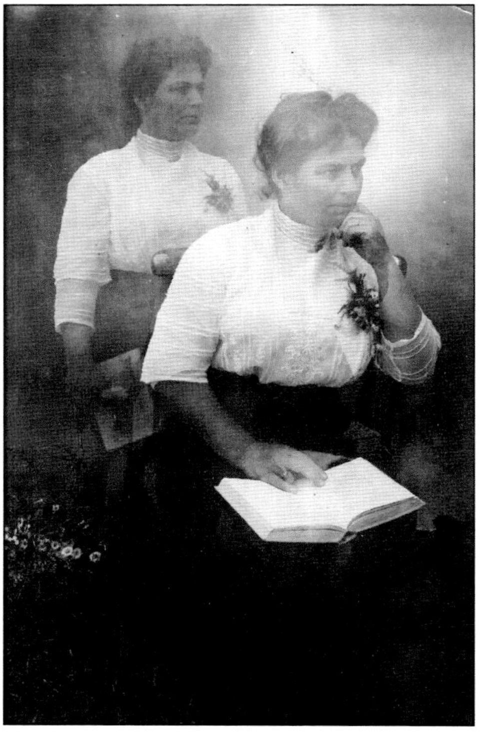

Fashionable Ladies, c. 1910. Ladies in small towns and rural areas kept up on the latest fashions and could be seen around town in their finery, such as the smartly tailored suits worn by the two ladies shown below. These suits would have been made from linen, wool, or black silk. Their hats are made from wool, feathers, and fur and trimmed with ribbon, lace, and flowers. Rose (last name unknown) is pictured at left in a simple gored skirt and an intricately embroidered cotton or linen blouse as the subject of a lovely double-exposure photograph. (Both images courtesy of the Quincy Valley Historical Society.)

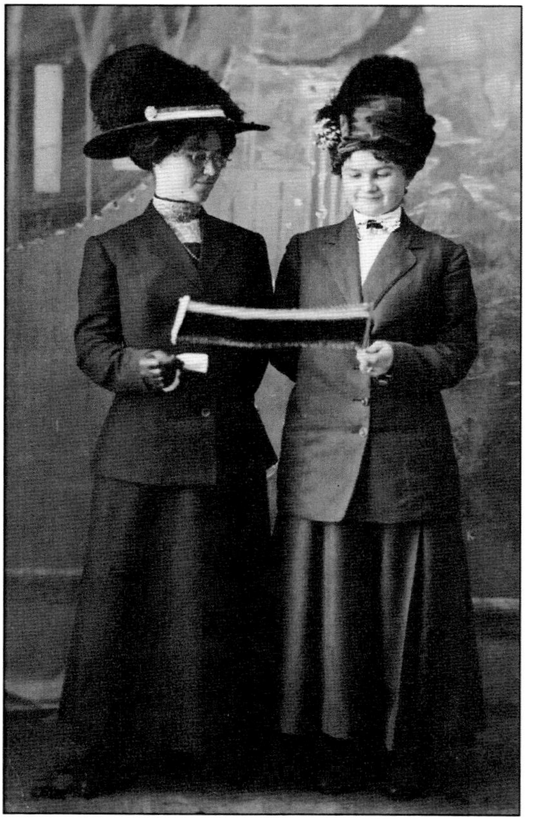

Fashionable Babies, c. 1910. Helin Reiman is the baby on the right. She is the daughter of William and Lydia Reiman, niece of Samuel and Katharina Reiman. The baby on the left cannot be identified. Both are wearing gowns trimmed in delicate handmade lace, typical of the era. (Courtesy of the Quincy Valley Historical Society.)

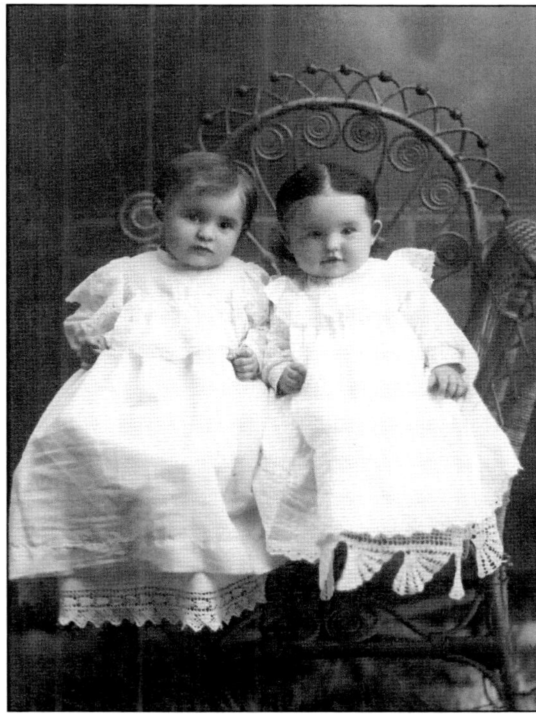

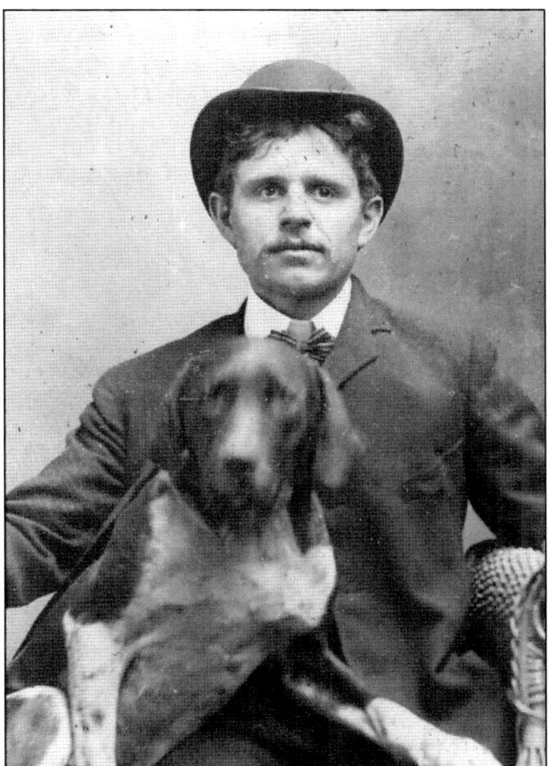

Man's Best Friend. Not to be outdone by the fashionable ladies and fashionable babies of the day. John Bauer shows off his favorite hunting dog. He was married to Regina Schorzman, one of the daughters of Jacob Schorzman. John bought the Hieb and Schatz General Store in 1910 from his brothers-in-law, all of whom were married to Schorzman sisters. He ran the store until his death in 1940, installing what were modern carbide gaslights in 1908. (Courtesy of the Quincy Valley Historical Society.)

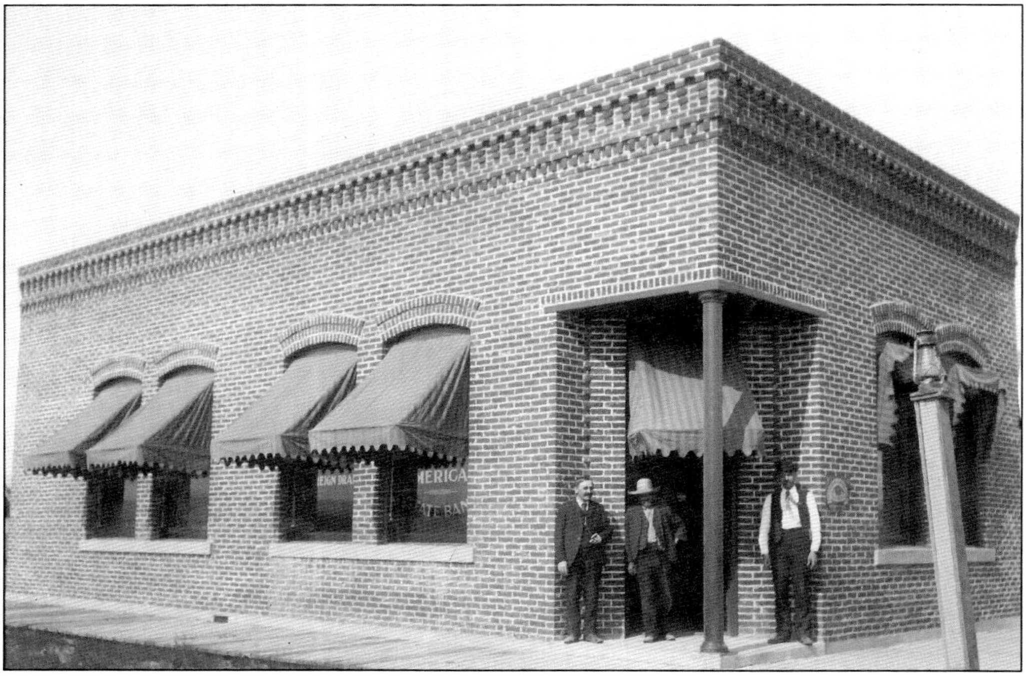

THE GREAT QUINCY BANK ROBBERY. The German American Bank, above, founded in 1906, became the scene of the first bank robbery in the Quincy Valley. In July 1931, a group of men entered the bank and stole over $4,000, taking Charley Simpson and Reinhold J. Baade hostage as they made their escape in a speeding car. Both hostages were dropped off at Rock Island, northwest of Quincy. The case remained unsolved until 1934, when one of the robbers was traced to a house in Vancouver, Washington. Only half the stolen cash was ever recovered. Below is the Bank of Quincy, founded in 1903 by David Richardson. From left to right are Ray Hunter, Leonard Rudberg, Raleigh Wightman, Jess Heaverlo, Dietrich J. Peters, H. S. Van Velsor, Christian Steinbach, and Jacob Roduner. (Both images courtesy of the Quincy Valley Historical Society.)

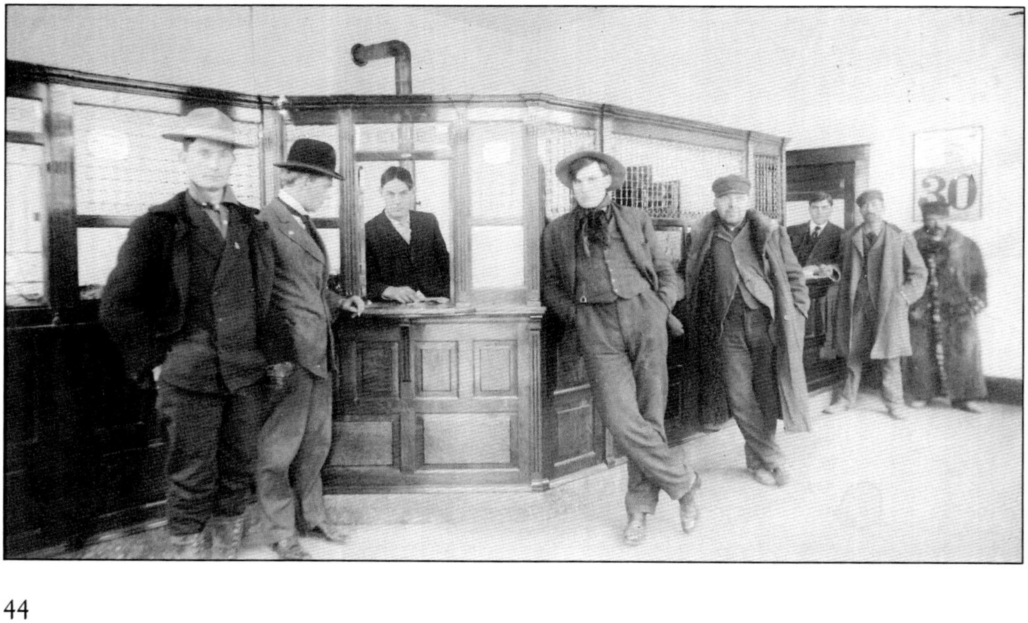

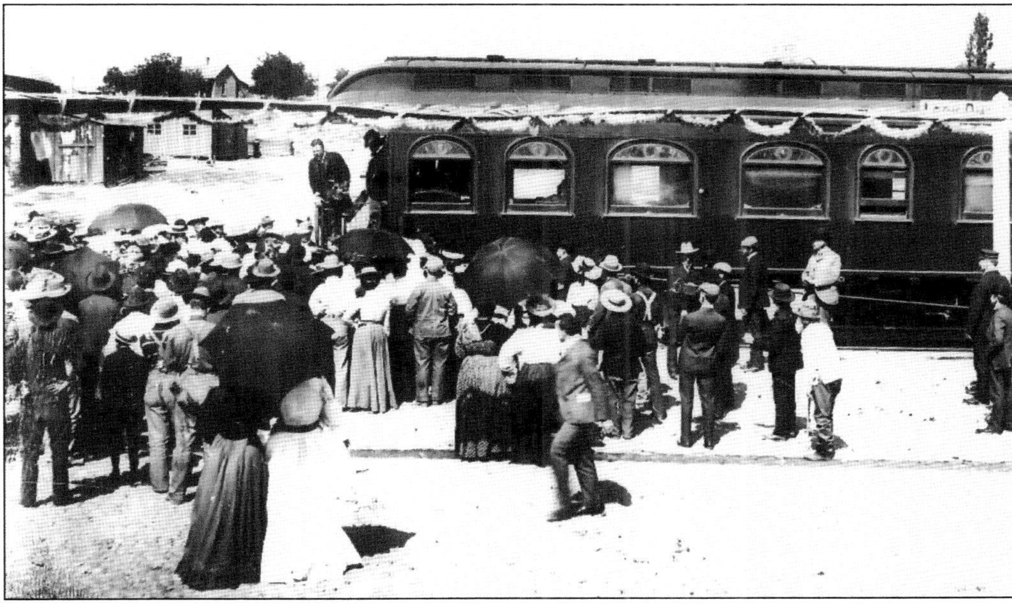

WHISTLE STOP CAMPAIGN, 1904. Pres. Theodore Roosevelt is seen here at the Quincy whistle stop during his 1904 campaign across the United States. He was running for president after having taken office following the assassination of Pres. William McKinley. Patriotism was an important value to these immigrants who no longer considered themselves Russian or German but American. (Otto Henderson photograph; courtesy of the Quincy Valley Historical Society.)

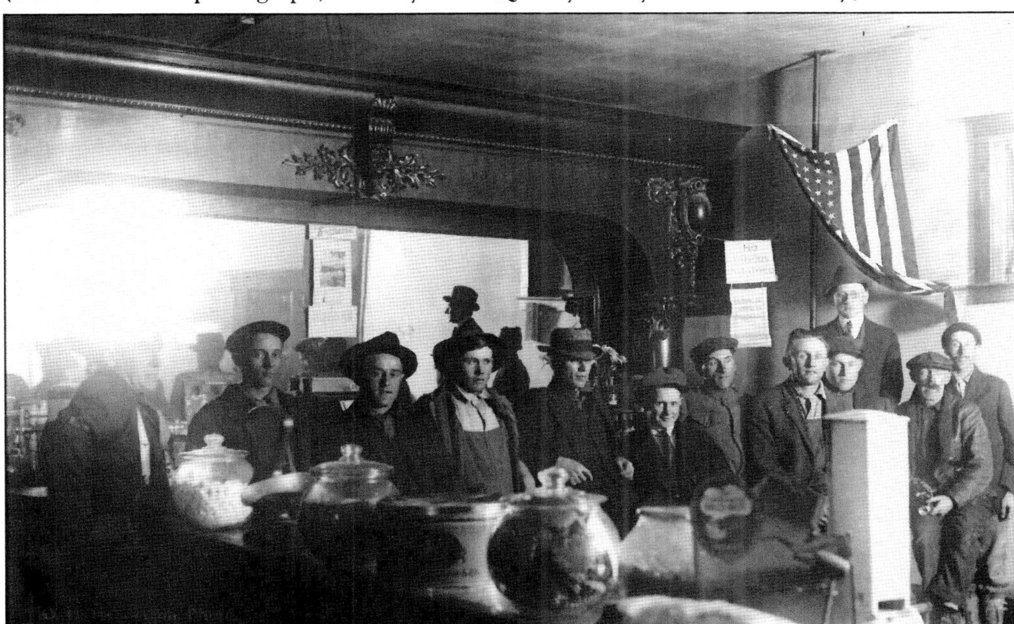

VICTORIA HOTEL BAR, 1923. Saloons and bars were where men gathered to talk about the things that mattered to them, including farming and politics. The bar at the Victoria Hotel was one of the oldest in town and was managed by Wendell Phillips from 1920 until 1929, when it burned to the ground. (Otto Henderson photograph; courtesy of the Quincy Valley Historical Society.)

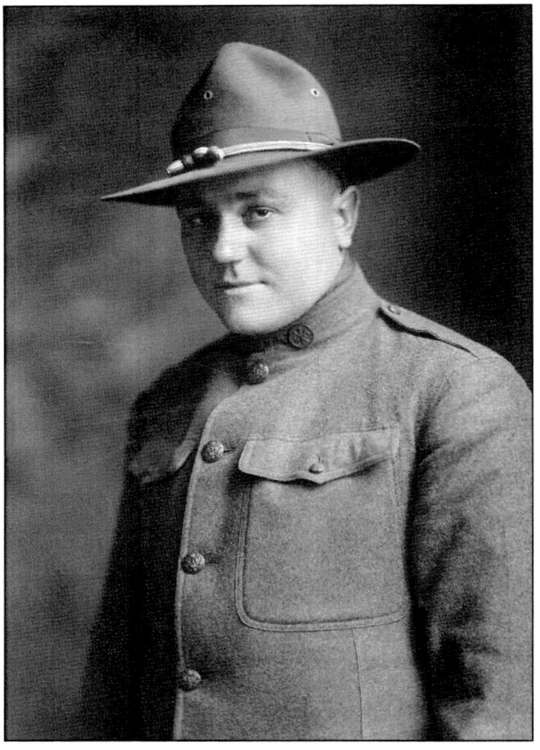

Julius Hieb, Veteran. Julius Hieb was one of many Quincy Valley sons to serve in World War I. He was born in South Dakota and was the adopted son of Balthasar and Katharina Schorzman Hieb. The Hieb family co-owned the Hieb and Schatz general store from 1903 until 1908. (Courtesy of the Quincy Valley Historical Society.)

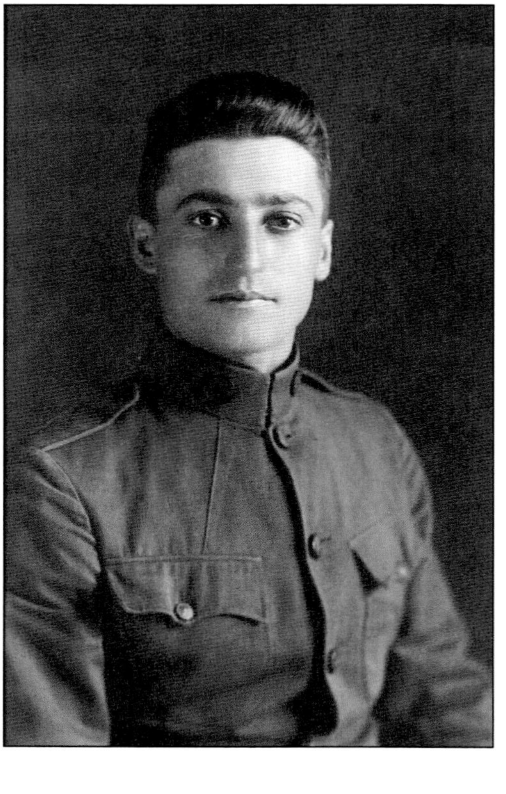

Phillip Tempel, Veteran. Phillip Tempel was a nephew of Phillip Schatz. This postcard was sent to the Schatz family from Camp Dodge, Iowa, where Private Tempel was stationed in 1918 with the U.S. Army in Company B, 527th Engineers Service Battalion. He then served with the 163rd Depot Brigade and Company A, 55th Division Machine Gun Battalion. (Courtesy of the Quincy Valley Historical Society.)

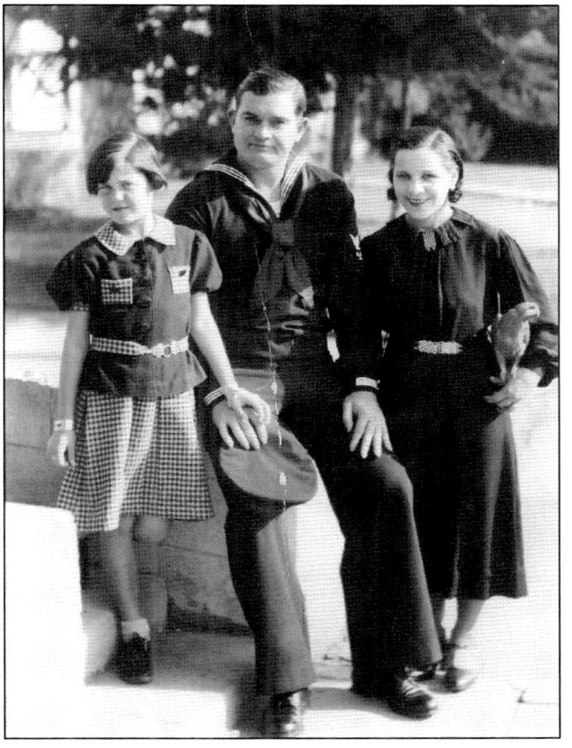

World War II. The men of the Quincy Valley have served in all American wars since the Civil War. Karl Coulson (center right) served in the U.S. Navy. He is seen here with his wife, Lillian Schulz Coulson, and their daughter, Peggy Jean Coulson. Below, three young soldiers can be seen in the yard of what is now known as the Reiman-Simmons House. The young man nearest the house is the nephew of then-owner Calvin Blanchett. He and his two friends are preparing to leave for war in the summer of 1942. Most of the farmers who settled the area after the completion of the Columbia Irrigation Project in 1951 were World War II veterans. (Both images courtesy of the Quincy Valley Historical Society.)

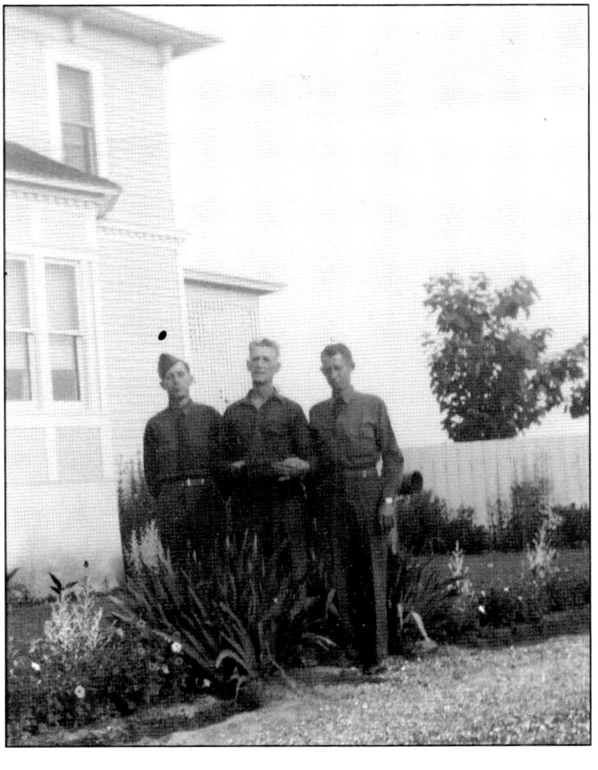

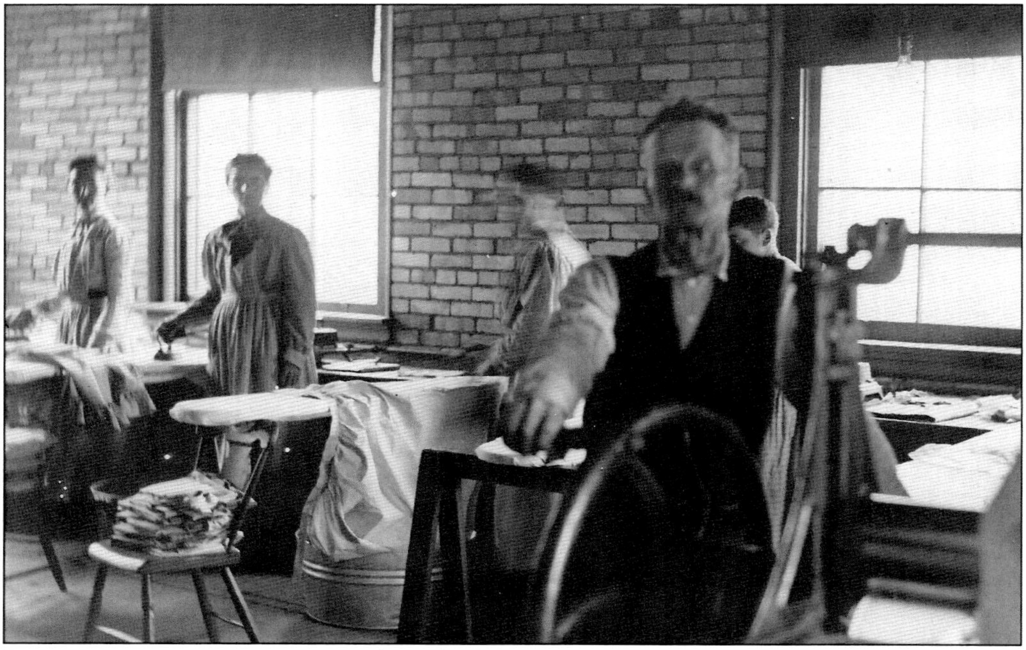

LAUNDRY DAY, C. 1902. Most people washed their own dirty linens at home, but for hotel guests and bachelors, laundry services would have been greatly appreciated. This laundry is most likely attached to one of the hotels in town. The irons would have been heated on a wood stove. (Courtesy of the Karl Schorzman Collection, Quincy Valley Historical Society.)

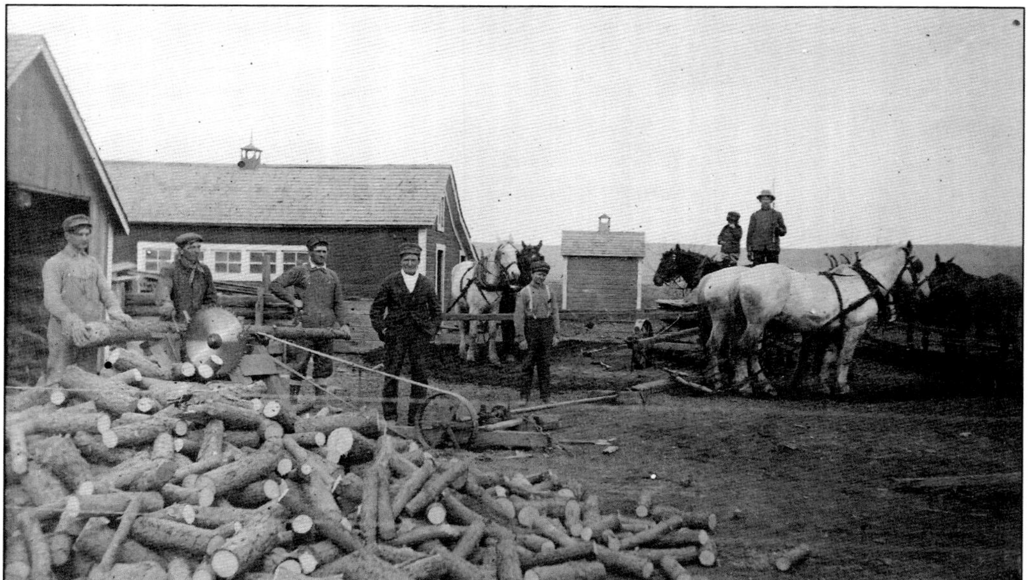

QUINCY WOODLOT. Wood was the main energy source for early settlers in Quincy. It provided fires used for cooking, laundry, housecleaning, bathing, steam engines, and locomotives. In this picture, the men of the Quincy Valley can be seen hauling logs into a common woodlot, where a circular saw cuts the wood into pieces small enough for a train boiler or wood stove. (Courtesy of the Quincy Valley Historical Society.)

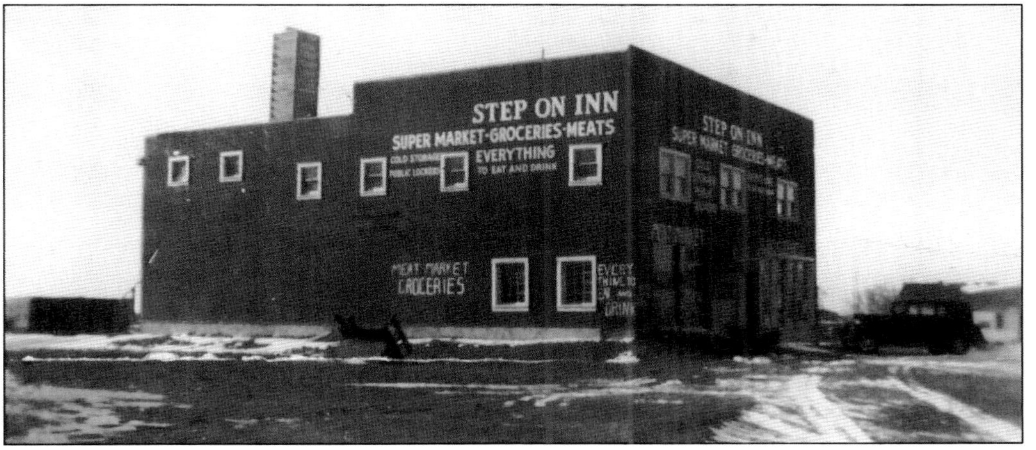

Stepon Inn. Stepon Inn is a great play on words. It was owned by Charles F. and Mary Petrak Stepon. Mary is the daughter of Anton and Anna Petrak. Like the Petraks, the Stepon family originated in Bohemia, immigrated to South Dakota, and eventually found their way to the Quincy Valley. Charles and Mary were the parents of eight children and are buried in East Wenatchee, Washington. Above, Stepon Inn invites the shopper to find "Everything to Eat and Drink" within its walls and advertises itself as a "Super Market." Below, Charles is seen behind his meat counter in 1935. (Above, courtesy of Fran Miller; below, courtesy of the Quincy Valley Historical Society.)

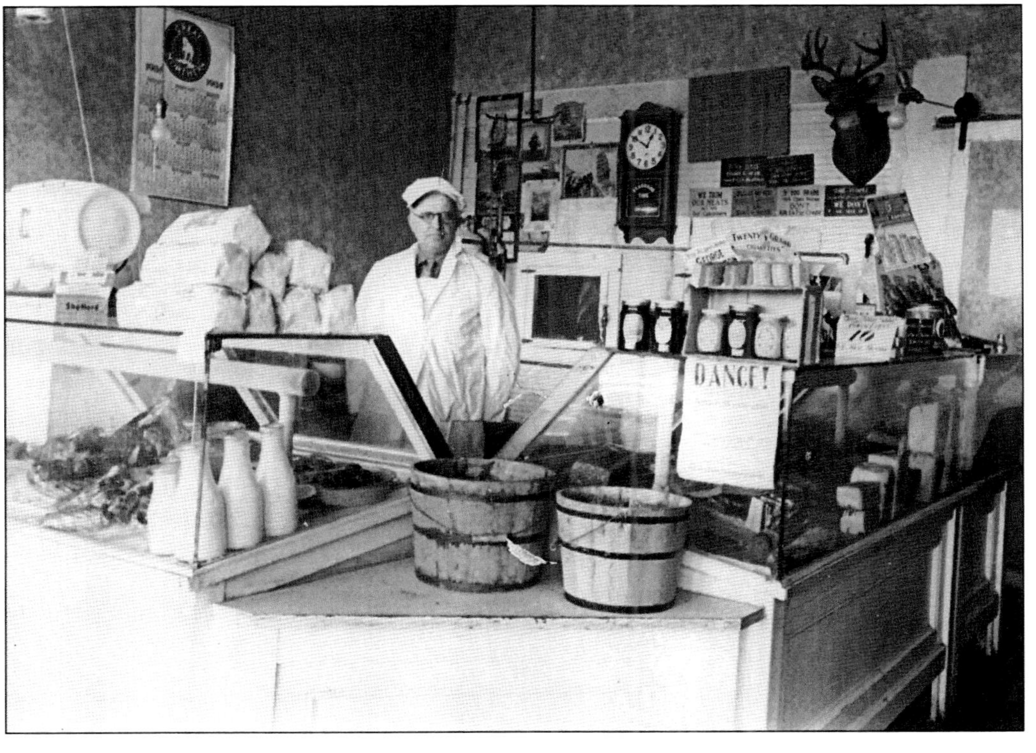

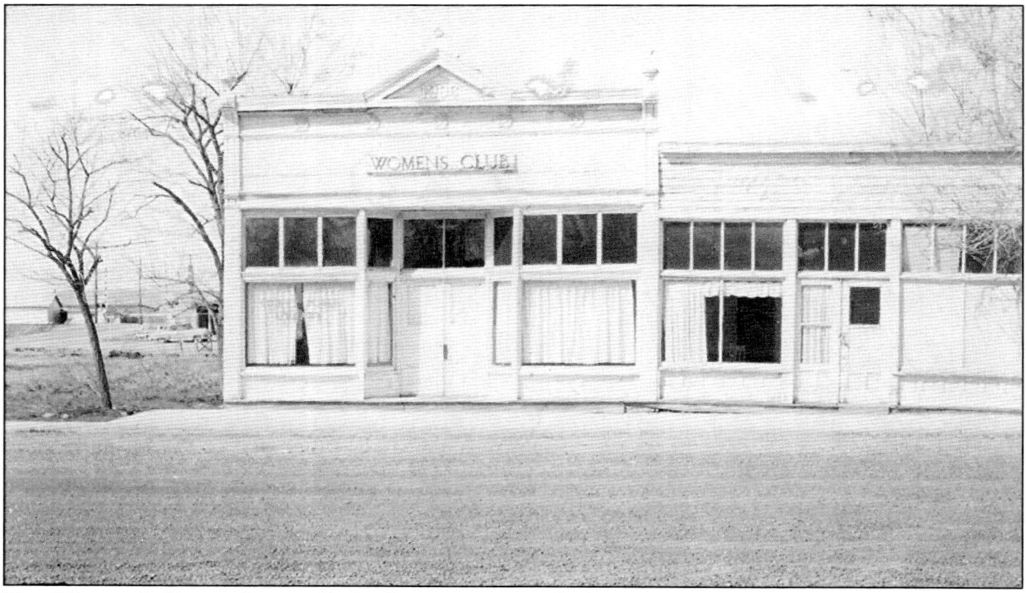

The Women's Club. Originally built in 1908 as a clothing store by E. K. Molden, this building later became the Women's Club. By the time this picture was taken, it also housed the Quincy Public Library. The library later moved to its current location on B Street SW. The building was torn down in the late 1970s. (Courtesy of Fran Miller.)

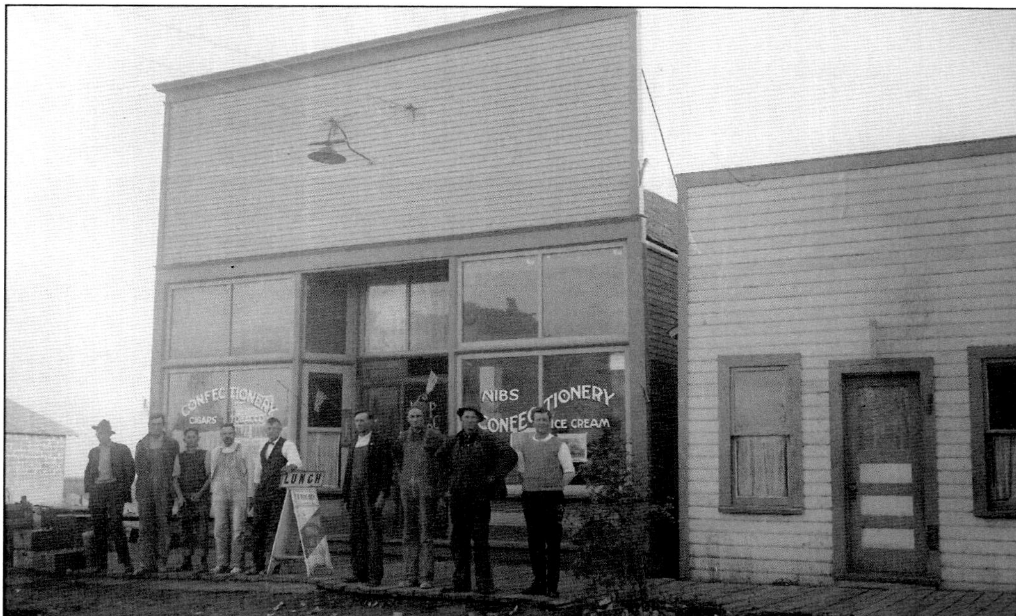

Nibs Confectionery. Ernest A. "Nibs" Niblack opened an ice cream parlor in 1919 after Prohibition shut down his Idle Hour Saloon pool hall. It would later become the Spud Shed and is now known as the Idle Hour Café. Some of the men pictured here are Jack Cather, George Petrak, Edward Petrak, Ilet Engelbretson, and Earnest A. Niblack. (Courtesy of the Quincy Valley Historical Society.)

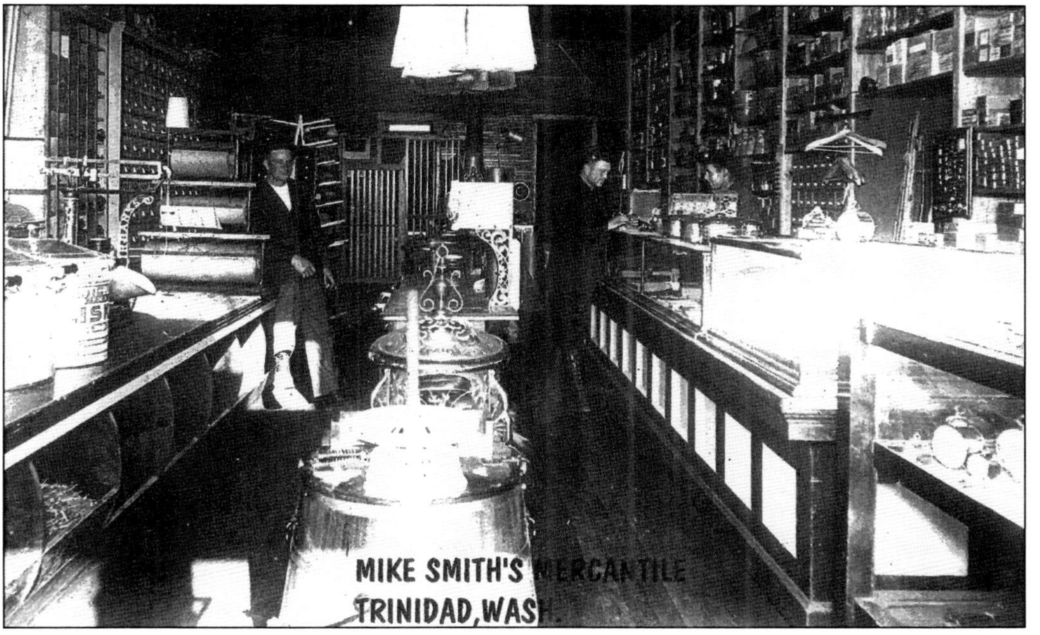

Mike Smith's Mercantile. In 1913, Michael D. Smith reopened Frank Kepple's general merchandise store in the Trinidad and Crescent Bar area, 7 miles west of Quincy. He built a new Smith Brothers store on the same site in 1926, doing business until the construction of the Wanapum Dam permanently flooded out farmers on Crescent Bar in 1961. It is now an antique store. (Courtesy of the Quincy Valley Historical Society.)

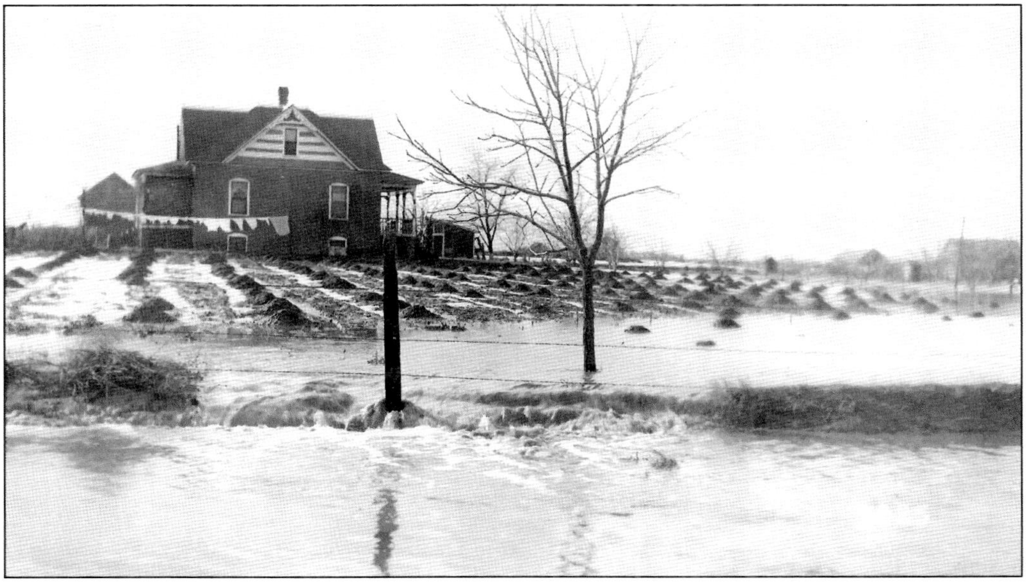

Heavy Snows and Floods. The Quincy Valley may be known as a dry land, but snowfalls in excess of 13 inches were not unknown. When a warm Chinook wind blew, the Quincy Flats would flood. This picture shows the Balthasar Hieb house during one of these Chinook floods. Sometimes the streets in town were navigable only by boat. (Otto Henderson photograph; courtesy of the Quincy Valley Historical Society.)

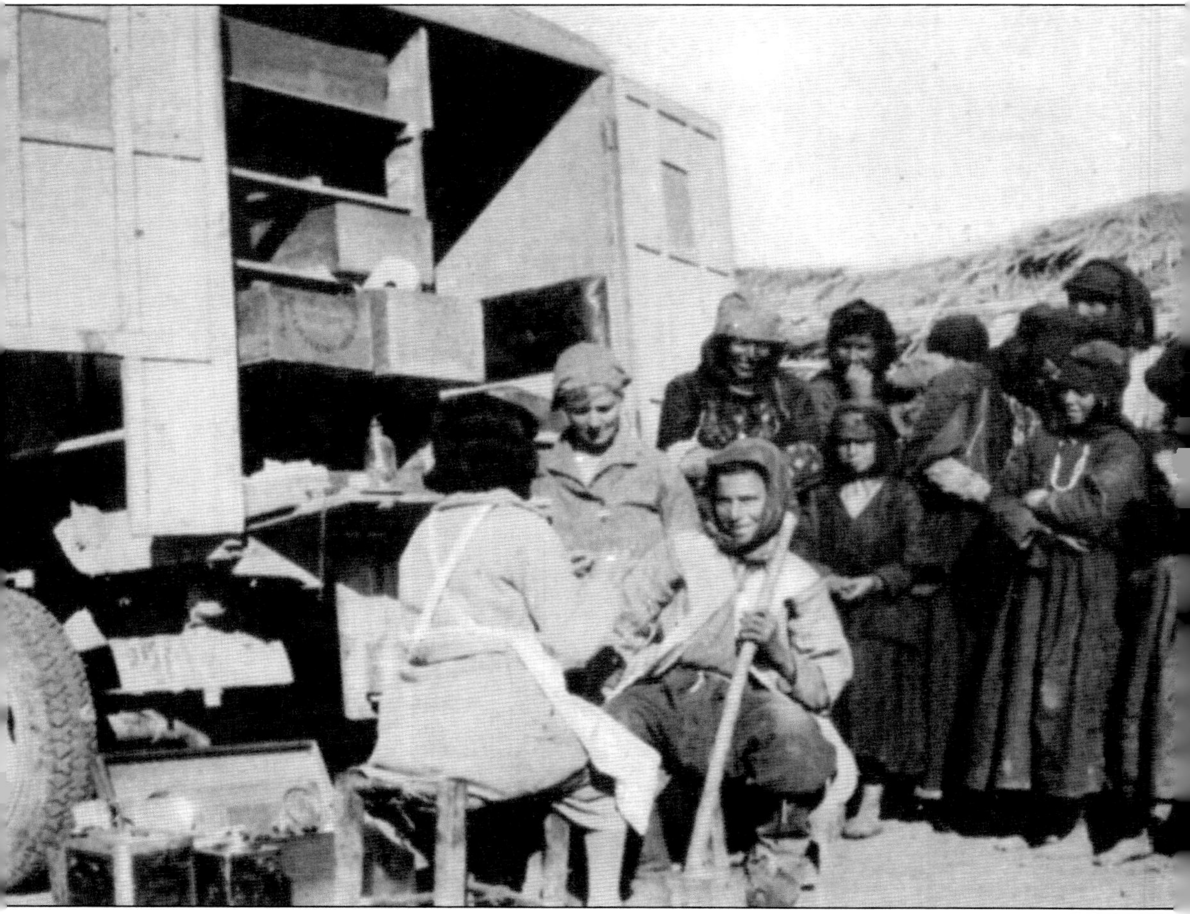

GYPSIES IN THE VALLEY. Gypsy bands, such as the one pictured here, were often seen in the Quincy Valley. Adults living today remember hearing stories about encounters between gypsies and residents of the Quincy Valley. Gypsy is a slang term used for the Romani people, a nomadic ethnic group with origins in the Punjab region of India. The Roma were often mistaken for Egyptians, hence the name "Gypsy." Many came to America from Serbia, Russia, and Austria-Hungary between 1880 AD and 1914 AD. Many early Quincy Valley settlers were also from Russia and Austria, as well as 20 other countries, so perhaps the Roma felt comfortable traveling through these communities. The Roma often used their skills as coppersmiths and handymen to make their living. An estimated one million Roma live in America today, including eastern Washington. (Courtesy of the Quincy Valley Historical Society.)

Five

Blossoming as a Rose

Water, or the lack of it, has always been the bane of life in the Quincy Valley. Early settlers got their water either from Willow Springs in the Beezley Hills northwest of town or from the Columbia River. Some carried it by the small barrelful, while others with horse and team hauled their own or contracted with others to do it for them. The first well was drilled by Fidd Cochran near the site of the present city hall. It came in at 198 feet. By 1904, some 12 wells had been drilled. Naturally the price of land rose, but more settlers came anyway.

Sometimes too much water was the problem. Periodic flooding would occur after large snowpacks were quickly melted off by a surprise chinook wind. A chinook wind is an out-of-season warm wind that melts everything it blows across. Downtown Quincy could only be navigated by boat when this would happen. Homesteaders would be stranded. In 1916, the flooding was so bad it undermined the railroad tracks, stranding three trains at Quincy for several days.

Drought was the other extreme. Many wells dried up in the years between 1908 and 1913. Many people moved away. The ground was so dry around one well that the wind eroded the soil around it, causing the casing to pull six feet out of the ground and topple the windmill over.

Wind is another natural resource in the Quincy Valley. Wind farms have sprouted on top of the hills to the west, providing power to the city of Seattle. Those who live here accept that wind will last in the spring until the snow is melted off the Colockum Ridge. Quincy residents know to batten down the hatches and hold on to their hats—it will blow again in the fall.

A band of government surveyors arrived in 1903, exploring and mapping the possibility of irrigation canals using water from the Columbia River. It was decided that it was not feasible to lift water from the river near Trinidad. Eventually water did come from the Columbia River, with the construction of the Grand Coulee Dam and the establishment of the Columbia Basin Irrigation Project. And so the people came, too.

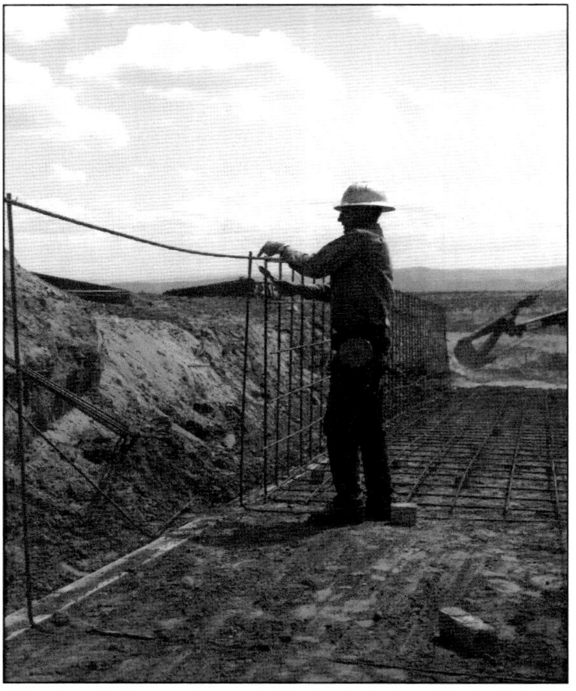

BUILDING THE CANAL SYSTEM. In 1908, a group of men formed the Quincy Valley Irrigation Association to petition the federal government to develop an irrigation project. Voters defeated a bond to fund the project locally in 1914. The federal project now maintains over 331 miles of main canals, 1,339 miles of smaller canals, and 3,500 miles of waste ways. (Courtesy of the *Quincy Valley Post-Register.*)

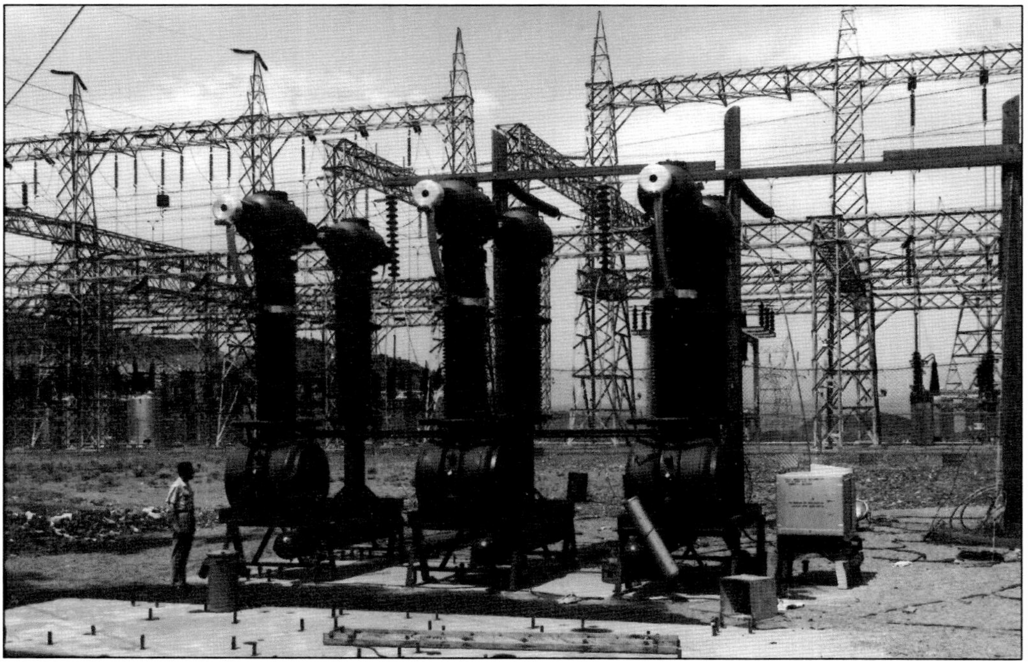

TURNING THE LIGHTS ON. Carbide gaslights provided by the Quincy Gas Company were the first form of artificial lighting available in the Quincy Valley. In 1907, the Quincy Power and Irrigation Company formed at Rock Island, but its attempts to harness hydropower failed. They were on the right track. Electricity is currently generated using the hydropower of both Rock Island and Wanapum Dams. (Courtesy of the *Quincy Valley Post-Register.*)

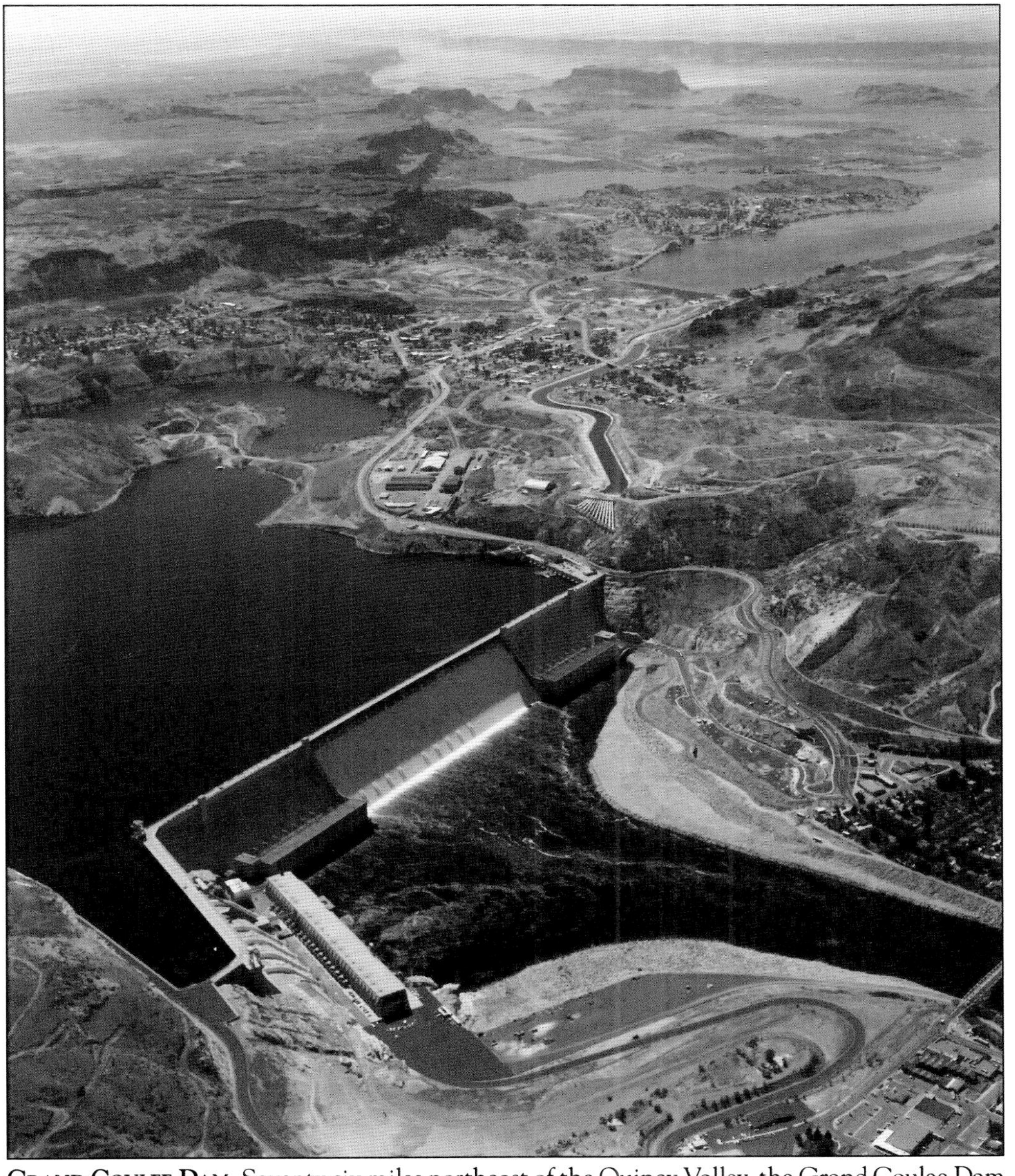

GRAND COULEE DAM. Seventy-six miles northeast of the Quincy Valley, the Grand Coulee Dam is the keystone of the Columbia Basin Irrigation Project, which annually produces $630 million in irrigated crops; $950 million in generated electricity; and $20 million in prevented flood damage, with over three million people participating in recreational activities each year. The dam also serves to control seasonal flooding. Surveyors arrived in 1903 to map the area for a proposed irrigation project. The dam was completed in 1922, and water began to flow into the canals in 1951. Irrigation opened up thousands of acres for cultivation, and a second great Quincy Valley migration began. Water issues had been the subject of discussions within the federal government since 1890. Until the problem was solved, water had to be hauled or raised from wells by windmills or gasoline generators. (Bureau of Reclamation photograph by H. S. Holmes; courtesy of the Quincy Valley Chamber of Commerce.)

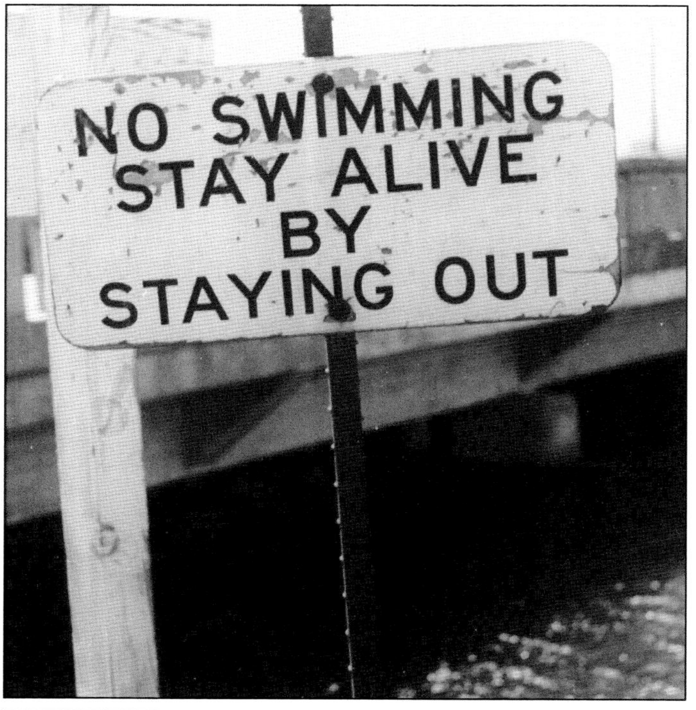

No Swimming Allowed. One of the dangers of flowing water is the possibility of drowning. The sign at left warns of the danger in 1967. Drownings have occurred but are relatively rare. The Winchester Waste Way section of the canal system remains a popular canoeing area. Below, water flows rapidly through a weir, or small dam, which controls the flow through the ditches in this 1966 picture. It is the job of the ditch rider to make sure the sluice gate is opened and closed to control the flow of water. The one pictured here is operated by hand. (Both images courtesy of the *Quincy Valley Post-Register.*)

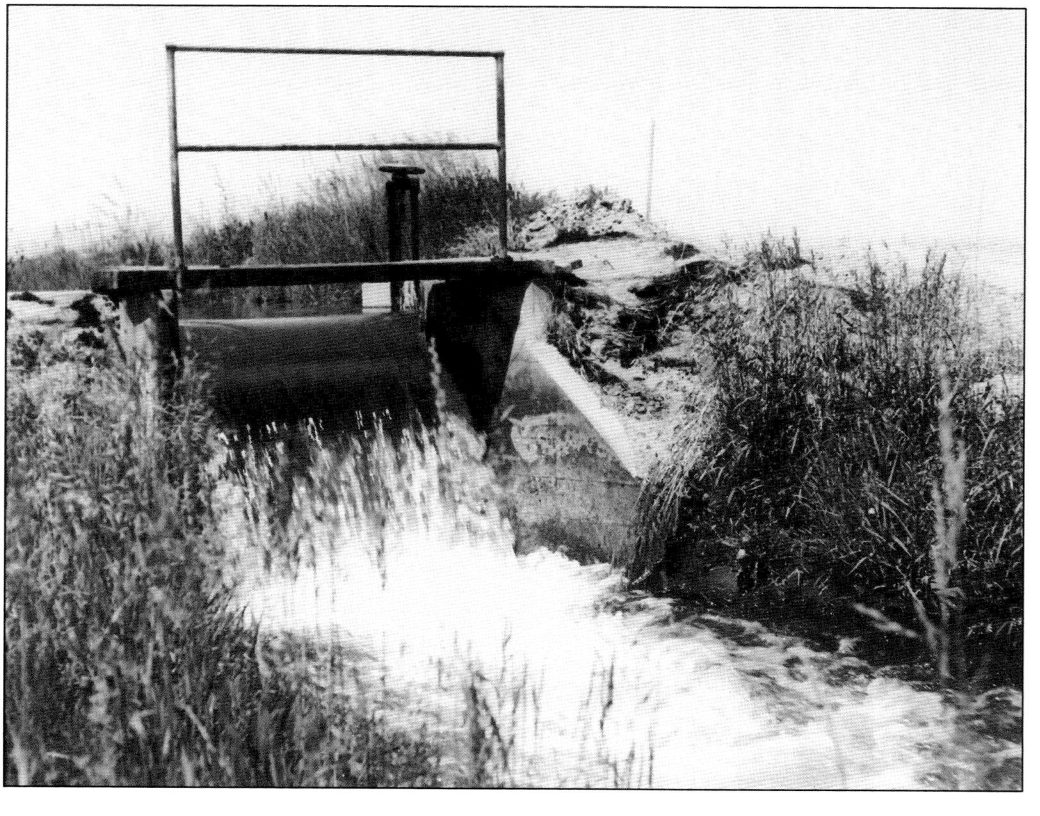

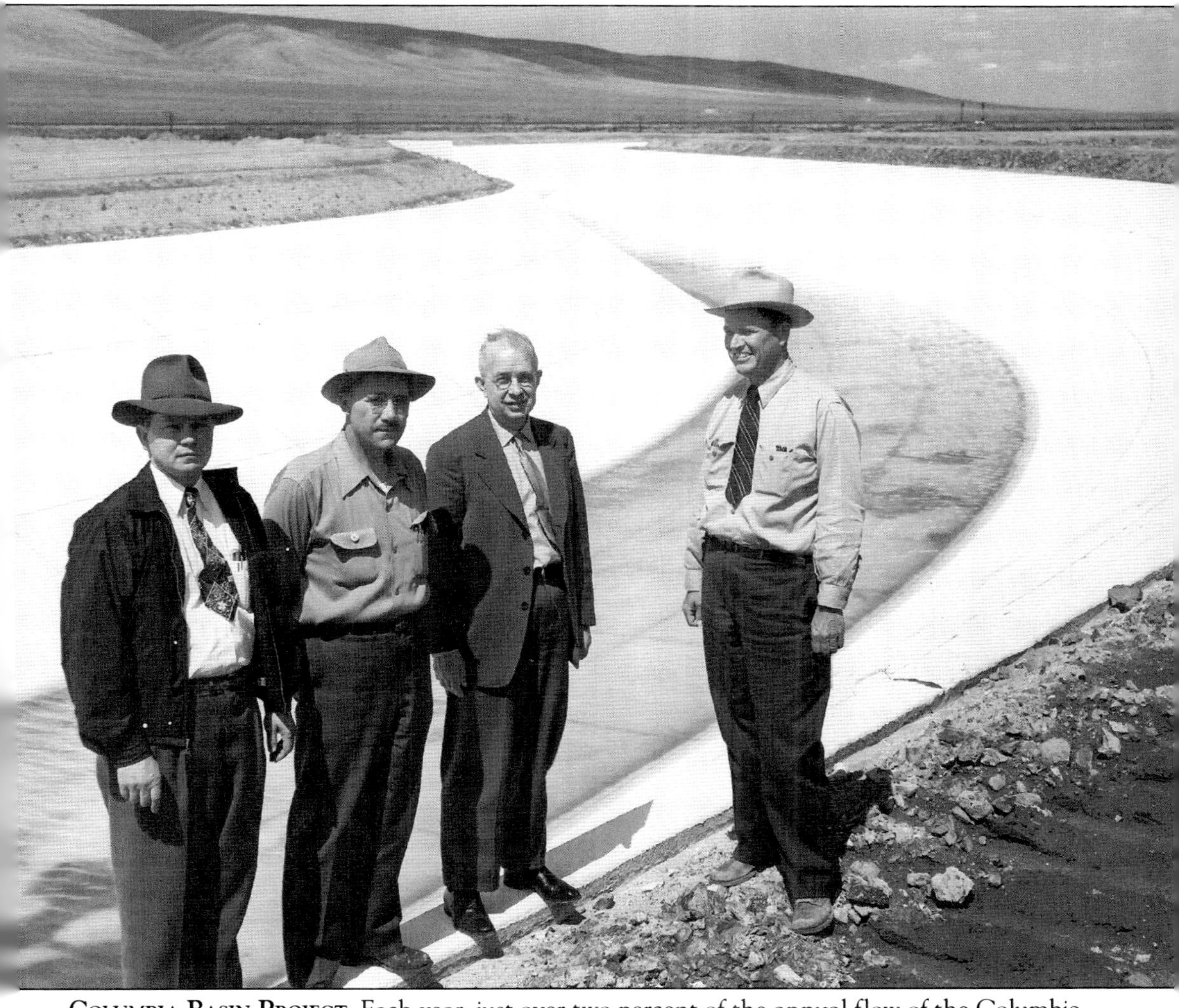

Columbia Basin Project. Each year, just over two percent of the annual flow of the Columbia River is diverted from Lake Roosevelt, behind Grand Coulee Dam, and pumped uphill into a 27-mile-long reservoir known as Banks Lake. Using gravity, water flows down into the Columbia Basin through a series of canals, reservoirs, and waste ways. The Quincy Valley receives its share from the West Canal. Irrigation water from the northern end of the project is collected through the drainage and waste ways system into the Potholes Reservoir and rerouted into the southern portion of the system so that the water is used twice. Of the 2.5 million acre-feet of water that enters the canals each year, approximately 1 million are recycled in this manner. From left to right, Vaughn Downs, Marvin J. Hawkins, an official from Washington, D.C., and Phil Noble stand by a completed West Canal, which is receiving its first water from the Columbia River Irrigation Project. (Bureau of Reclamation photograph; courtesy of the Quincy Valley Historical Society.)

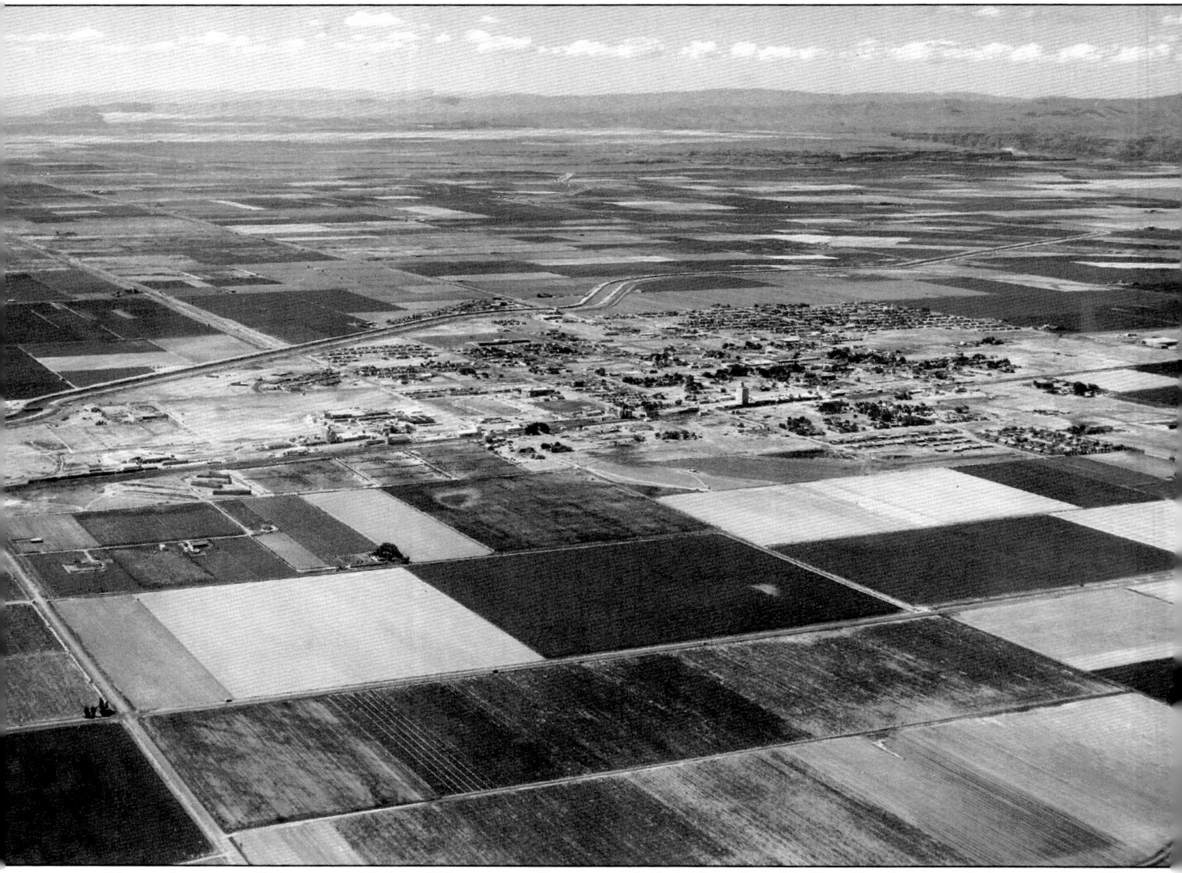

The Quincy Valley, 1957. This aerial view of the Quincy Valley looks southwest towards Ancient Lakes and the Columbia River. In the five years since irrigation began, the desert can be seen blossoming as a rose. The number of acres under cultivation has increased, as has the variety of crops grown. Gone are the endless miles of sagebrush and bunchgrass desert. In its place are many acres of crops, which feed not only the United States but people throughout the world. Today over $2 billion worth of crops are grown here, including alfalfa, apples, apricots, blueberries, corn, wheat, wine grapes, mint, potatoes, and many others. (Courtesy of the Quincy Valley Historical Society.)

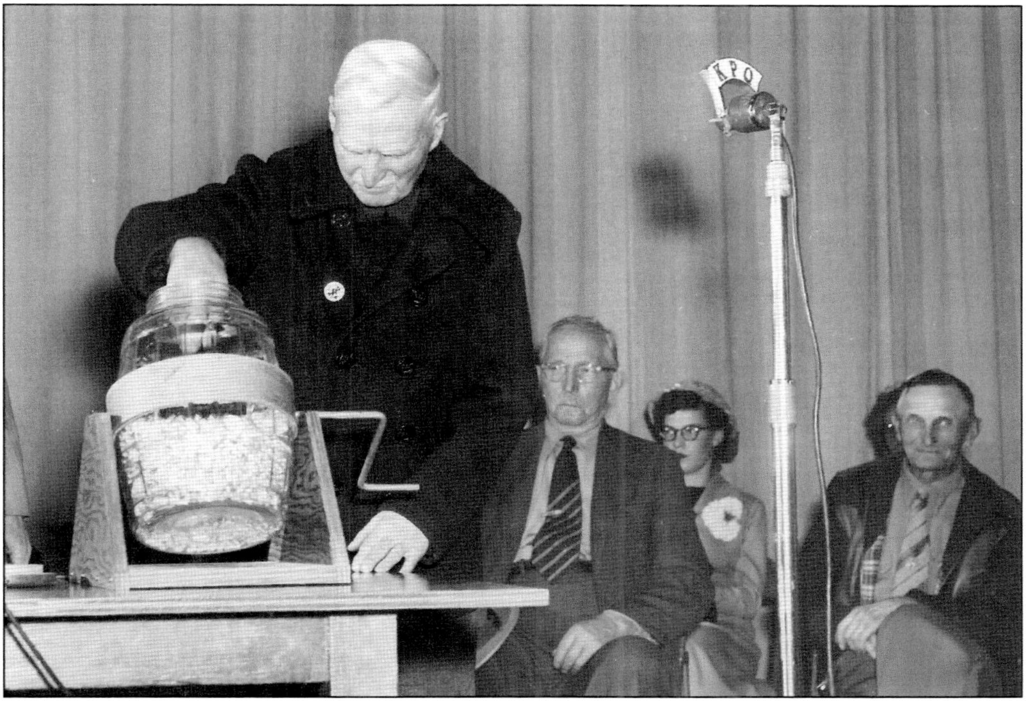

VETERANS' LAND LOTTERY. Land was distributed to World War II veterans by a lottery between November 15, 1948, and 1967. Veterans were eligible after submitting an application proving farming experience, physical and mental fitness, good character, and a net worth of $3,700. The first veteran number in Quincy is drawn by William Conlan, with Conrad Weber, an unidentified woman, and William Schorzman (right) looking on. All were early settlers of the valley. (Courtesy of the Quincy Valley Historical Society.)

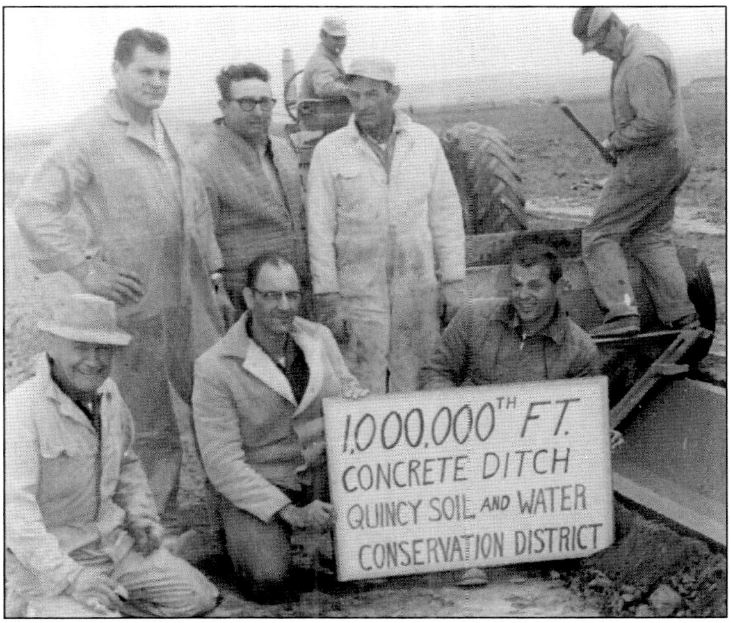

ONE MILLION DITCH FEET. In 1968, the Quincy Soil and Conservation District reached a milestone of one million feet of concrete ditch completed and ready for use. Ditches are used to feed the water from the West Canal along the edge of a farmer's field so he can draw his allotment of water. (Courtesy of the *Quincy Valley Post-Register*.)

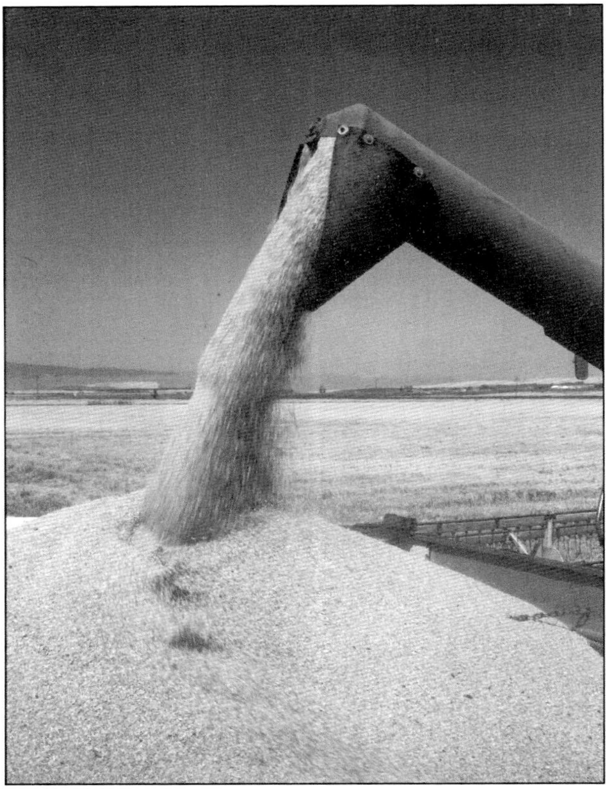

Modern Wheat Harvesting. The picture to the left shows wheat flowing into great heaps of golden grain from which the world is fed. Beginning in the 1930s and 1940s, self-propelled combines (such as the New Holland TR95 shown below) began to replace horse-powered threshing machines. One farmer could now adjust the height of the cutter, control the direction of the combine, and dispose of the grain alone, eliminating the need of work crews and horse teams. Many farm animals were sold at auction, and men had to seek employment elsewhere, or begin their own farms. An easier harvest did not diminish the need for water, however, and farmers continued to push for irrigation. (Both images courtesy of the Quincy Valley Chamber of Commerce.)

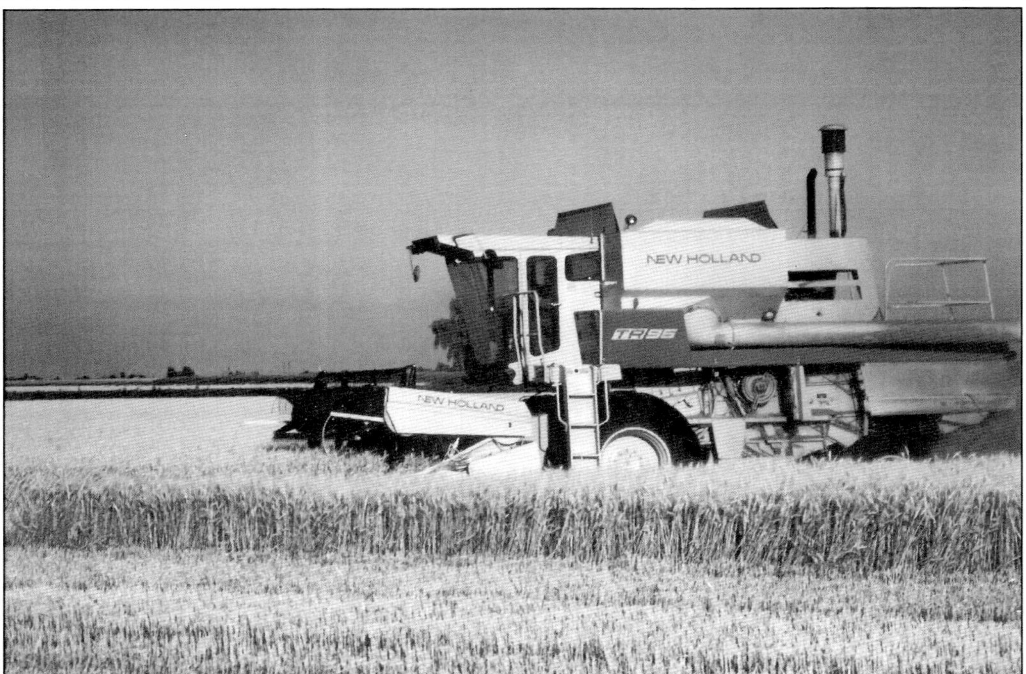

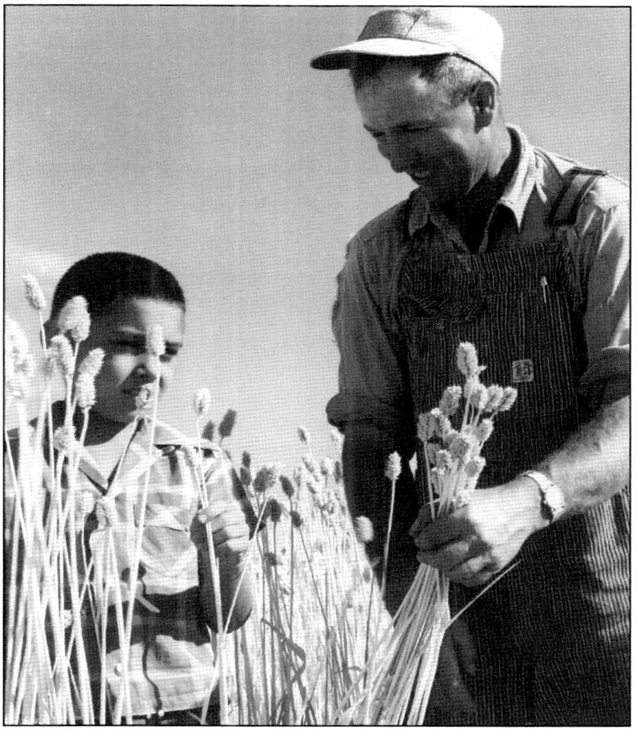

Training the Next Generation, 1966. William Grigg passes on his knowledge of wheat farming to his son Phillip. This picture symbolizes the family farm where one generation mentors the next generation in the mysteries of producing food for survival and profit. This scene is as timeless as the wheat they are inspecting. (Courtesy of *Quincy Valley Post-Register.*)

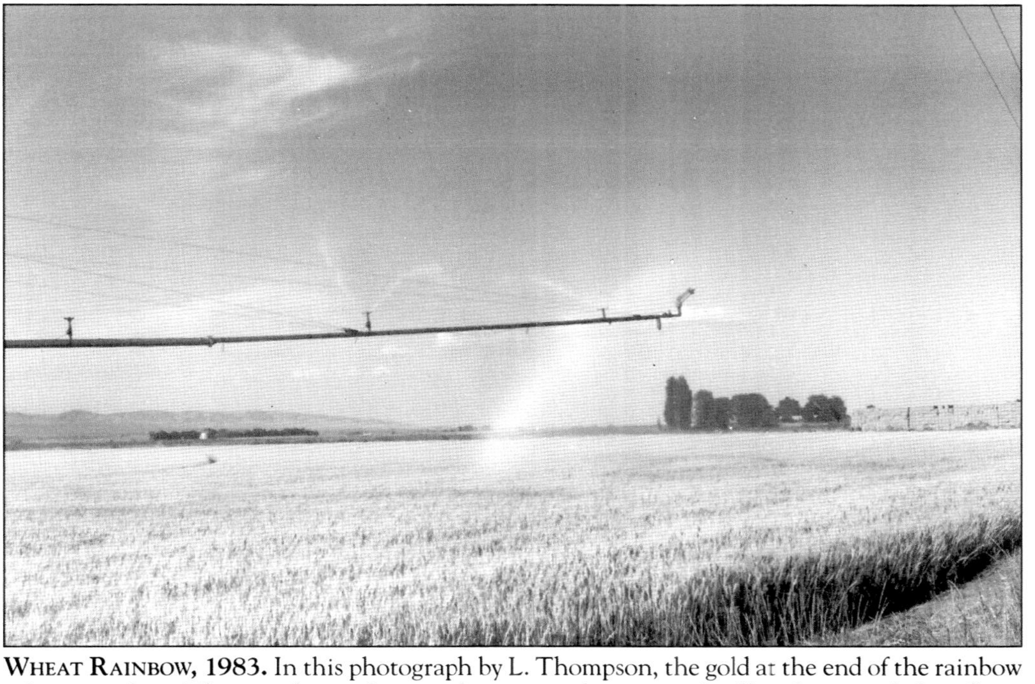

Wheat Rainbow, 1983. In this photograph by L. Thompson, the gold at the end of the rainbow is luscious wheat. The casual passerby can often see rainbows on a cloudless day as sunlight reflects off water droplets sprayed from irrigation systems. (Courtesy of the Quincy Valley Chamber of Commerce.)

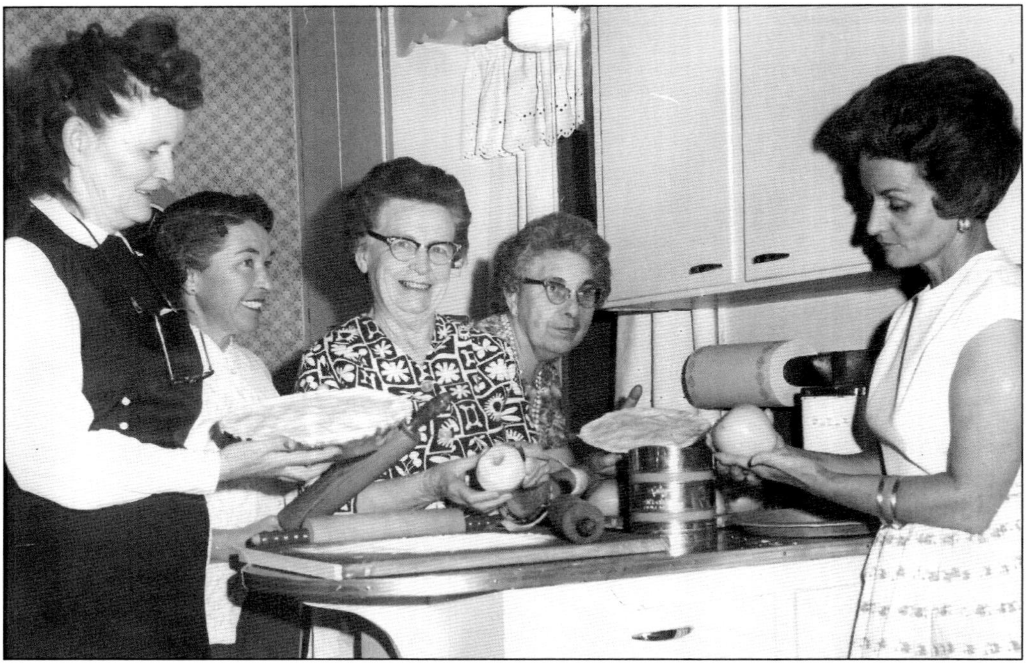

Baking Apple Pie, 1966. The scent of apples baking with cinnamon and sugar is a hallmark of fall harvest. Above, the ladies of the Quincy Democratic Club have gathered to bake pies for the annual Candidate Testimonial Dinner. From left to right are Mary Weber, Clare Larson, Irene Bepple, Ann Rau, and Allyne Gile at work on the 50 pies they have committed to bake. Below, local girl Cynthia Scott showcases a beautiful crop of apples. The most common varieties grown in Washington are Red Delicious, Golden Delicious, Gala, Fuji, Granny Smith, Braeburn, Honeycrisp, Cripp's Pink, and Cameo, with Red Delicious accounting for 30 percent of the total crop. (Above, courtesy of the Quincy Valley Post Register; below, Public Utility District of Grant County photograph, courtesy of the Quincy Valley Chamber of Commerce.)

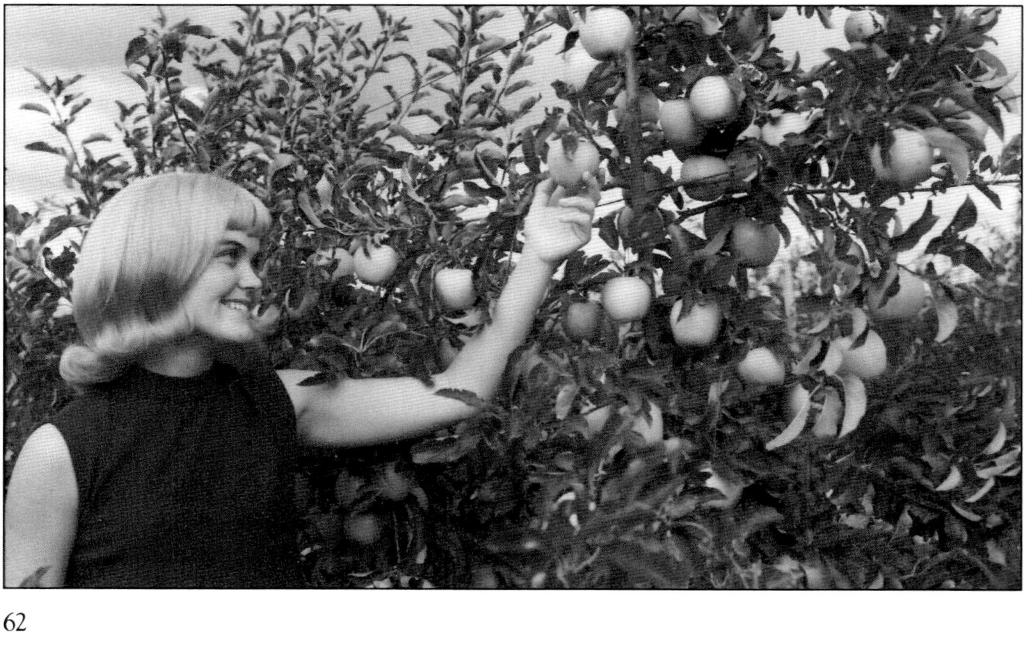

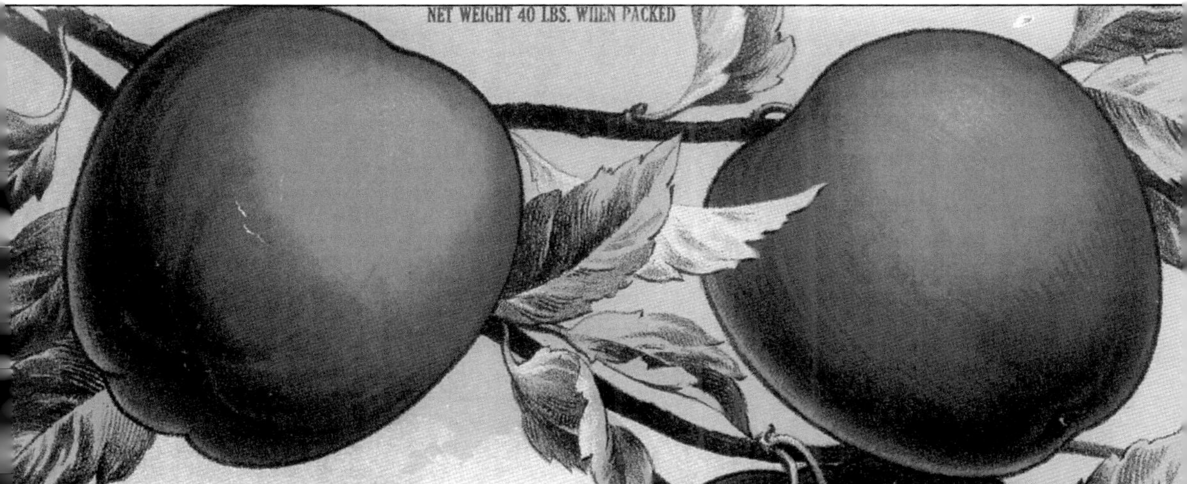

WENATCHEE-QUINCY ORCHARD. Fred B. Keigley was the first to try his hand at apple growing in the Quincy Valley, planting 50 acres. Balthasar Hieb was second, with an orchard of 15 acres. Soon the Wenatchee Apple Land company formed in 1911. By 1914, they had 520 acres in apple trees and boasted of the largest pumping plant in the Pacific Northwest. Bankruptcy struck in 1918. This did not end apple production in the Quincy Valley, however. The Apple Lane Orchard owned by Charles Simpson produced a record crop of 158,130 boxes of apples from his 157 acres of trees in 1930. Apple harvesting would be a boost to the local economy, both in terms of bringing dollars to the area and also in providing seasonal employment opportunities. Currently workers in the state of Washington pick 10 to 12 billion apples each year. (Courtesy of the Quincy Valley Historical Society.)

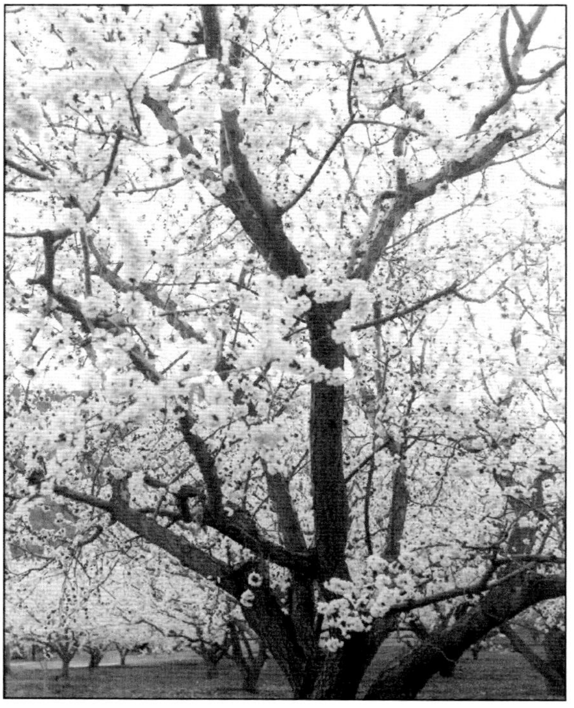

Quincy Valley Cherries, 1966. The state of Washington produces the most sweet cherries in the nation and is the fourth largest producer of tart cherries. The Quincy Valley town of George, Washington, named its streets after different varieties of cherries, such as the Montmorency and the Bing. (Courtesy of the *Quincy Valley Post-Register.*)

The Guy Willard Orchard, 1960. This Quincy Valley orchard uses an environmentally friendly method of controlling weeds by interplanting the trees with alfalfa grown for seed. The concrete-lined head ditch with siphon tubes helps to conserve precious water by controlling the amount of water used and minimizing seepage. (Courtesy of the *Quincy Valley Post-Register.*)

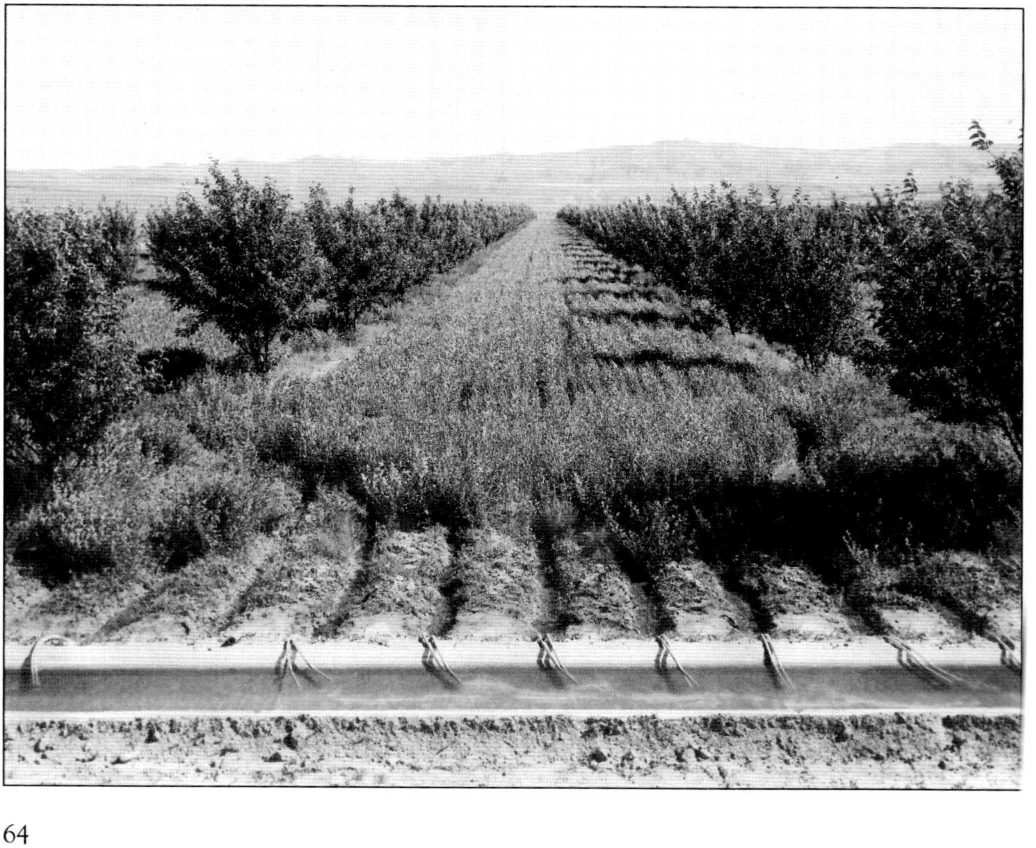

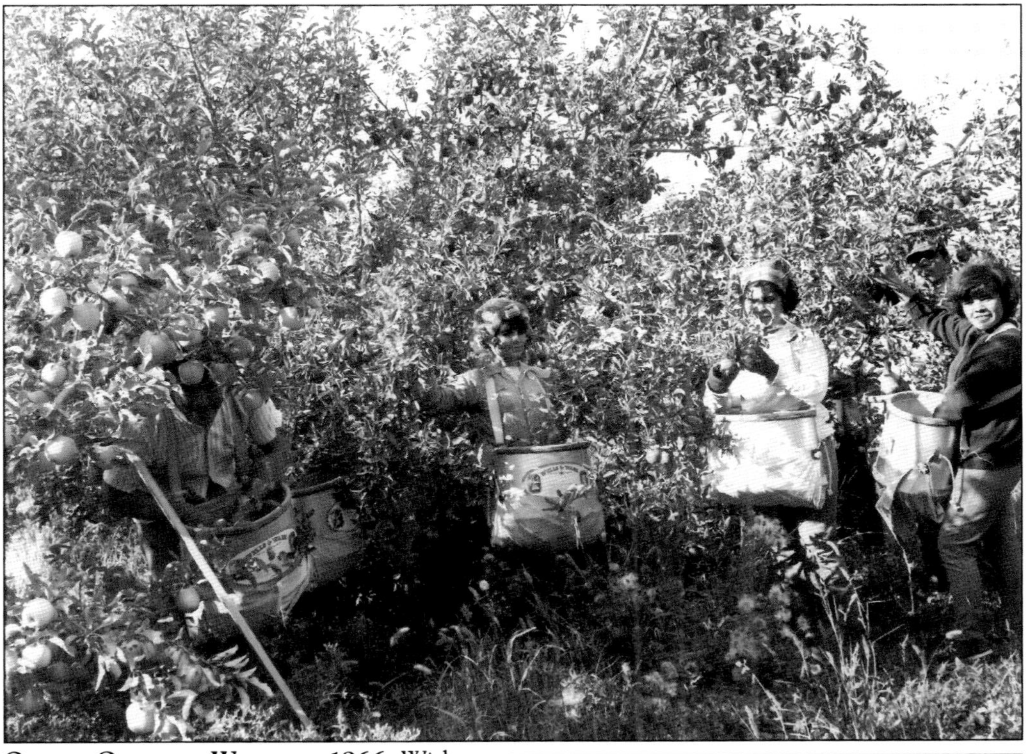

QUINCY ORCHARD WORKERS, 1966. With the coming of irrigation and the increase in agricultural production, there arose a labor shortage. Independent labor contractors recruited Mexicans and Mexican Americans to till the crops and work the harvest in the Pacific Northwest. The U.S. government also entered into an agreement with the Mexican government to provide contract workers, known as *braceros*. The Quincy Valley saw its first Mexican fiesta in 1957. Above, young Hispanic women are harvesting apples. One has curlers in her hair, perhaps in anticipation of a date that evening. At right, a woman harvests grapes. (Above, courtesy of the *Quincy Valley Post-Register*; right, courtesy of the Quincy Valley Chamber of Commerce.)

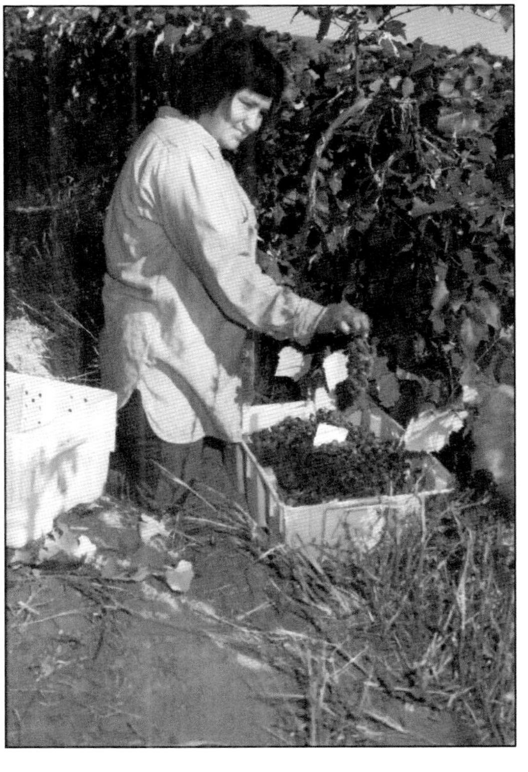

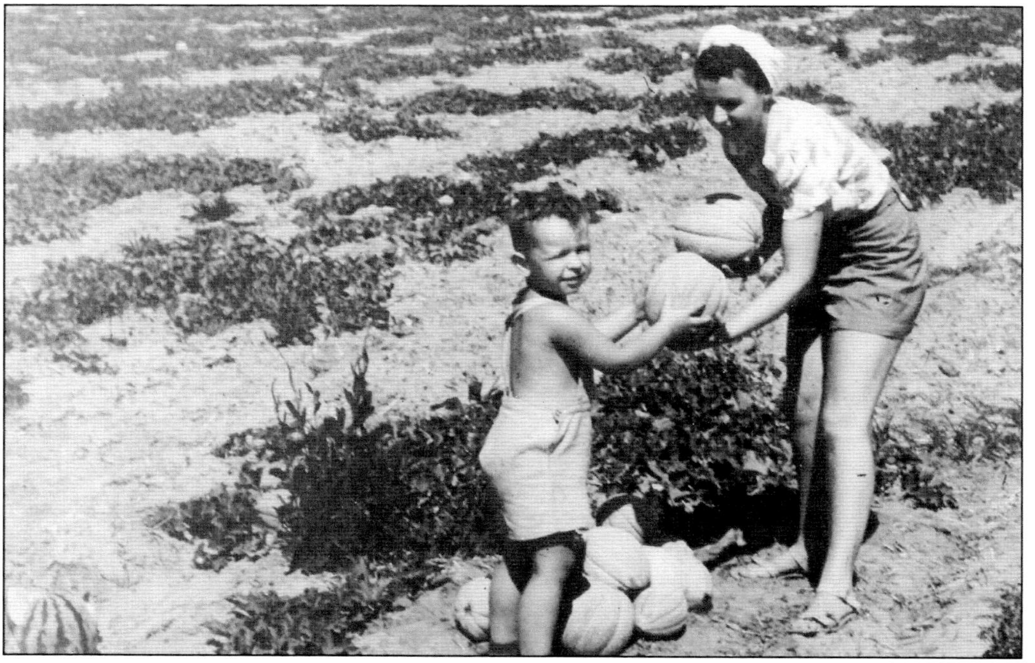

HARVESTING MELONS, C. 1965. Janice Gibson and Dale Gibson Jr. harvest melons in the summer heat. Watermelons were a favorite of early Quincy settler Louie Mullerheile, known as "the Watermelon King," as well as the coyotes who regularly visited his patch. Teenagers often went on moonlight safaris to "borrow" a melon or two for a party. (Courtesy of the Quincy Valley Historical Society.)

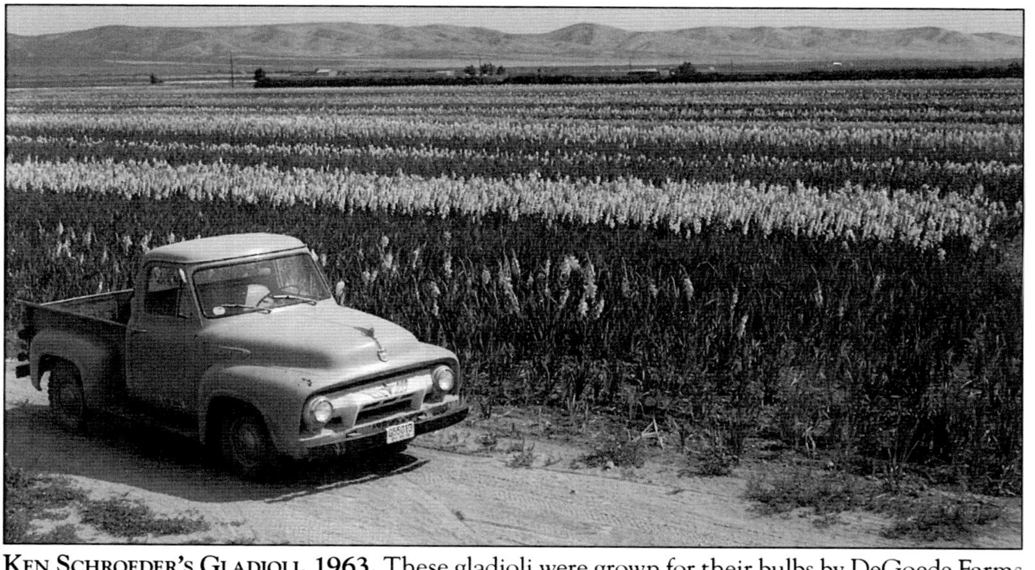

KEN SCHROEDER'S GLADIOLI, 1963. These gladioli were grown for their bulbs by DeGoede Farms based in Mount Vernon, Washington. Quincy Valley farmer Ken Schroeder was first approached by his friend Henry (Hank) DeGoede in 1955, and a partnership was born. Along the far edge of the field a multiflora rose hedge was planted as cover for upland birds. (Ken Schroeder photograph; courtesy of the Quincy Valley Historical Society.)

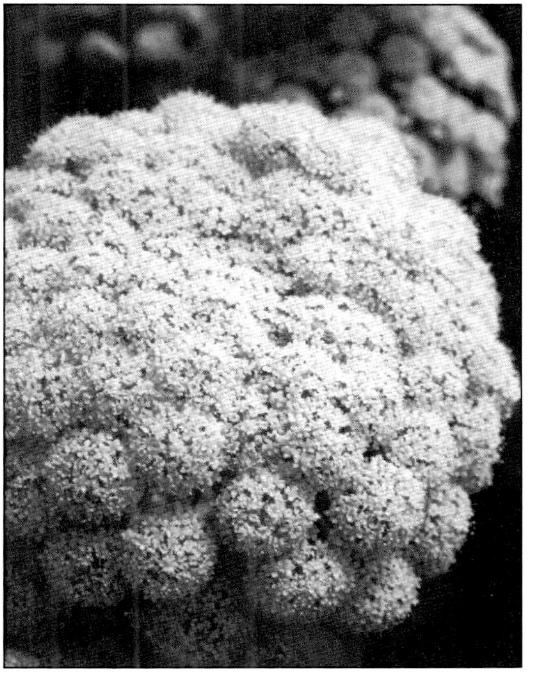

Seed Crops. The Quincy Valley has the ideal combination of weather and soil conditions for growing seed crops. Radish seed is thought to be the first type of small vegetable seed raised in the valley, beginning in 1953. The picture below shows Roger Hughes and Zene Flinn inspecting radish seed on the Ker Farm in 1967. Fifty percent of the world's small vegetable seeds are grown in Washington. In early June, many acres of beautiful flowering seed crops, like the carrots pictured to the right, can be seen blanketing the valley floor. (Right, courtesy of the Quincy Valley Chamber of Commerce; below, courtesy of the *Quincy Valley Post-Register.*)

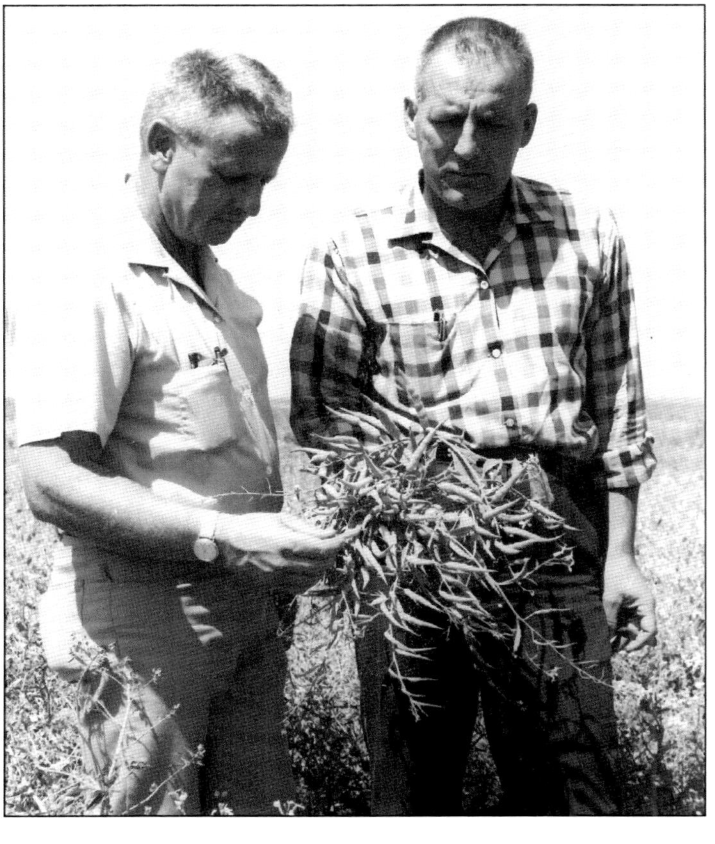

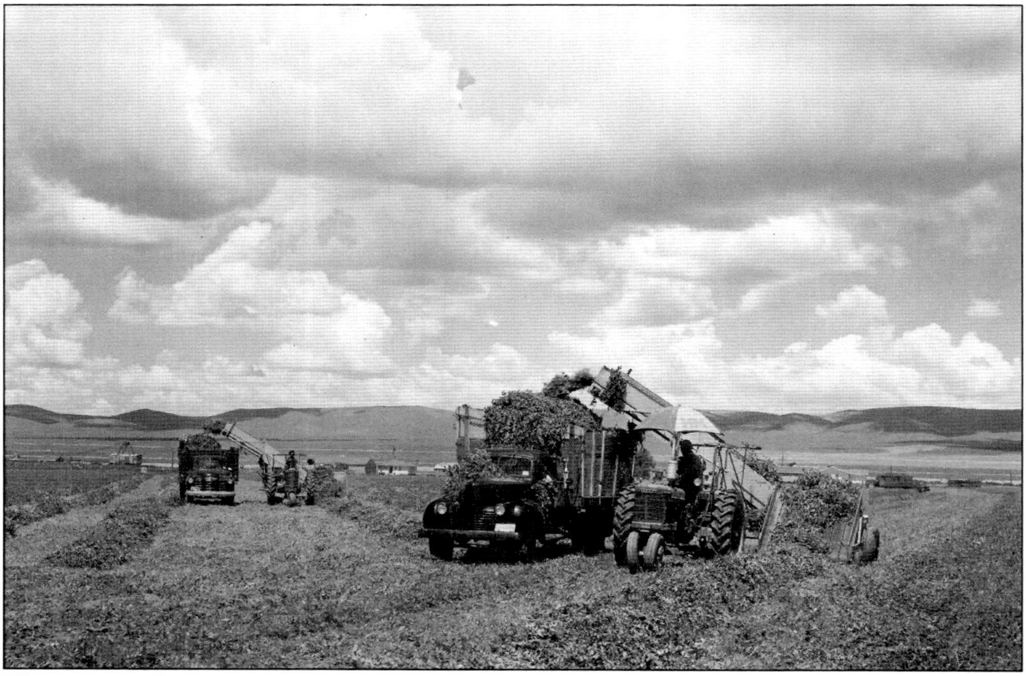

Winchester Pea Harvest, 1952. Loaders pick up windrowed pea vines near Winchester, a community east of Quincy. Peas grown for seed yielded about 2,800 pounds per acre, while fresh peas yielded about 4,000 pounds per acre in the Quincy Valley. Grant County now produces about 435,000 pounds per year. (Courtesy of the Quincy Valley Historical Society.)

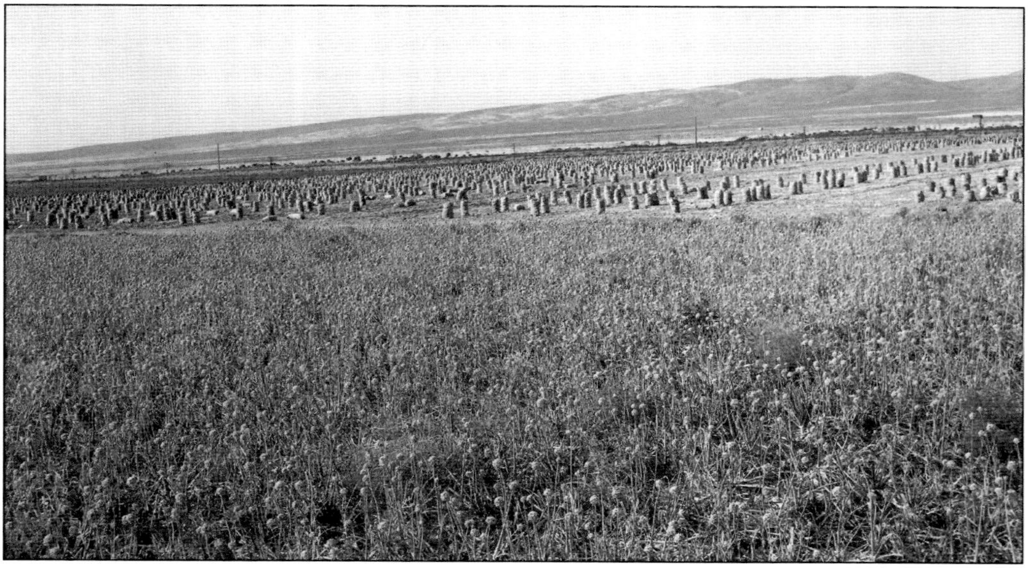

Onion Field, 1953. Onions grown for seed are seen in the foreground of this picture taken two years after water began flowing through the canals. Yields were about 20 tons per acre. In the background, harvested onions stand sacked and ready for sorting and re-sacking for market. Onions were considered a speculative crop, with prices widely fluctuating year to year. (Courtesy of the Quincy Valley Historical Society.)

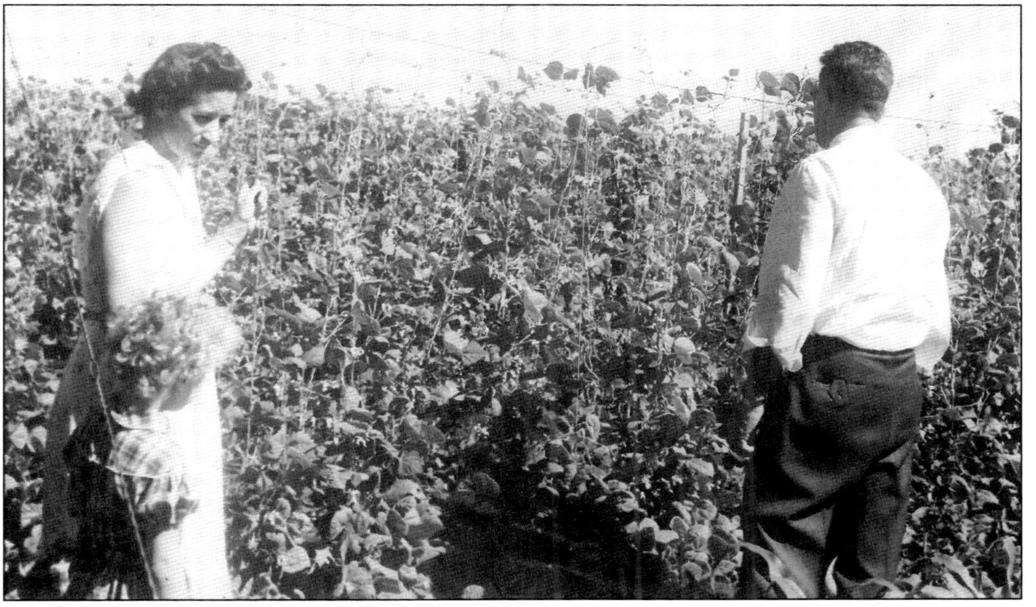

Growing Beans, 1955. Bonnie Ker and Chuck Haraugh examine a field of green beans while one of Bonnie's daughters looks on. Fresh green beans and dry beans such as Mexican reds, pintos, and great northern varieties became an important cash crop. The Ker family continues to farm in the Quincy Valley. (Courtesy of the Quincy Valley Historical Society.)

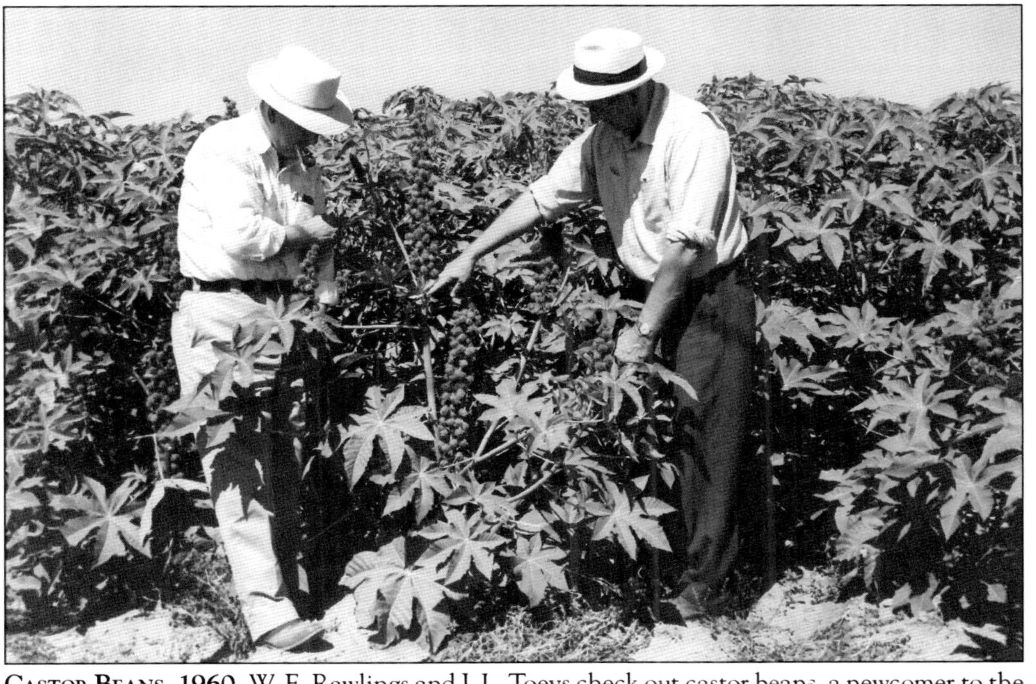

Castor Beans, 1960. W. E. Rawlings and J. L. Toevs check out castor beans, a newcomer to the Quincy Valley's list of crops. Although castor beans contain ricin and are considered poisonous, they have been used as cattle and swine feed and in nylon, motor oils, and medicines. (Courtesy of the *Quincy Valley Post-Register*.)

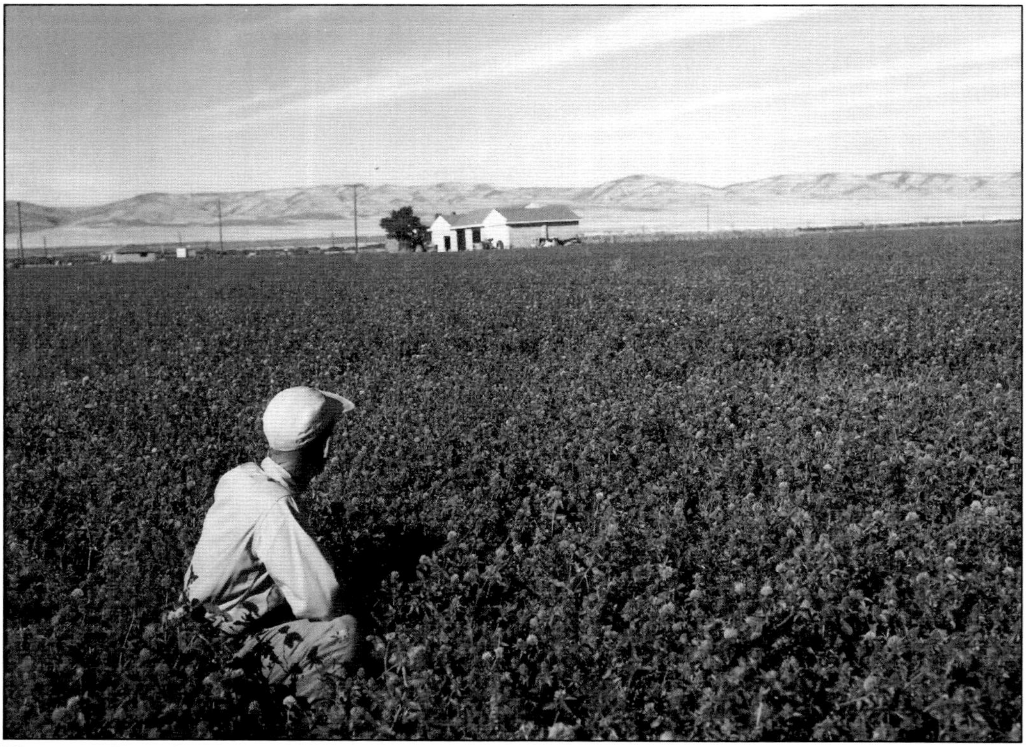

KENLAND RED CLOVER, 1952. This man takes in a beautiful field of Kenland red clover one year after irrigation began in the Quincy Valley. Red clover is a legume used for pasture and hay. It is also used as green cover crop because it helps maintain the fertility of the soil. (Courtesy of the Quincy Valley Historical Society.)

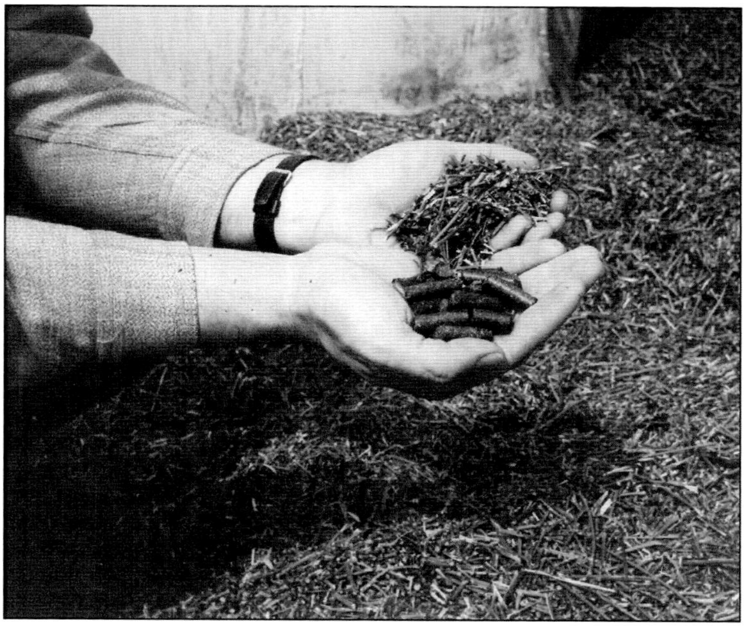

ALFALFA PELLETS, 1960. Neiderost Dehydrating Company between Quincy and George made alfalfa pellets for animal feed from chopped alfalfa hay. The mill capacity was 48 tons of finished pellets in a 24-hour day. Alfalfa continues to be grown in the Quincy Valley. (Bureau of Reclamation photograph by Gene Hertzog; courtesy of the *Quincy Valley Post-Register.*)

THE BEEKEEPER'S ART, 1965. Bees are essential to farmers and orchardists. Most plants and trees must be cross-pollinated in order to produce fruit. This beekeeper is using a Langstroth hive, which has movable frames for easy honey extraction and inspection of the hive. (Bureau of Reclamation photograph; courtesy of the *Quincy Valley Post-Register.*)

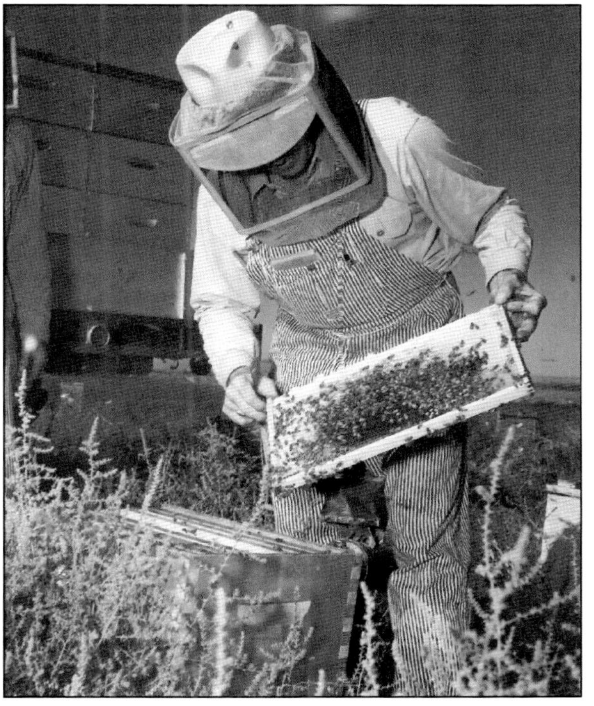

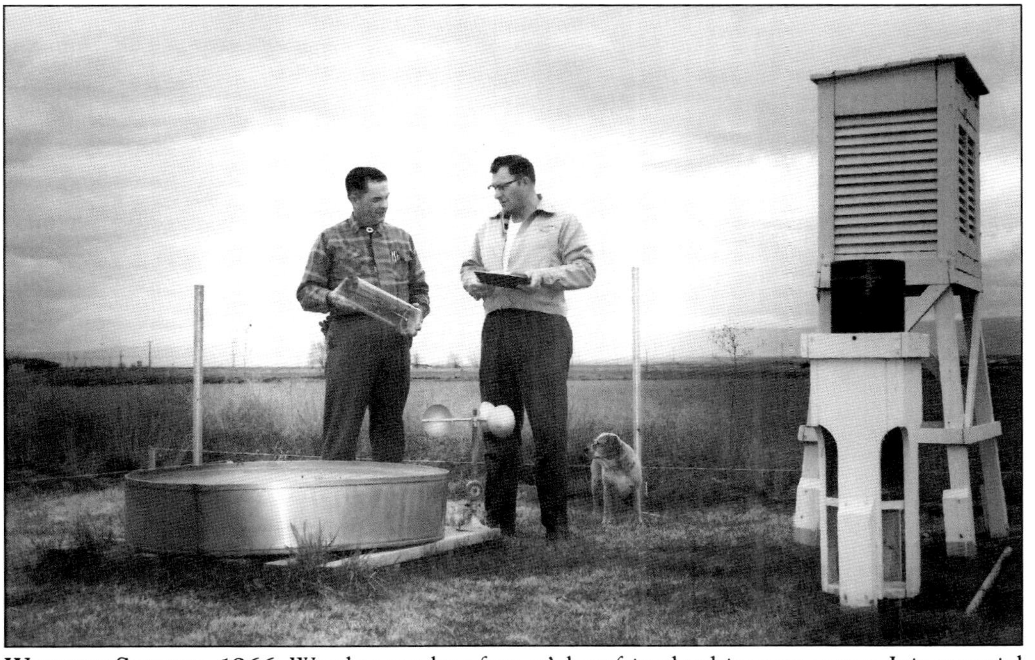

WEATHER STATION, 1966. Weather can be a farmer's best friend or his worst enemy. It is essential to be able to predict an early or late frost or foresee drought conditions so that crop losses can be minimized by preparation. This station is a typical station that could be found in various locations in the Quincy Valley. (Bureau of Reclamation photograph; courtesy of the *Quincy Valley Post-Register.*)

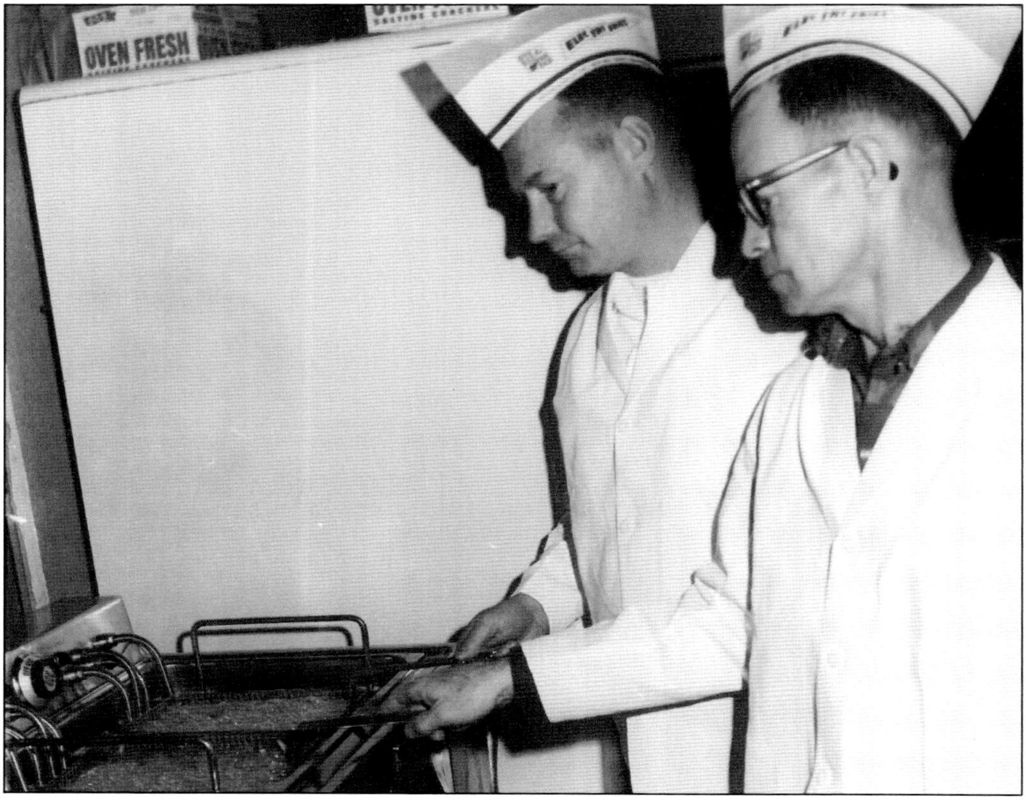

LAMB-WESTON PROCESSING PLANT, 1965. Erroll Brown and Percy Kelly established the first french fry plant in the Quincy Valley. F. Gilbert Lamb purchased it a year later in 1966. A new plant was added in 1972. Expansion of both size and product offerings continued when ConAgra took over in the late 1990s. ConAgra remains one of the largest employers in Quincy. In 2007, Grant County led the state and the world in having the largest yield of potatoes per acre. The picture above shows Quincy Valley resident Delmar Read (right) and a coworker test-frying french fries, checking for taste, appearance, and food safety. Below is a ramp of freshly washed potatoes in line for processing. (Both images courtesy of the *Quincy Valley Post-Register.*)

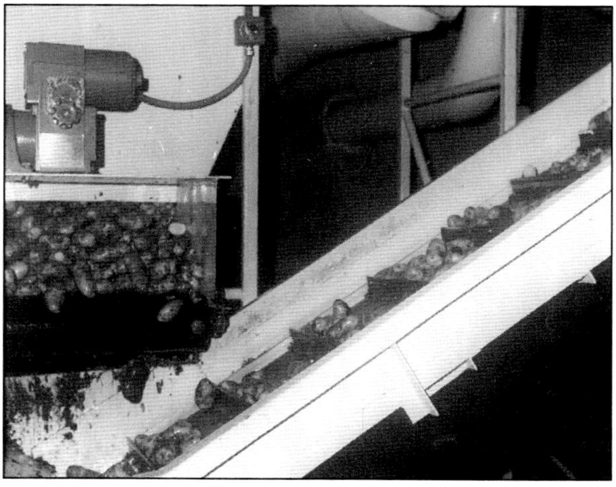

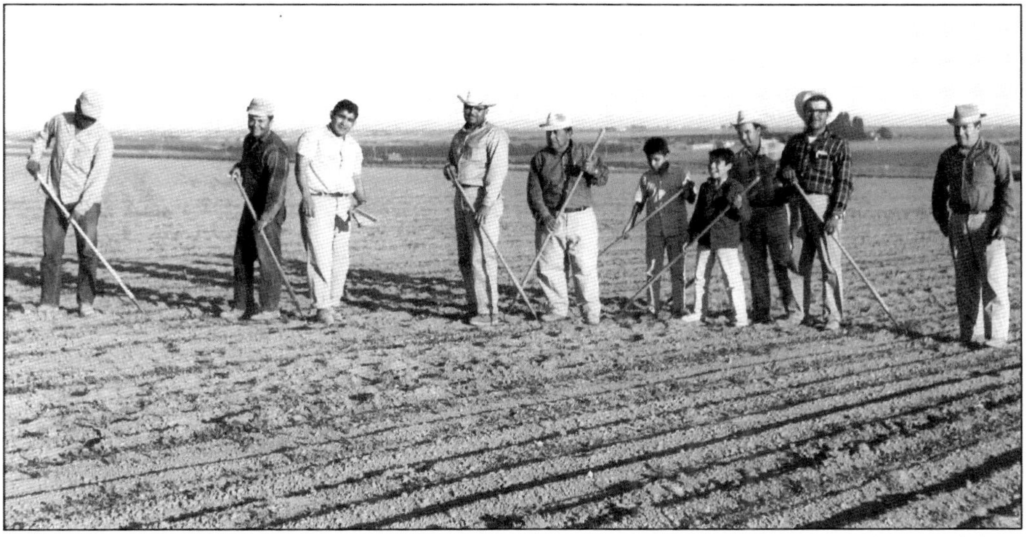

Sugar Beet Farming. When the Utah-Idaho Sugar Company (known as U and I) opened their Moses Lake facility (below) on October 23, 1953, it was the largest sugar beet processing plant in the United States. By the time the picture below was taken in 1967, over 800 farmers were cultivating 33,000 acres yielding 800,000 tons of sugar beets, including those from the Quincy Valley. The farmworkers seen above are "blocking," or thinning, sugar beets in May 1965. Many Hispanic families came to the Quincy Valley during this time, set down roots, and have been woven into the diverse fabric of the community. (Both images courtesy of the *Quincy Valley Post-Register.*)

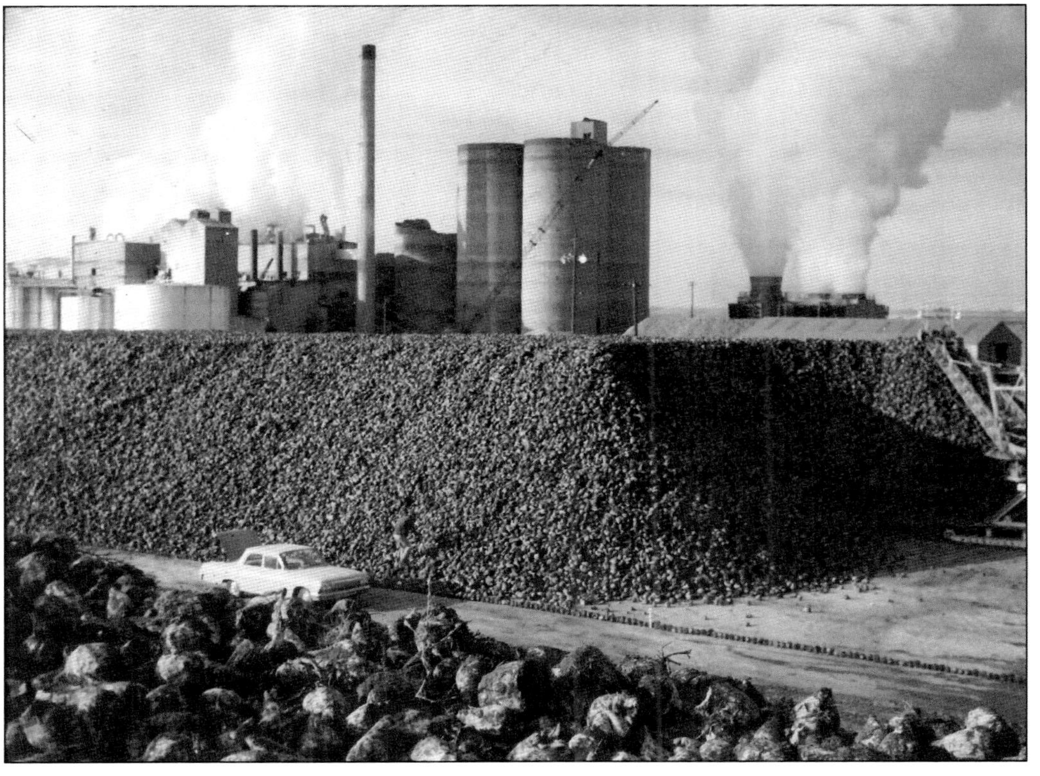

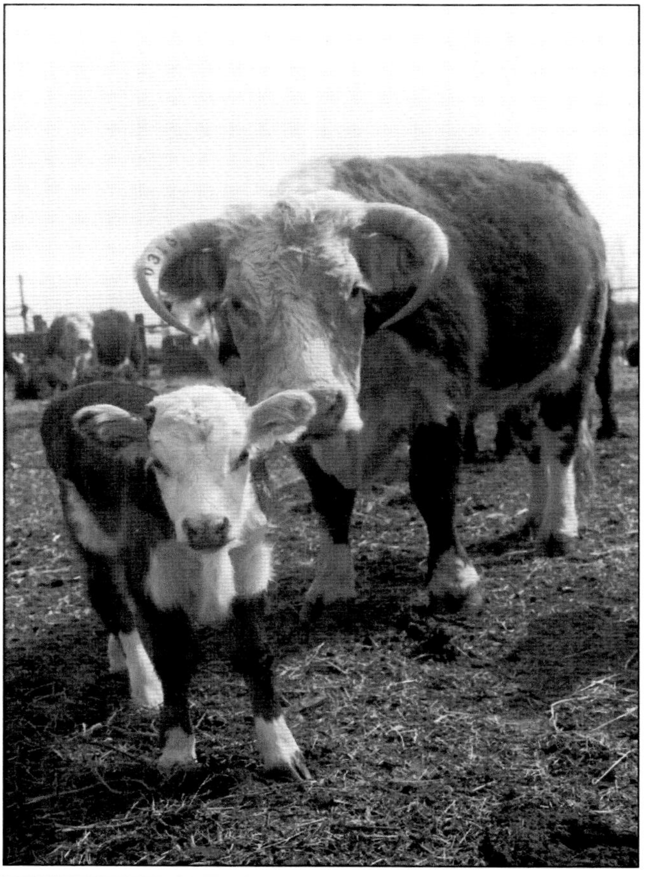

Hereford Beef Cattle, 1966. Beef cattle arrived in the Quincy Valley before most settlers. Thomas S. Blythe had the largest herd of the cattle owners in the area. Herefords originated in Herefordshire, England, and now dominate the world market in beef cattle. (Bureau of Reclamation photograph by Ron York; courtesy of the *Quincy Valley Post-Register.*)

Jerseys and Holsteins, 1952. Dairy cattle also arrived early, as the settlers had need of milk and cheese. Irrigation water made pasture and hay more abundant, increasing herd sizes and milk production. In 2007, Grant County had 16,500 head of milk cattle, with numbers declining. (Courtesy of the *Quincy Valley Post-Register.*)

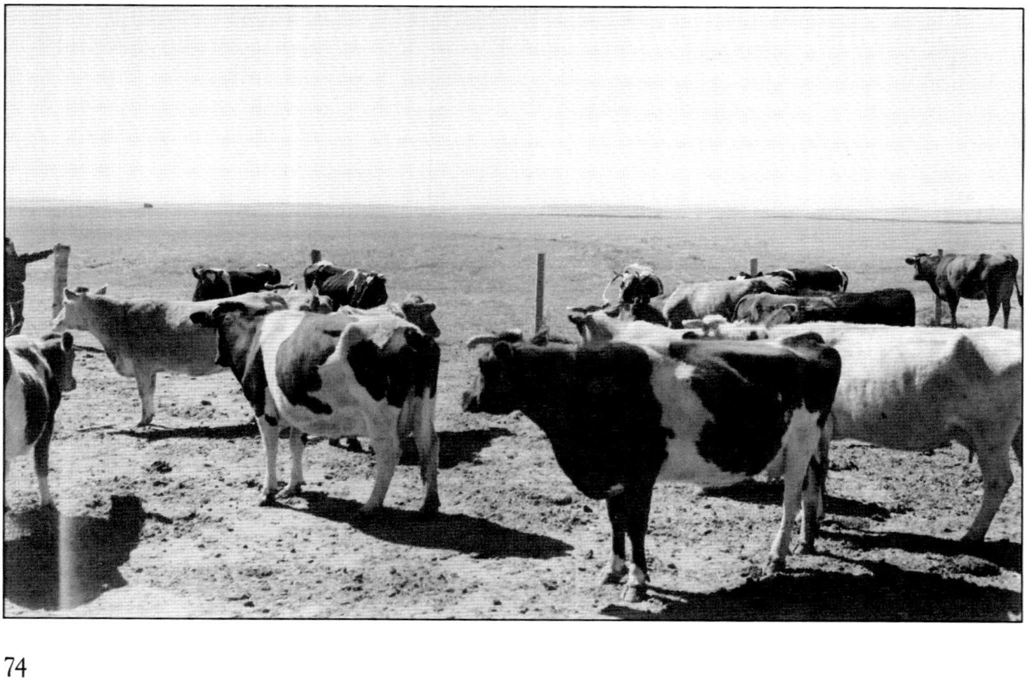

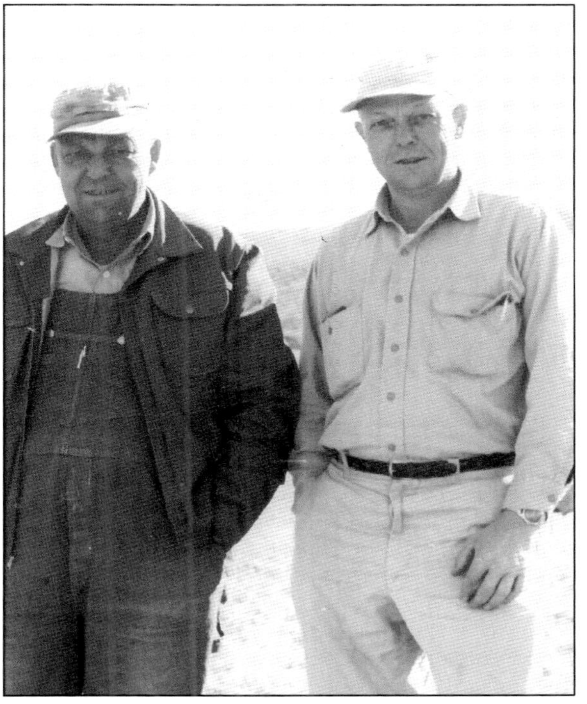

CATTLEMAN OF THE YEAR. In May 1966, the Grant County Cattlemen's Association chose brothers Ivan and Clarence Overen to share their Cattleman of the Year award. Ivan (left) and Clarence, sons of Ole and Agnes Larson Overen, were born on the family homestead about 12 miles north of Quincy. (Courtesy of the *Quincy Valley Post-Register*.)

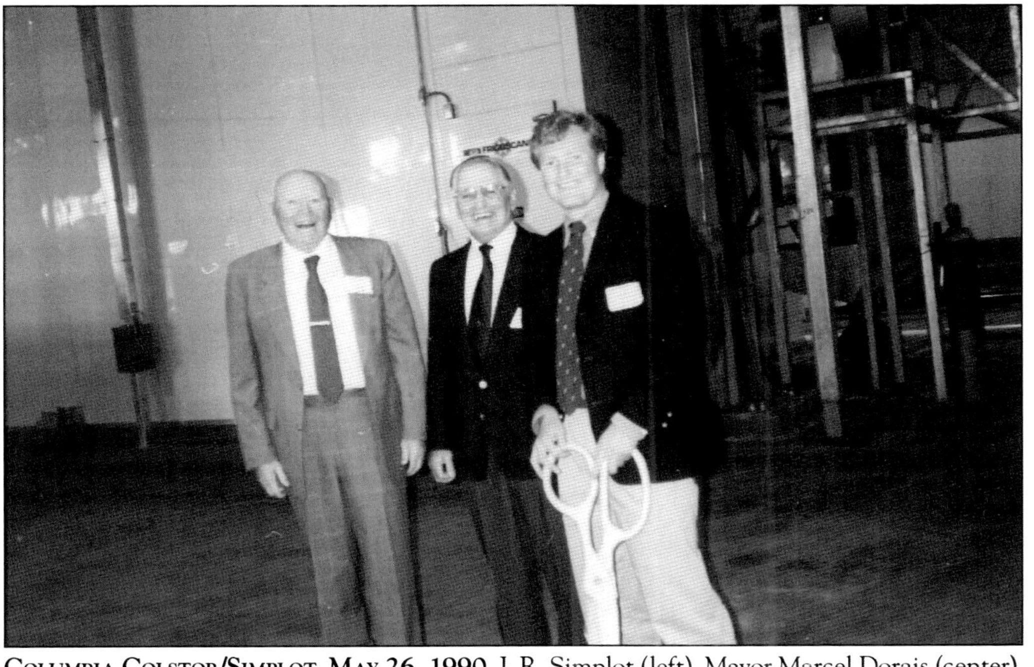

COLUMBIA COLSTOR/SIMPLOT, MAY 26, 1990. J. R. Simplot (left), Mayor Marcel Dorais (center), and Don McGraw are shown at the grand opening of the Columbia Colstor facility, which stores frozen food products awaiting shipment to faraway places. The McGraw family has been in the frozen food storage business over 70 years. Simplot once owned a nearby processing plant that is now owned by Quincy Foods. (Courtesy of the Quincy Valley Chamber of Commerce.)

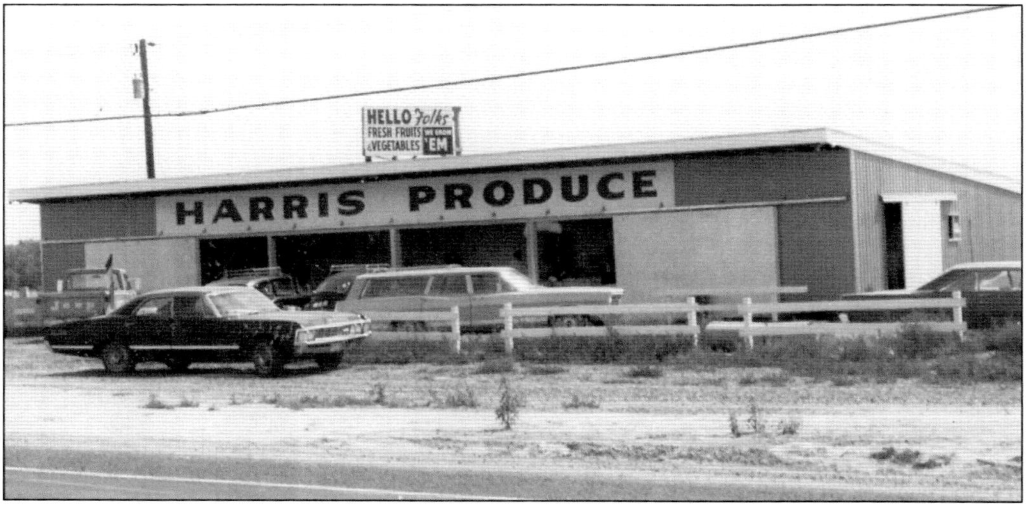

HARRIS PRODUCE, 1967. A popular place to get fresh local produce, Harris Produce was owned by the Edward Harris family and was located on Highway 28, west of Quincy. It is no longer in use. Wife 'N' I was another produce stand on Adams Road, operated by Martin and Lucille Bushman. Today White Trail Produce, also west of Quincy, is the place to go. (Courtesy of the *Quincy Valley Post-Register.*)

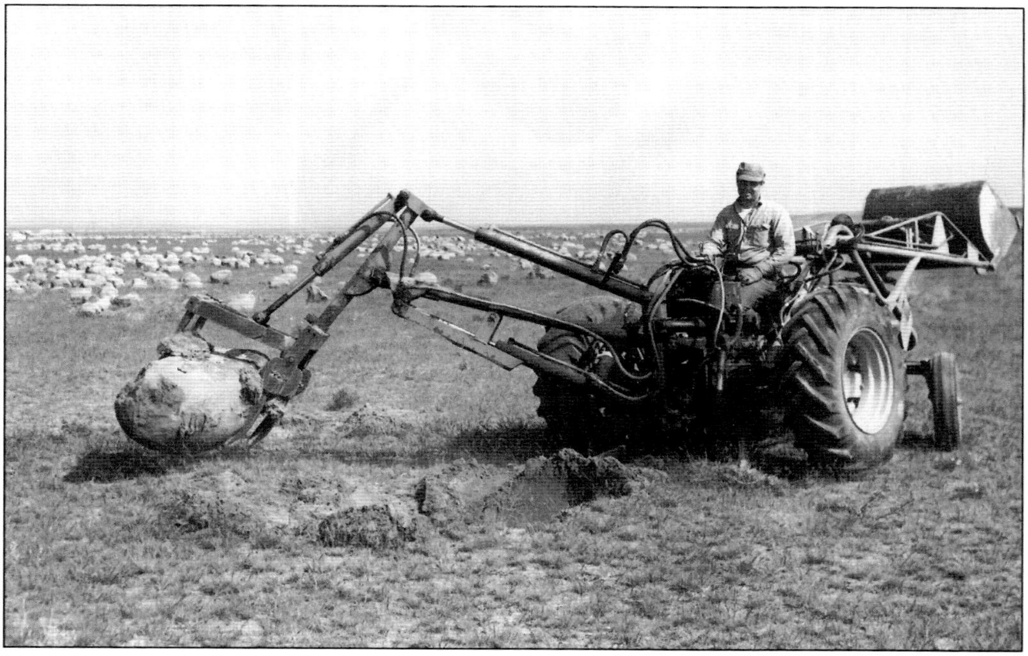

ROCK FARMING, 1967. This farmer is harvesting the most abundant crop in the Quincy Valley—rocks. In some areas of the valley, rocks are the hardiest of crops, often appearing each spring like weeds. Many of Quincy's children have memories of long days spent clearing rocks before spring planting could begin. (Columbia Basin Irrigation Project photograph; courtesy of the *Quincy Valley Post-Register.*)

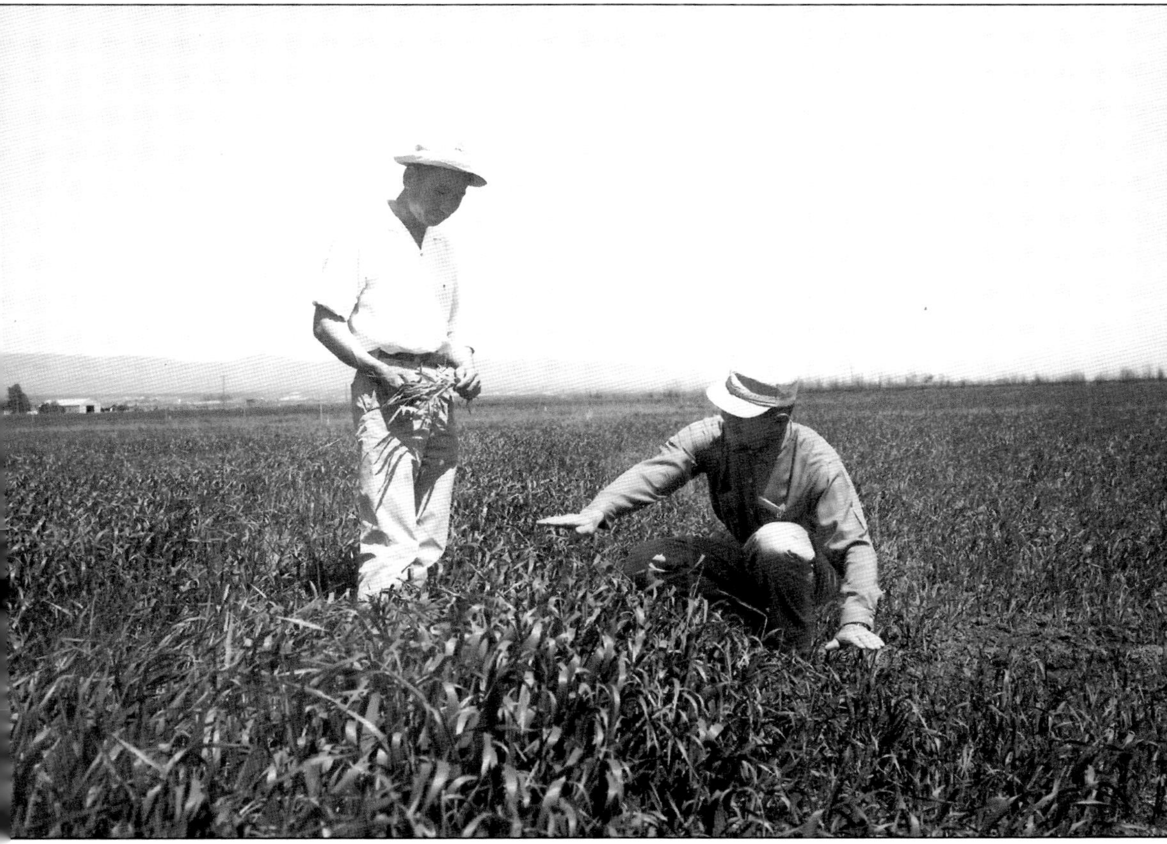

JAPANESE FARMERS, 1965. Quincy Valley farmer Mike Mano (left) is seen here discussing the crop with another farmer. During World War II, many Japanese people had their civil rights suspended when President Roosevelt signed Executive Order 9066, seizing the property and businesses of Japanese living west of the Columbia River. Some were sent to internment camps farther east, while others, like Joseph Tokunaga, came to work on farms in the Quincy Valley or for Cedergreen Frozen Foods. Mike Mano was invited to the Quincy Valley by the Cedergreen family but chose to join the army. He served in Europe with the 442nd Regiment Combat Team, the most decorated unit for its size, according to combat records. The Japanese community continued to grow once the irrigation project began. The earliest Japanese family in Quincy, listed on the 1920 census, was Michita and Tommaso Akagi and their daughter Setsuko. (Courtesy of the *Quincy Valley Post-Register.*)

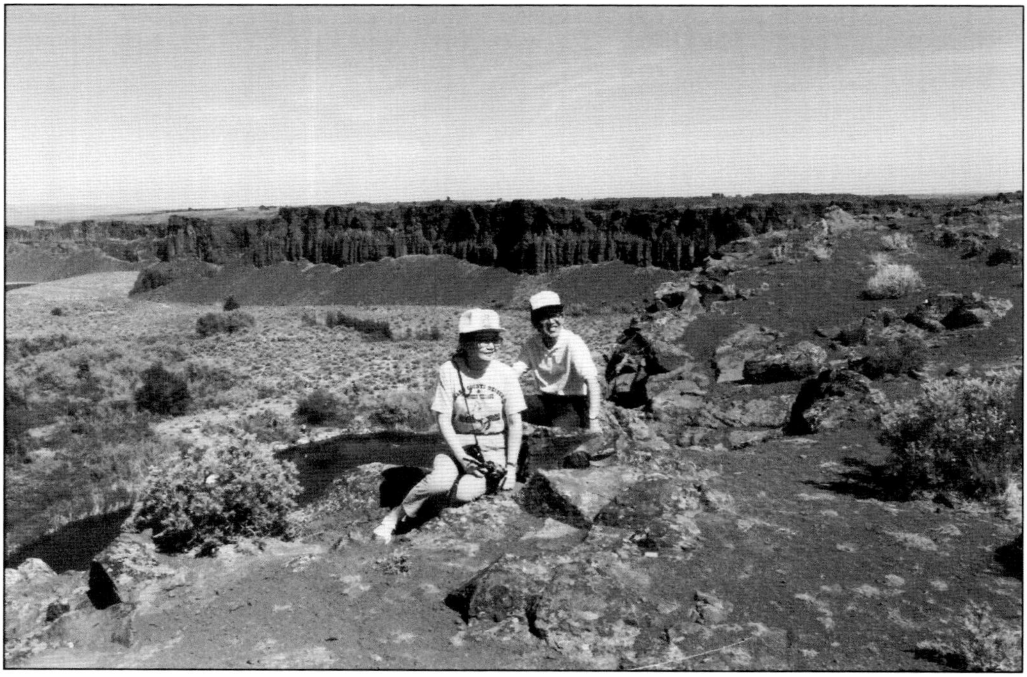

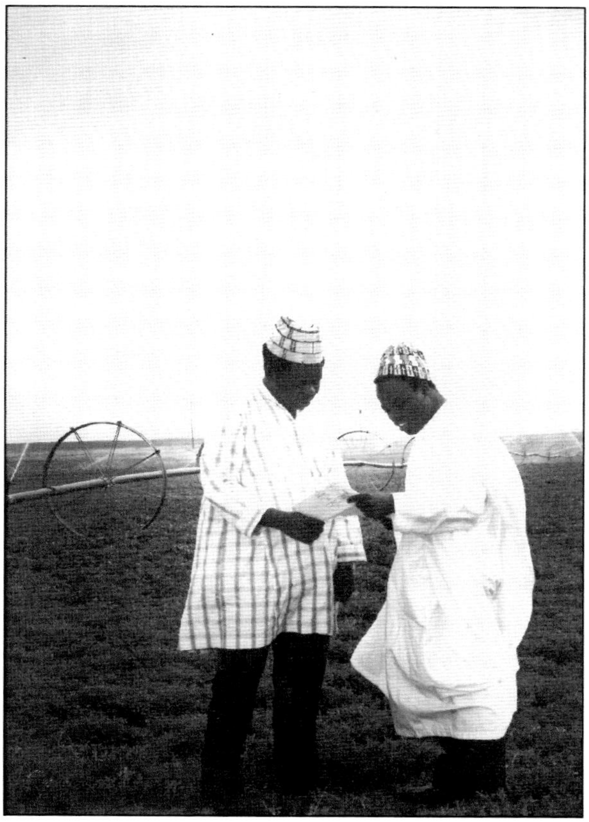

Visitors from Faraway Places. Many people come to Quincy—to live, learn, or simply to visit. In 2007, the Taste of Quincy Festival identified 27 different ethnic groups with ties to the Quincy Valley. In the picture on the left, two visitors from Africa in 1966 are learning about farming and irrigations techniques so that they can improve crop production in their nation. In 1988, the Burke Museum of Natural History and Culture conducted one of its regional tours (the Farm Tour) through the Quincy Valley. They visited the Champs de Brionne Winery tasting room near George, were served a catered lunch with delicious delicacies provided by the Spud Shed, and made a trip to the Quincy Lakes. Two tour members from China are seen above enjoying the view from their perch above a basaltic cliff. (Above, courtesy of the Quincy Valley Chamber of Commerce; left, Bureau of Reclamation photograph by Ron York, courtesy of *Quincy Valley Post-Register*.)

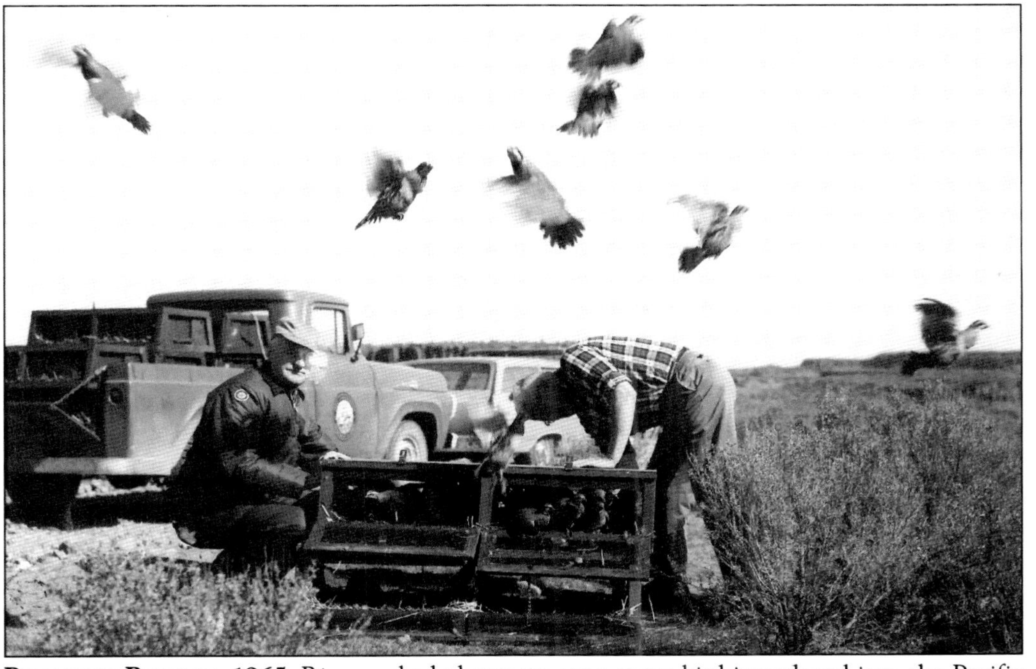

Pheasant Release, 1965. Ring-necked pheasants are a game bird introduced into the Pacific Northwest about 1883. They are well adapted to the sagebrush steppe of the Quincy Valley, which is similar to their original Eurasian habitat. Numbers began to decline as farming increased after the formation of the Columbia Basin Irrigation Project. Birds are released periodically to rebuild the population. In the above photograph taken by Ron York for the Bureau of Reclamation, wildlife officials release birds in 1965. Below, a hunter and his dog happily display their trophy. (Above, courtesy of the *Quincy Valley Post-Register*; below, courtesy of the Quincy Valley Chamber of Commerce.)

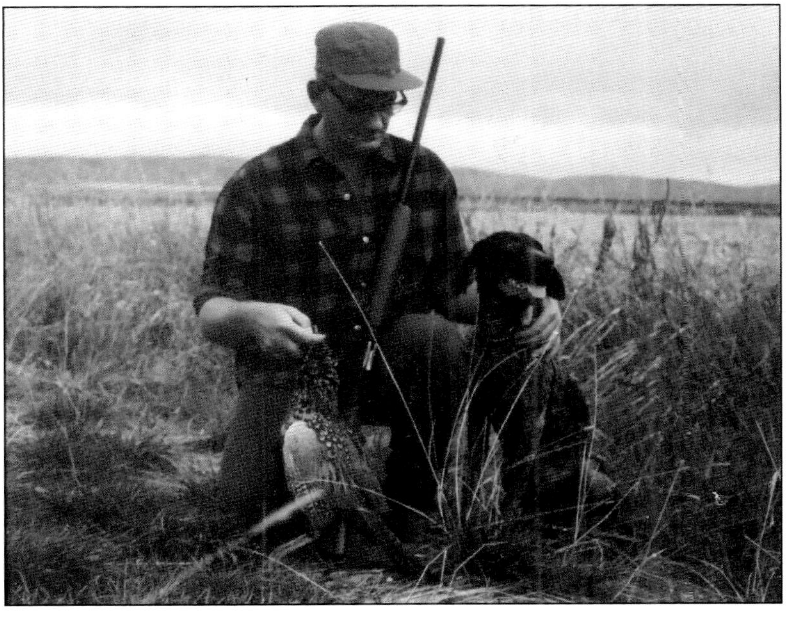

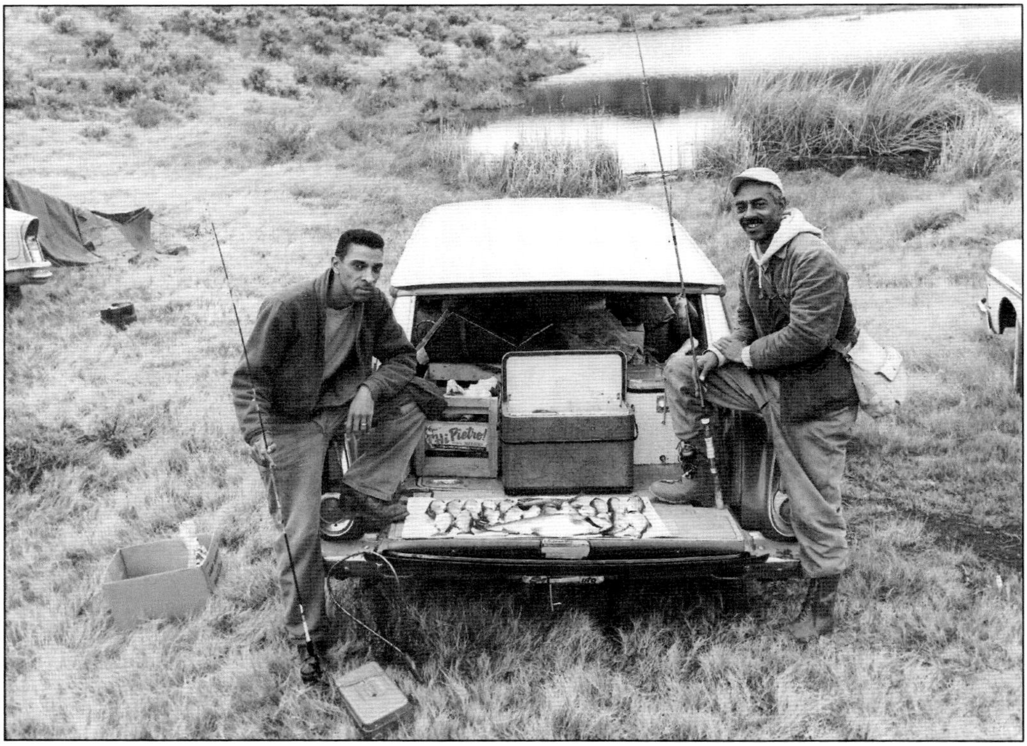

Fishing Season, 1961. Above, Seattle residents Bernet Williams and Albert Nicholas made the long trek across the Cascades to catch their limit on opening day—including a 20-inch, 3-pound trout—at one of the Ancient Lakes in the southwest area of the Quincy Valley. Below, opening day at Burke Lake calls dozens of anglers to take to the water. Ancient Lakes is a 15,266-acre wildlife area filled with upland game birds, desert wildflowers, hiking trails, three lakes, and several potholes that are filled by the irrigation runoff from the Quincy Valley on the plateau above the area. The area was formed by the erosion of basaltic lava flows by glacial floodwater, which periodically swept the area about 18,000 years ago. (Both images courtesy of the Quincy Valley Historical Society.)

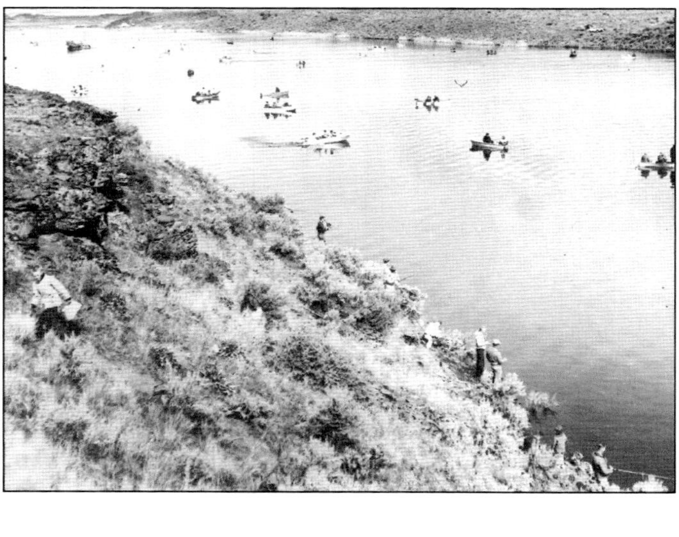

Six

Diversity and Growth

With irrigation water flowing in the canals and ditches, more people began to arrive in the Quincy Valley to share in its abundance. With more people came more challenges and more diversity. Hispanics began to arrive in greater numbers to work the fields and orchards, though they were part of the early settlers, mostly as sheepherders. Japanese farmworkers arrived with the advent of World War II and the internment camps.

Faith continued to play a role, with many new churches being built for a variety of faiths, including Free Methodists, Latter-day Saints, Catholics, Lutherans, Assembly of God, Baptists, Quakers, Seventh-day Adventists, and more.

Families still needed schools, and more were built. Akins Grocery Store, Kissell's Variety Store, the Spud Shed, the Turf, a new post office, hardware stores, a library, and more were built.

Farms grew a greater variety of crops than ever before, including sugar beets, potatoes, corn, peas, seed crops, apples, grapes, and wheat. Food production plants like Cedergreen Frozen Foods and Lamb-Weston provided greater employment opportunities.

Health issues arose when it was revealed that the Hanford Nuclear Reservation had been using American citizens as unknowing guinea pigs for experiments involving the release of radioactive iodine into the atmosphere, contaminating food and water supplies, as well as the people, farm animals, and wildlife.

Quincy's children participated in Future Farmer's of America, 4-H, scouting, sports, and many other educational and fun activities. Adults enjoyed bowling and other pastimes. Everyone spent time at Crescent Bar, enjoying the outdoors, or attending Canal Days, Farmer Consumer Awareness Day, the Fourth of July at George, and other events.

Quincy was not without its whimsical side, as evidenced by its passion for all things jackrabbit, headless horsemen, and the tooth fairy. Christmas, Presidents' Day, the Fourth of July, dog shows, and high school variety shows were among the favored celebrations and distractions available to all.

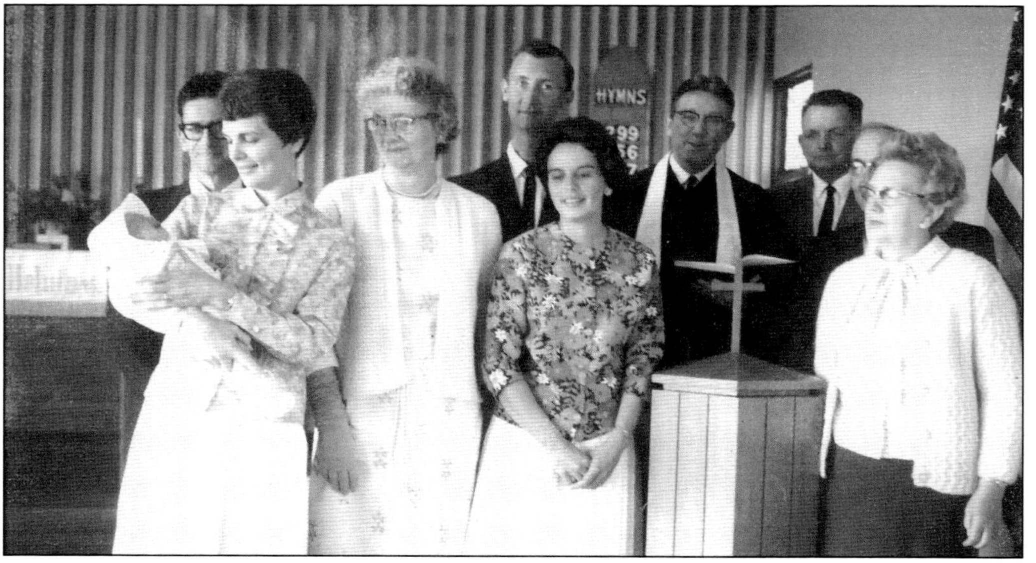

BABY CHRISTENING, 1967. The rites of Christendom begin with the blessing and naming of a baby. John and Bertha Doebler christen their newborn son, Scott Daniel Doebler, at Christ the Savior Lutheran Church in George, about 10 miles south of Quincy. George was originally called Allouez in honor of the first settler in the area, Allouez Domberger. In 1907, it was renamed Burke. (Courtesy of the *Quincy Valley Post-Register.*)

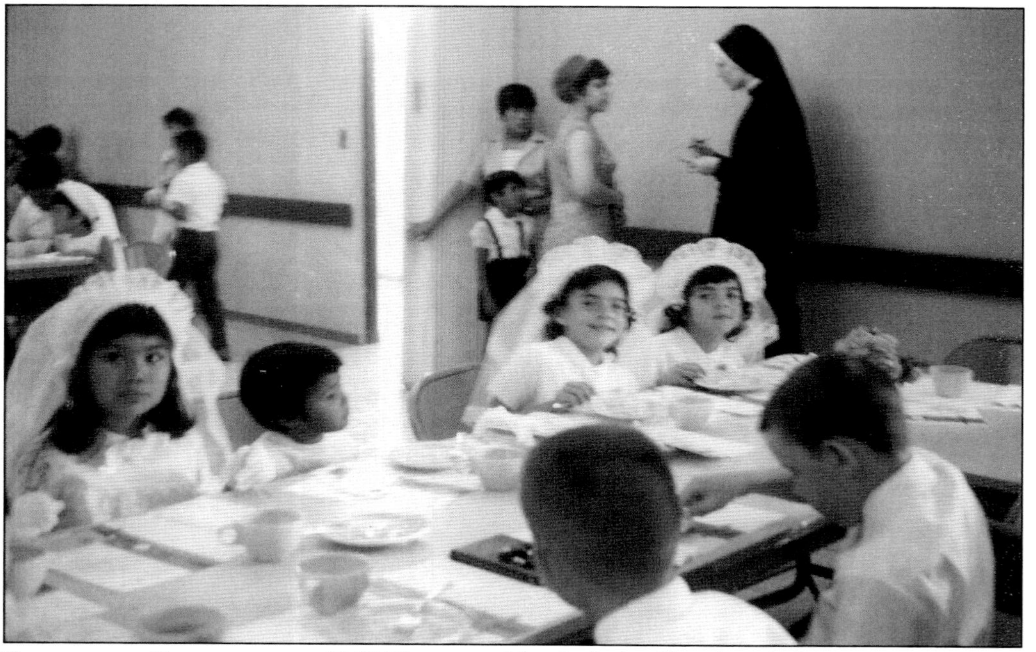

BAPTISM AND CONFIRMATION, 1967. The rites of the Catholic Church include confirmation at the age of seven. On the day pictured here, 35 children received their first Holy Communion at St. Pius X Church in Quincy. An annual day of prayer is held at Escure Farms, owned by descendants of early sheepherders Ramon and Martina Escure. (Courtesy of the *Quincy Valley Post-Register.*)

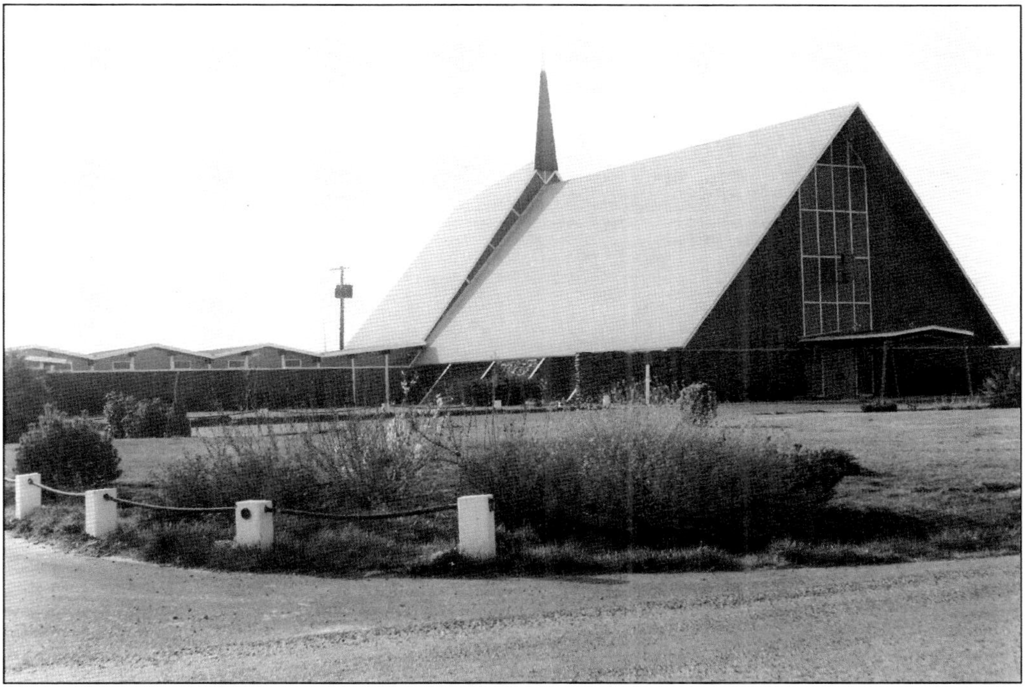

St. Pius X Catholic Church. St. Pius X was not the first Catholic church in the Quincy Valley. St. Anthony's in Burke (George) was founded in 1905 when the Jesuit father Folchi conducted the first services outdoors in German, English, and Spanish. As the Burke community dwindled, St. Anthony's moved to Quincy. It burned in 1959 and was rebuilt as St. Pius X. (Courtesy of the *Quincy Valley Post-Register.*)

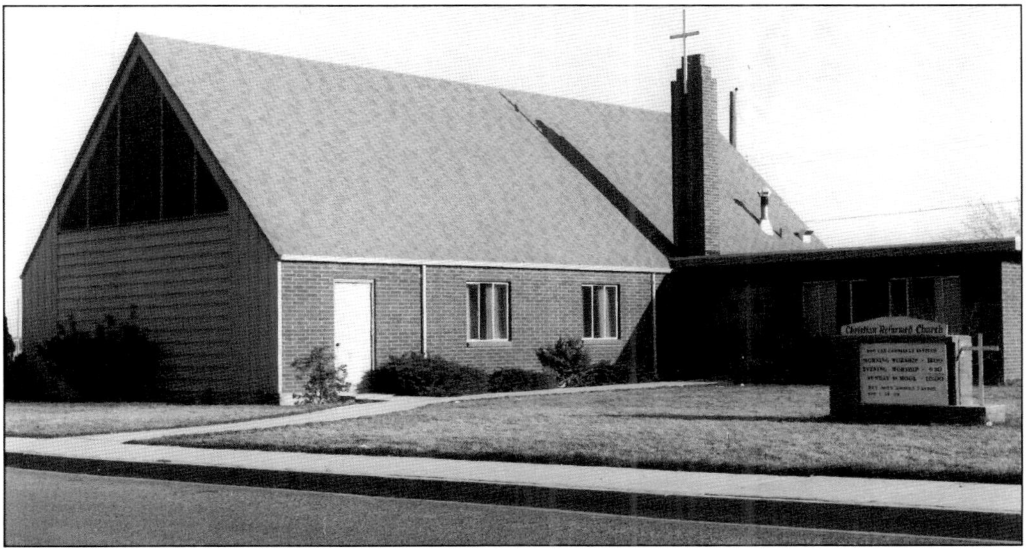

Christian Reformed Church. The Quincy Christian Reformed Church is part of the North American group of Reformed churches who stem from the Dutch Reformed Church, which traced its roots back to the teachings of John Calvin. It is one of the many faces of Christianity in the Quincy Valley. (Courtesy of the *Quincy Valley Post-Register.*)

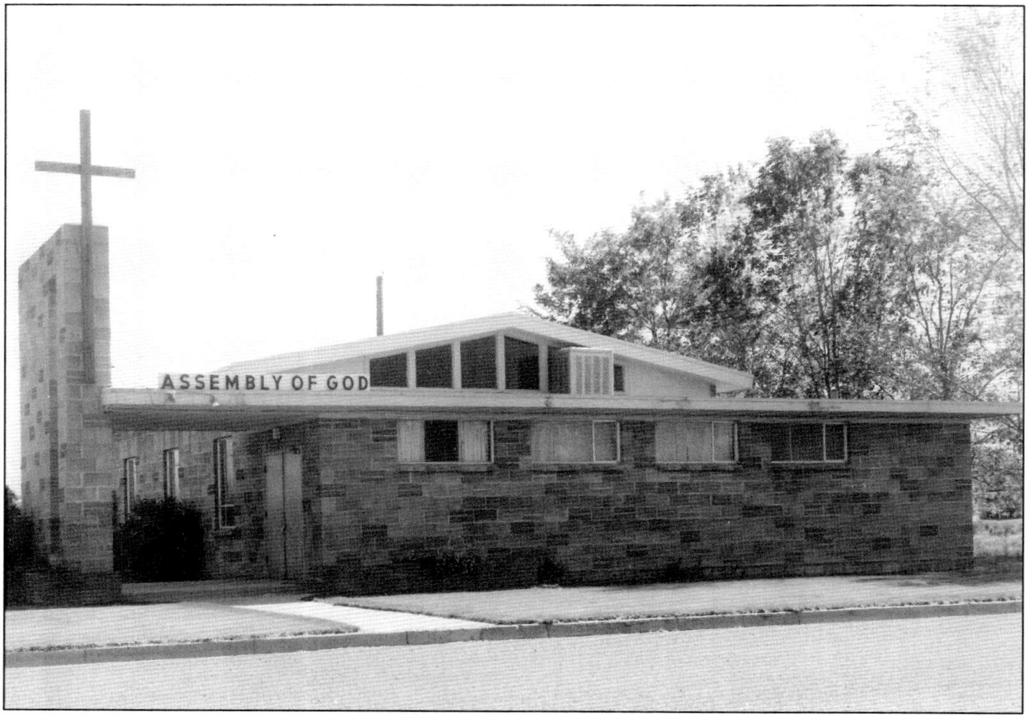

ASSEMBLY OF GOD CHURCH, 1966. Also known as the Pentecostal Church, the Assembly of God Church grew out of the movement known as the Azuza Street Revival. The church was established in Quincy by the 1950s, and there are now two congregations: one conducted in Spanish and the other in English. (Courtesy of the *Quincy Valley Post-Register.*)

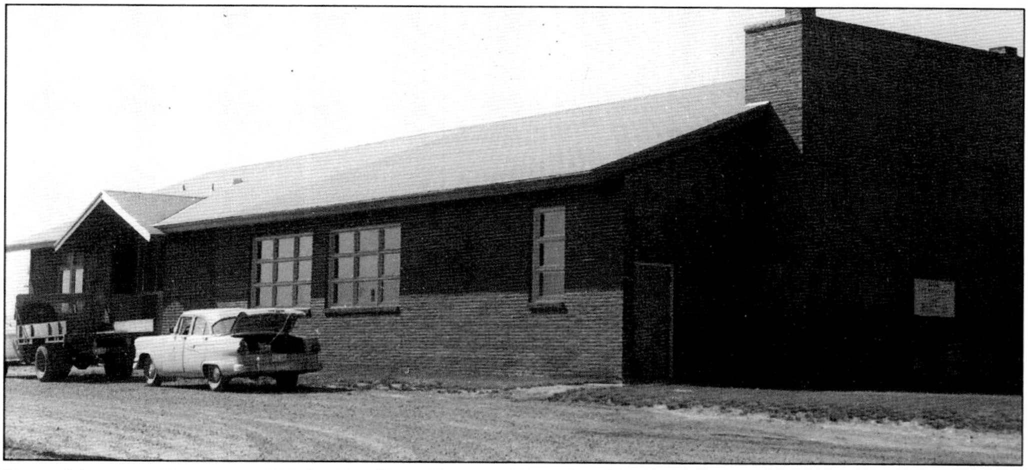

FIRST BAPTIST CHURCH, 1966. The First Baptist Church of Quincy, part of what was the Northwest Fellowship of Regular Baptist Churches, is just finishing up construction in this picture. One well-known Christian singer who has performed here is Bryan Duncan. Bryan is the son of the late Rev. Daniel Duncan, pastor of the Quincy Assembly of God Church in the mid-1950s. (Courtesy of the *Quincy Valley Post-Register.*)

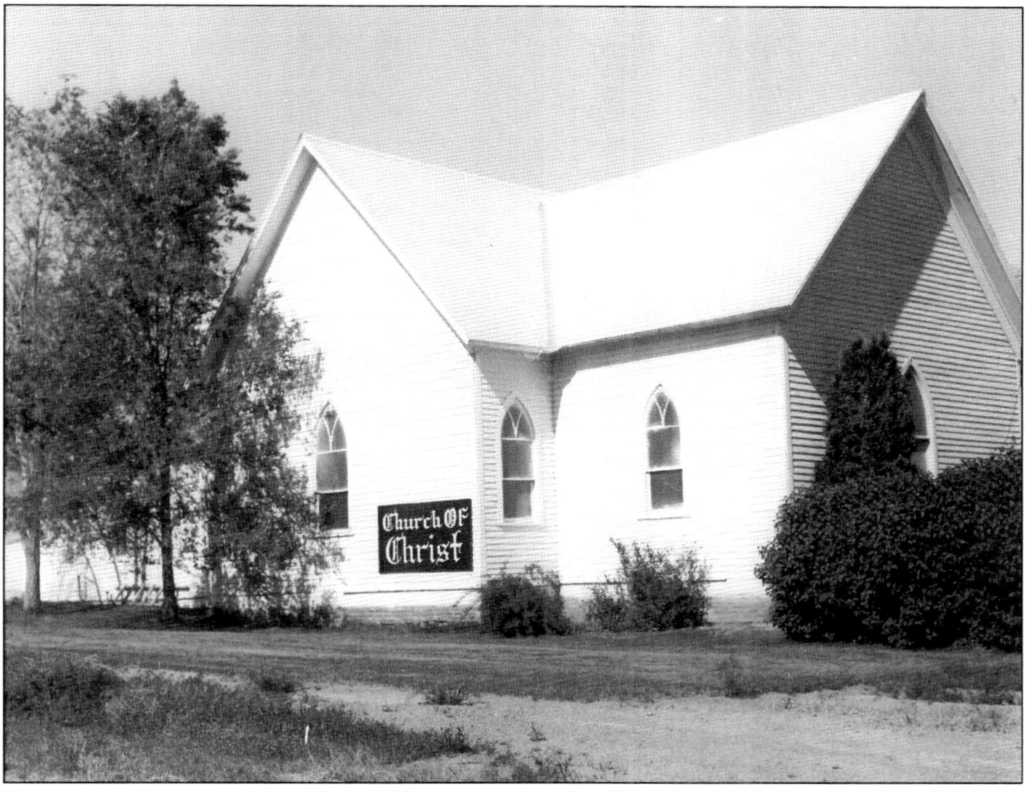

Church of Christ, 1966. This building is much older than this 1966 photograph and did not always house the Church of Christ congregation. The Church of Christ is a Restoration movement that believes in restoring the doctrines of the Primitive Church, as established by Jesus Christ during his lifetime. (Courtesy of the *Quincy Valley Post-Register.*)

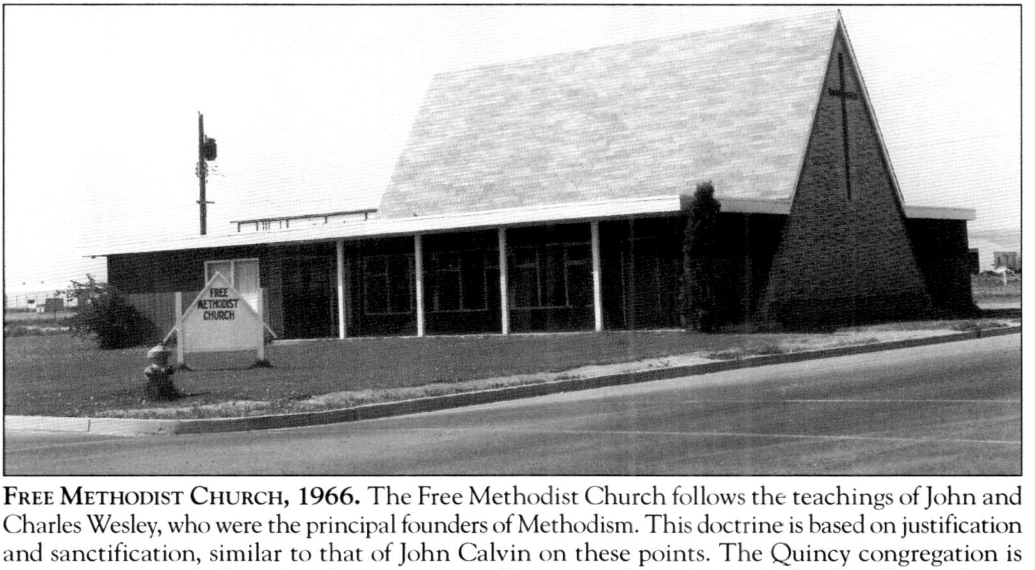

Free Methodist Church, 1966. The Free Methodist Church follows the teachings of John and Charles Wesley, who were the principal founders of Methodism. This doctrine is based on justification and sanctification, similar to that of John Calvin on these points. The Quincy congregation is very active in its faith and in the community. (Courtesy of the *Quincy Valley Post-Register.*)

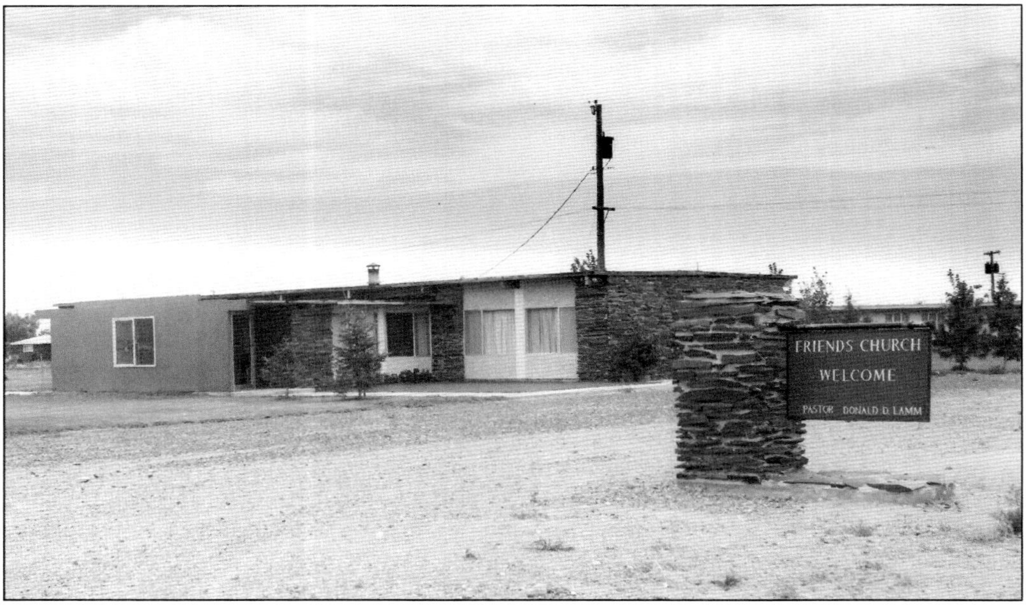

THE FRIENDS CHURCH, 1966. The Friends Church is also known as the Quaker Church. They originated in England during the 1600s and established the colony of Pennsylvania in 1681. When Quakers arrived in Quincy, they built their meetinghouse on a lot next to the Quincy hospital. (Courtesy of the *Quincy Valley Post-Register*.)

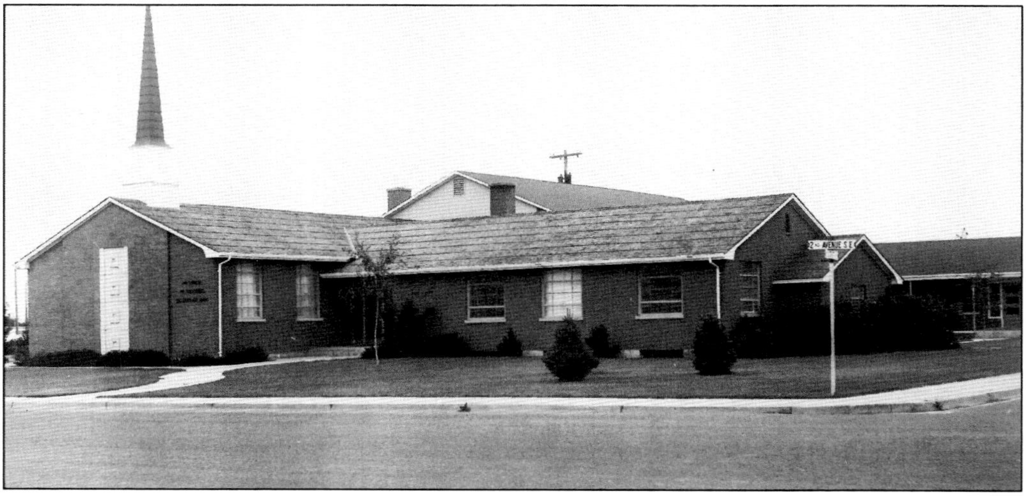

THE LDS CHURCH, 1966. Although there were a few members of the LDS Church in the Quincy Valley before irrigation, an influx of veterans from Idaho and Utah brought enough members to form a ward. This building was erected by the construction firm of Westover and Hope. (Courtesy of the *Quincy Valley Post-Register*.)

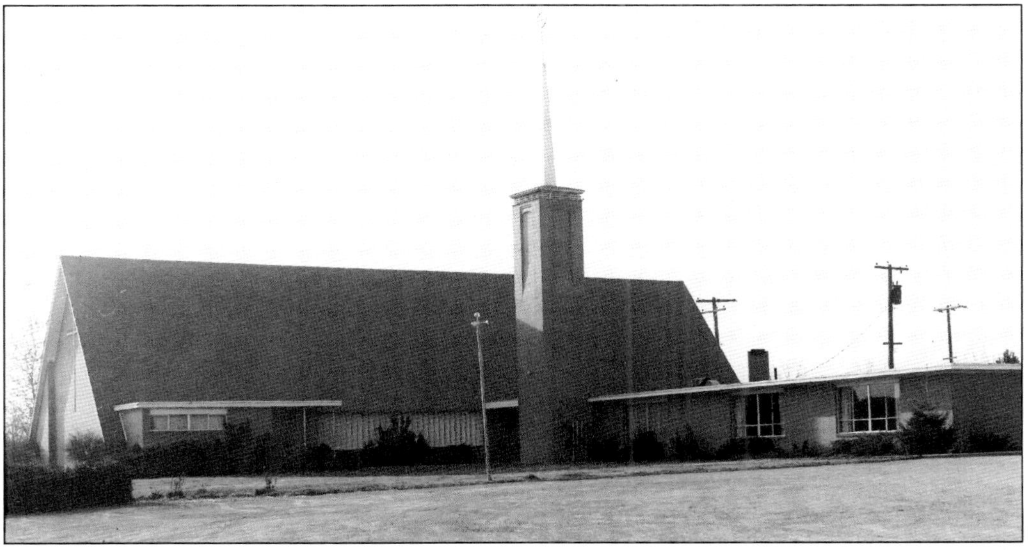

Presbyterian Church, 1966. The Presbyterian church was organized in 1905 as the first English-speaking congregation and the second church in Quincy. Six months later, the building was open for business and debt-free. The Presbyterians met every other Sunday, alternating Sundays with the Methodists. (Courtesy of the *Quincy Valley Post-Register.*)

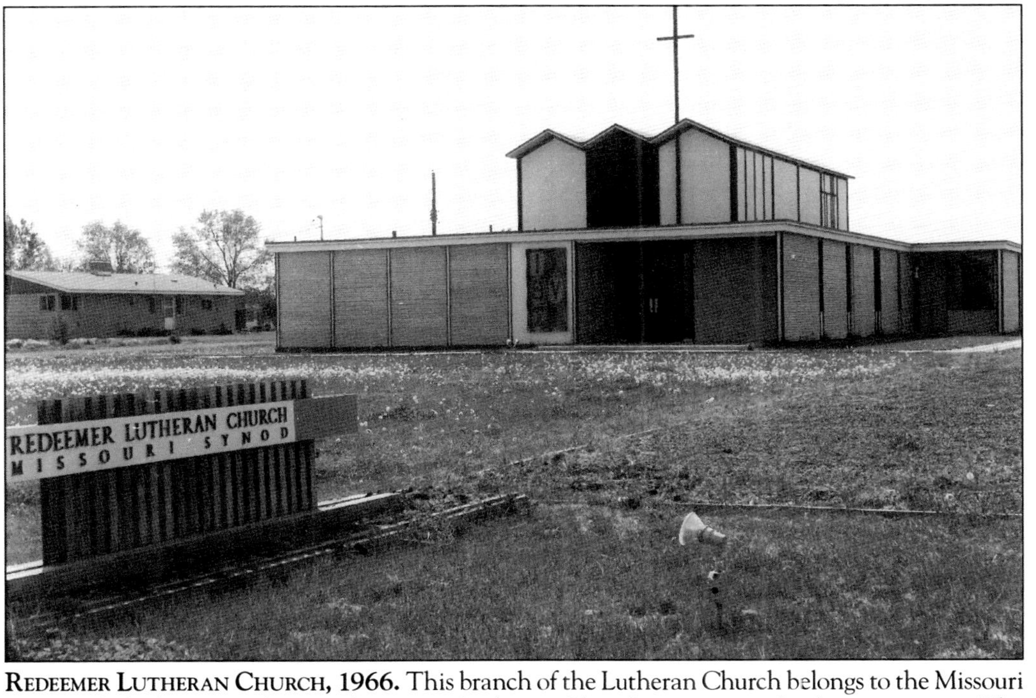

Redeemer Lutheran Church, 1966. This branch of the Lutheran Church belongs to the Missouri Synod, while the original St. Paul German Lutheran Church is an evangelical congregation. The building is now used to house the Quincy Migrant Head Start program run by the Washington State Migrant Council. (Courtesy of the *Quincy Valley Post-Register.*)

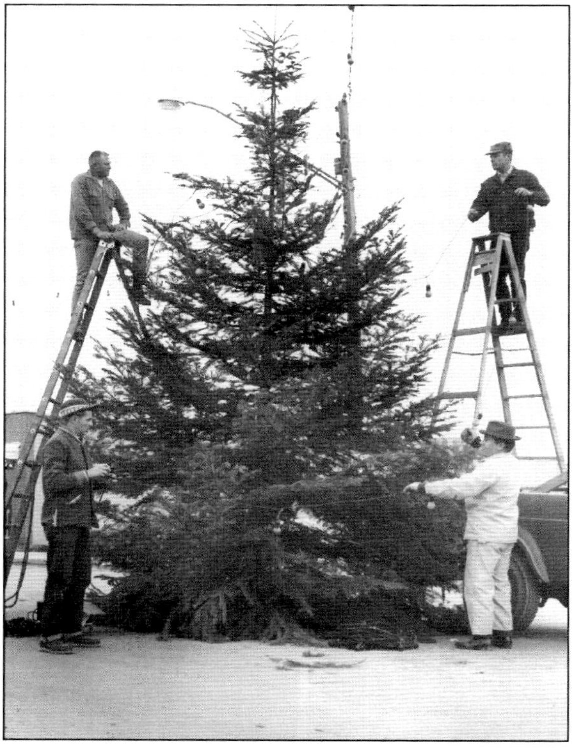

Christmas in the Quincy Valley. Christmas is very special place in the life of the Quincy Valley. It has been celebrated over the years with an annual tree-lighting ceremony and Christmas parade, with Santa arriving in a sleigh or a fire engine. A Christmas bazaar, Christmas caroling downtown, and a concert by the combined choirs of local churches often rounds out the season. At left, townsmen set up and decorated the tree for Christmas 1965. More recently, the restored Reiman-Simmons house has been the scene of the Old-Fashioned Christmas event, complete with Christmas caroling accompanied by an antique pump organ and real candles burning on the Tannenbaum in the old German tradition. Below, Pastor Al Montgomery is seen giving the invocation at the tree-lighting ceremony in 1989. (Left, courtesy of the *Quincy Valley Post-Register*; below, courtesy of the Quincy Valley Chamber of Commerce.)

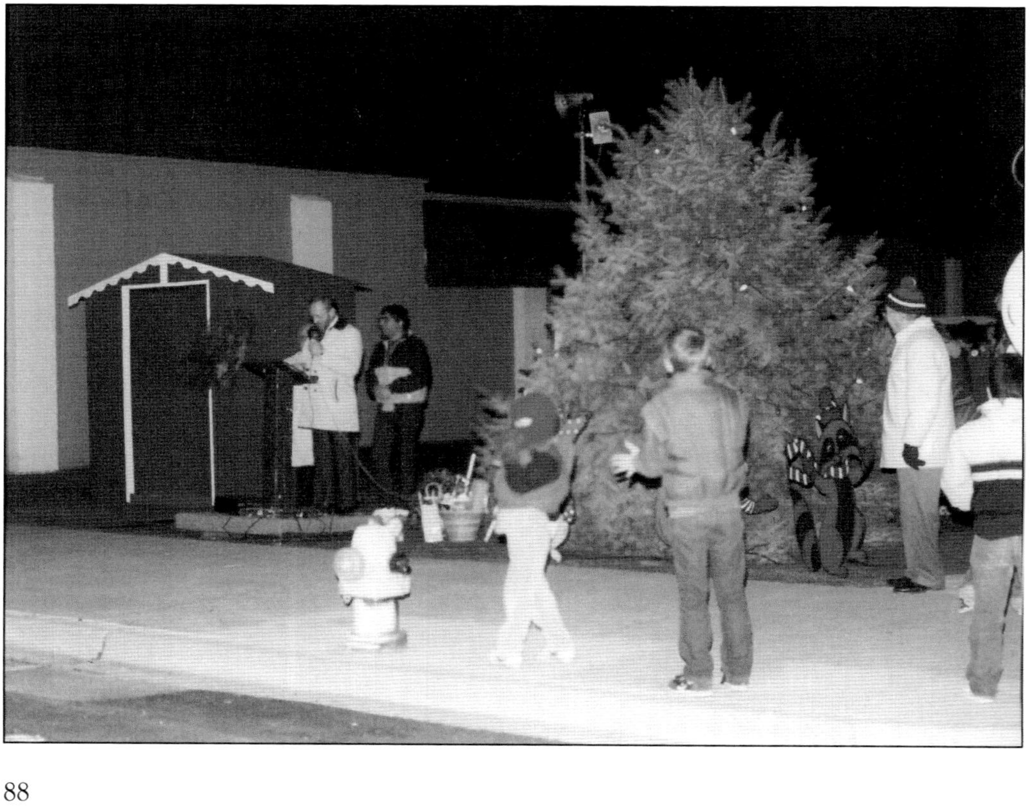

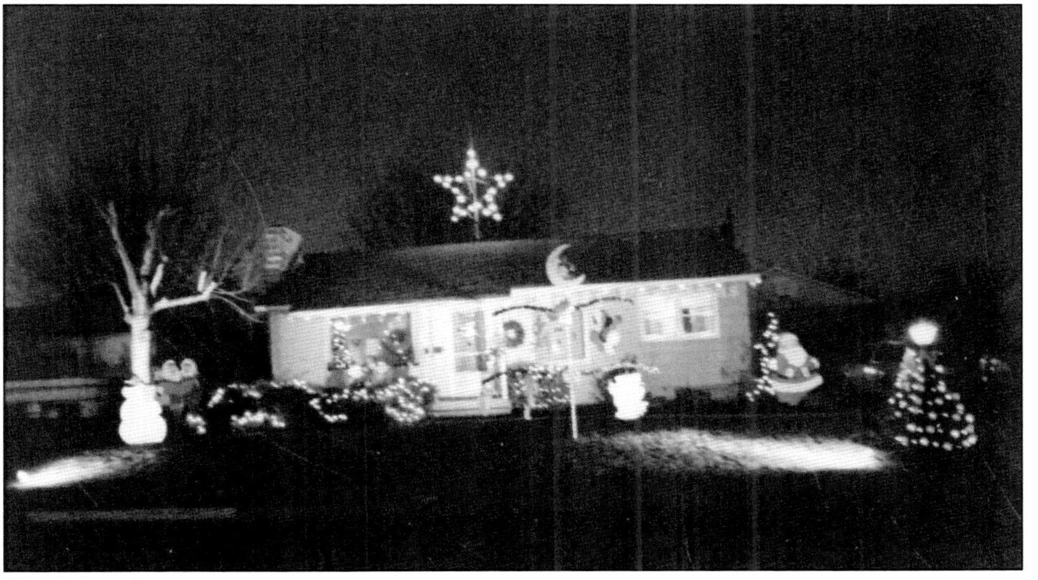

Christmas Lights. Decorating one's house at Christmas has been a long-standing tradition in Quincy. In 1989, the Ron Lindemeier house was selected as first honorable mention in the Christmas lights contest. Motorists along Interstate 90 are treated to the Quincy Valley Christmas lights, created by Scott Lybbert. The electricity from irrigation motors is used to power the designs, which range from the serious to the whimsical, often animated. (Courtesy of the Quincy Valley Chamber of Commerce.)

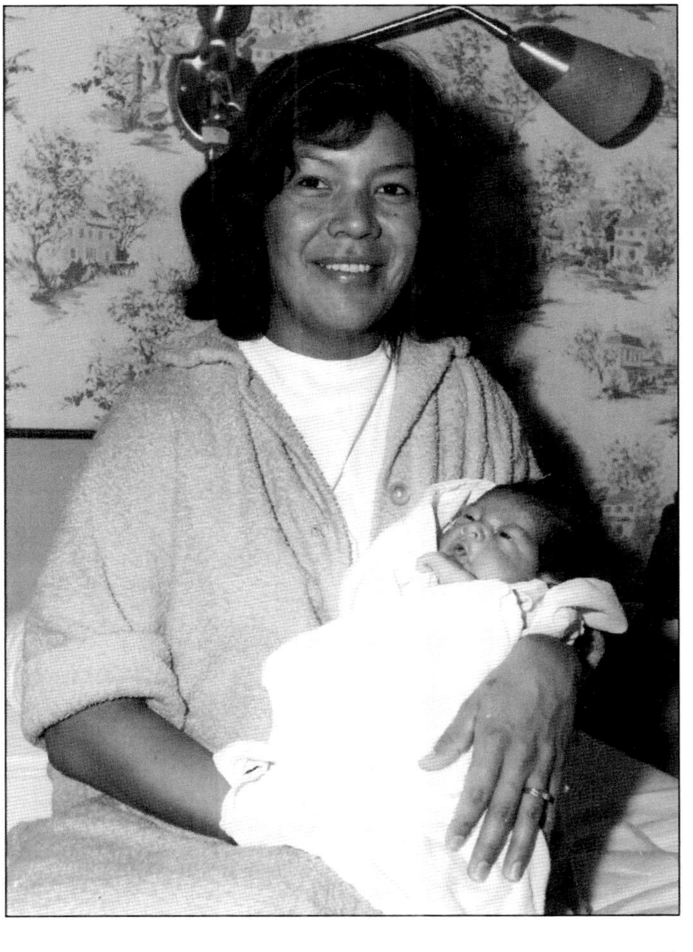

New Year's Baby, 1966. The first baby of the year is always an eagerly anticipated event. In January 1966, the honor fell to the Jesse and Margarita Luna family. Jesse Luna worked for a local Quincy Valley farm owned by the Child family. (Courtesy of the *Quincy Valley Post-Register*.)

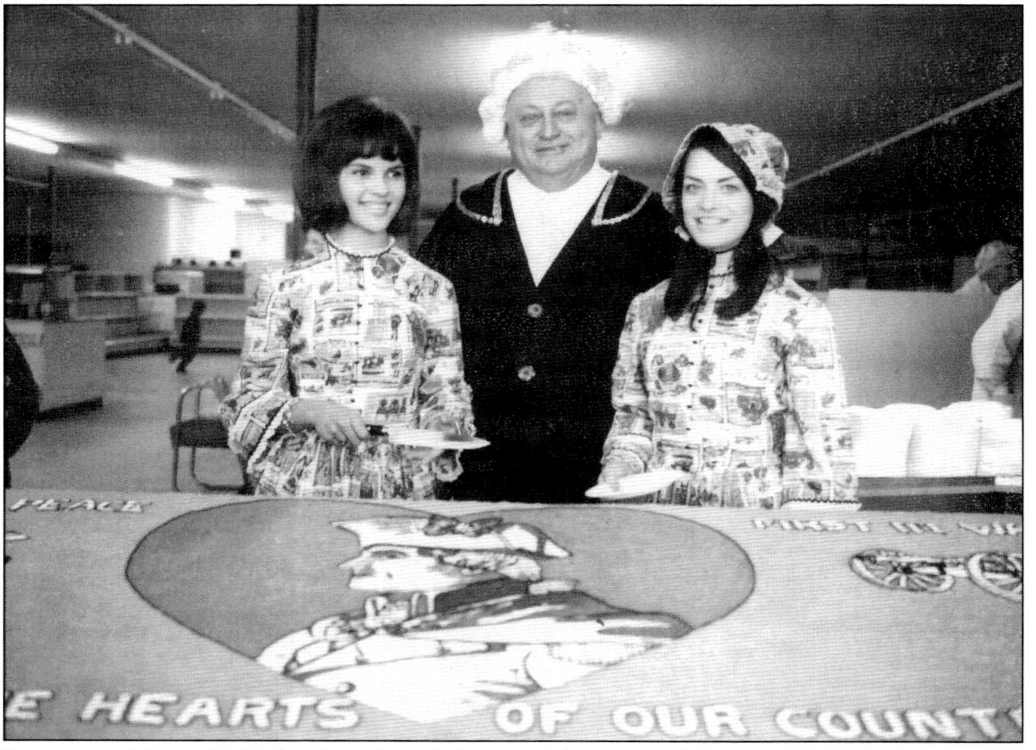

PRESIDENTS' DAY, 1967. In the colonial theme of the town of George, Washington, a special program is held each Presidents' Day to celebrate the birthday of the first president of the United States. The Colonial Market is the backdrop for this spectacular birthday cake. Mayor Charles Brown stands in the center with Linda Kniep on the left and Kathy Wilson on the right. (Courtesy of the *Quincy Valley Post-Register.*)

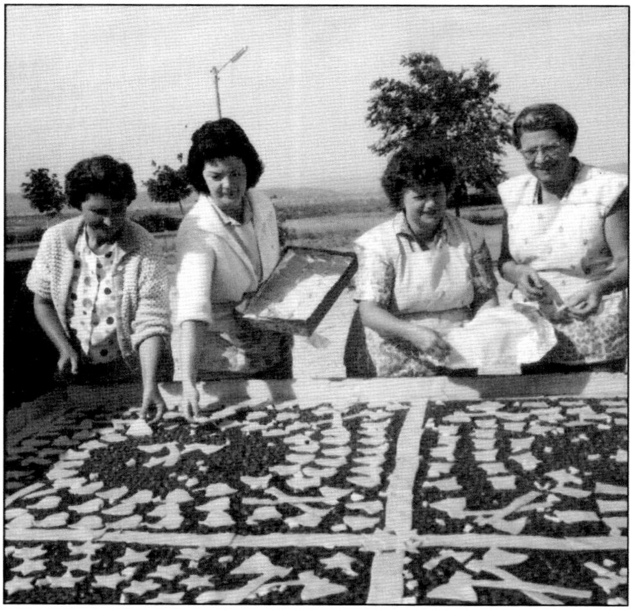

WORLD'S LARGEST CHERRY PIE, 1966. An estimated 800 pounds of cherries went into the baking of this pie. Charlie Brown, founder of George, Washington, a community on the southern reaches of the Quincy Valley, had a special brick oven made to bake it. Each Fourth of July in George, people gather from far and wide for a taste of this spectacular pastry. (Courtesy of the *Quincy Valley Post-Register.*)

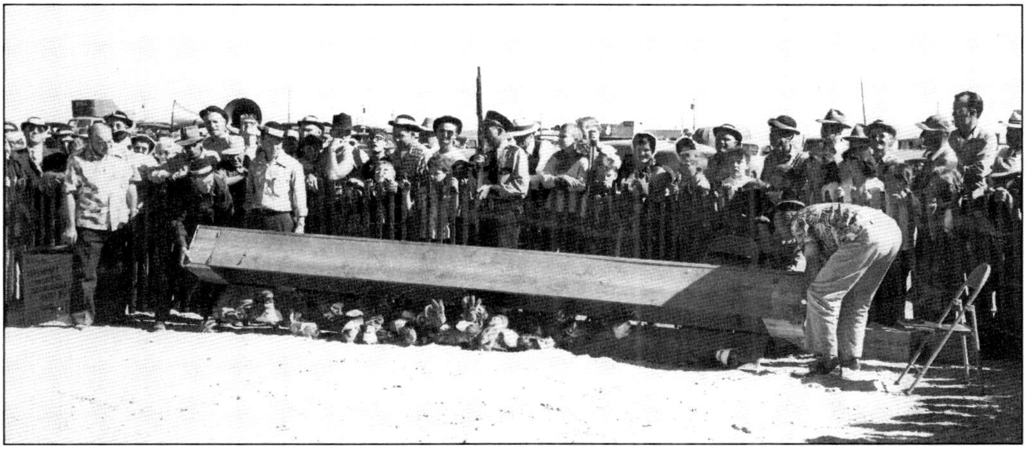

JACKRABBIT TALES. By the 1950s, jackrabbits were no longer hunted but gathered for racing. Here the crowd watches in anticipation while the chosen few are unceremoniously dumped from their box as the local police officer readies his firearm for the starting shot. (Courtesy of the Quincy Valley Historical Society.)

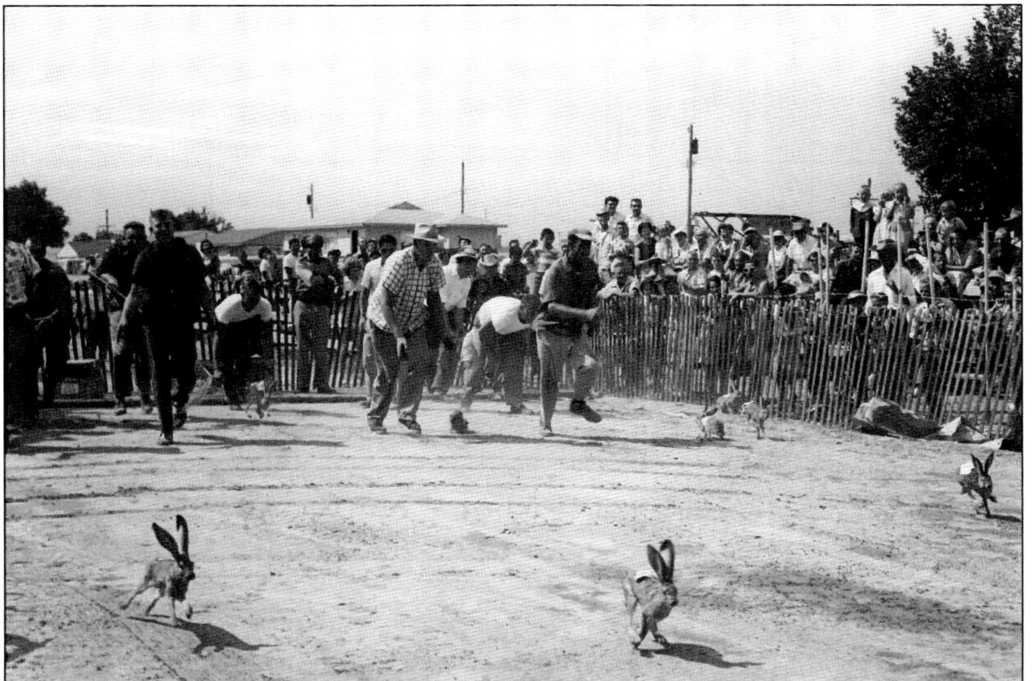

AND THEY'RE OFF. Rabbit wranglers and onlookers laugh as the racers go backwards or refuse to run and cheer for the three front-runners who just want to head for the hills. This scene is reminiscent of Mark Twain's *The Celebrated Jumping Frog of Calaveras County.* (Courtesy of the Quincy Valley Historical Society.)

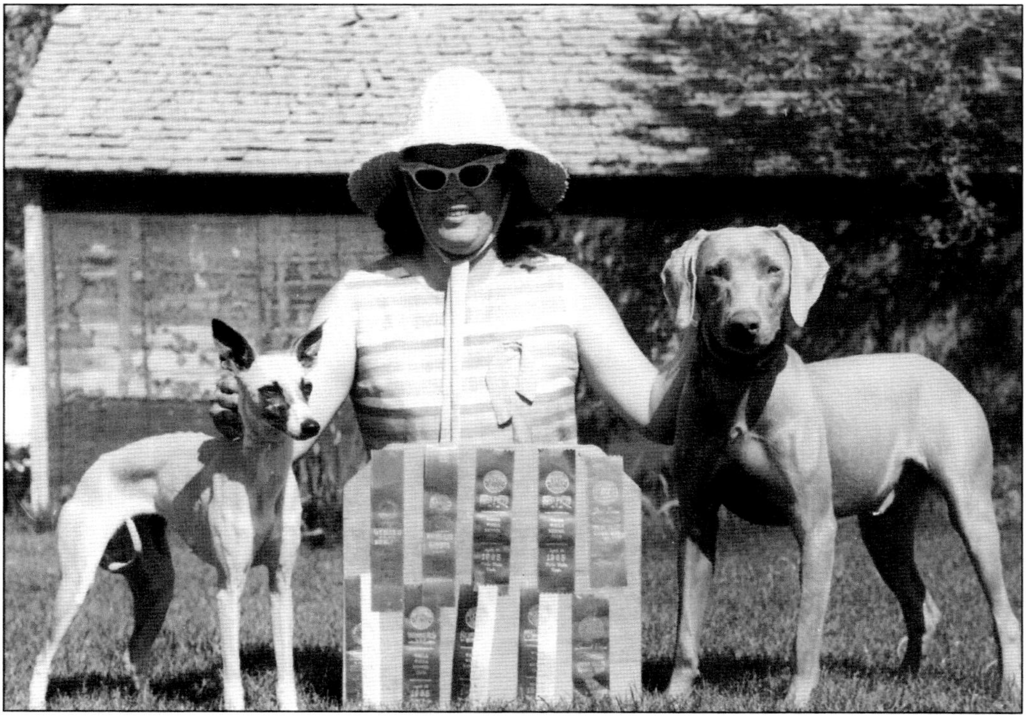

YEAR OF THE DOG, 1965. Everyone loves their dogs, including the people of Quincy Valley. The unidentified dog lady above shows off her prize pets. Below, children stand in line for the opportunity to prove what they already know in their hearts, that their dog is the best ever. This community event was sponsored by Ken-L-Ration Dog Food, which often served up hot dogs and T-shirts with the company logo. This brand was known for its snappy jingle, "My dog's better than yours," and they sponsored local dog shows so children could prove that their dog was the best. The company also sponsored the pet kennel at Disneyland until 1968, as well as presenting an annual Ken-L-Ration Dog Hero of the Year award. (Both images courtesy of the Quincy Valley Historical Society.)

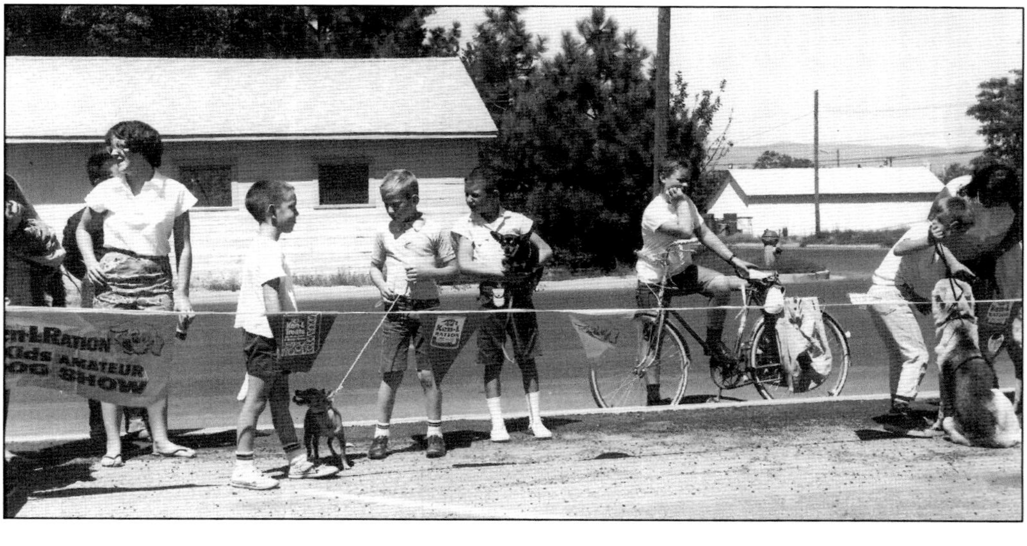

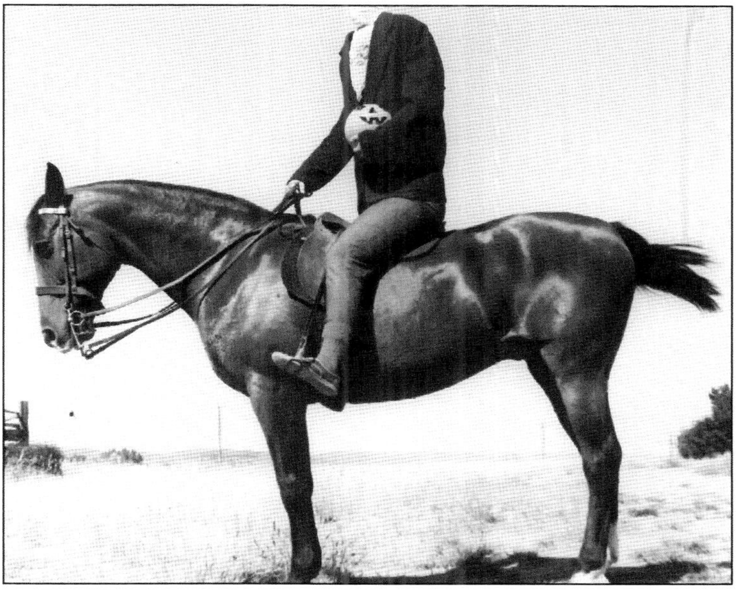

HEADLESS HORSEMAN, 1967. The identity of this mysterious headless horseman remains unknown to this day, much like the one in Washington Irving's story "The Legend of Sleepy Hollow." This rider was a participant in the costume class of a gymkhana event held near Quincy Farm Chemical Company, demonstrating that the theatrical side of Quincy runs as deep as its love of horses. (Courtesy of the *Quincy Valley Post-Register*.)

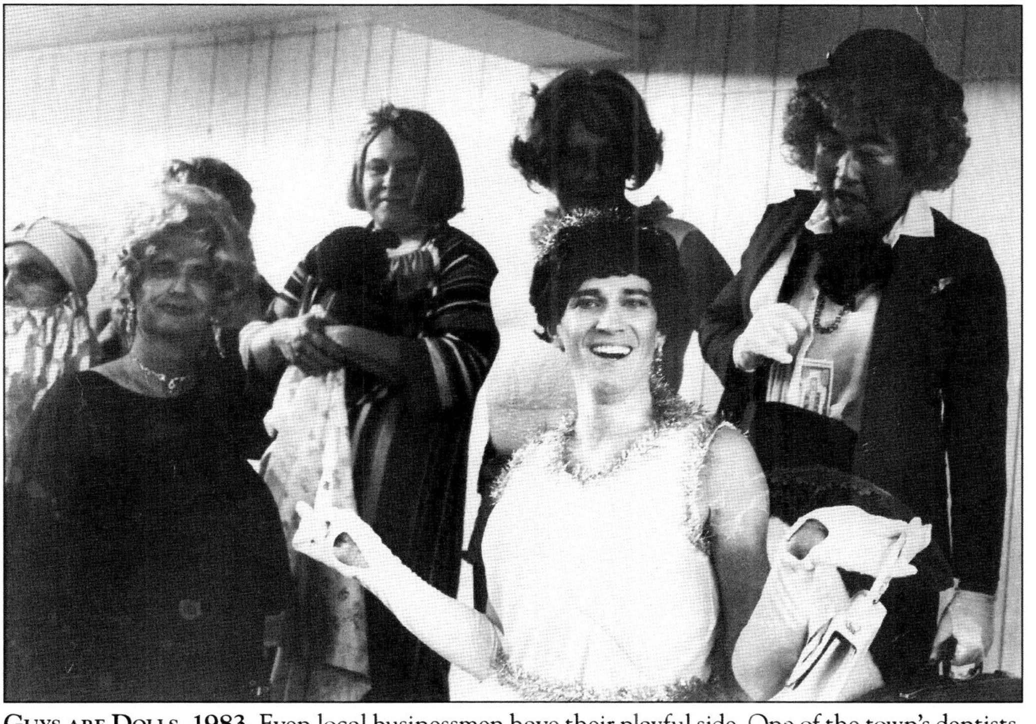

GUYS ARE DOLLS, 1983. Even local businessmen have their playful side. One of the town's dentists, Dr. Phillip Seaberg, models his tooth fairy outfit during a chamber of commerce event in the basement of the Turf restaurant. The restaurant is a frequent scene of Halloween breakfasts, Jail and Bail events, and other chamber frolics. Andrew Goto looks on in a stylish coat and hat. (Courtesy of the Quincy Valley Chamber of Commerce.)

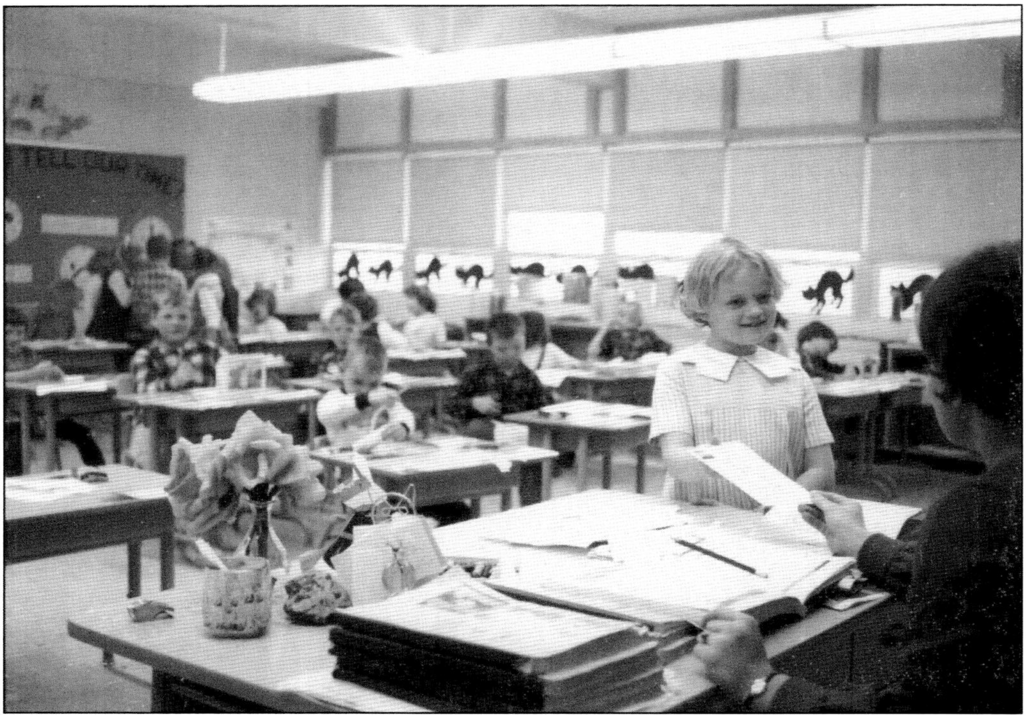

SCHOOL DAYS, 1966. Black cats on the windowpanes show that Halloween will soon be celebrated at the George Elementary School. Second-grade student Lisa Marcusen hands an assignment to her teacher, Mrs. Brooks. Lisa is the daughter of George area farmers Duane and Joy Marcusen. (Courtesy of the *Quincy Valley Post-Register*.)

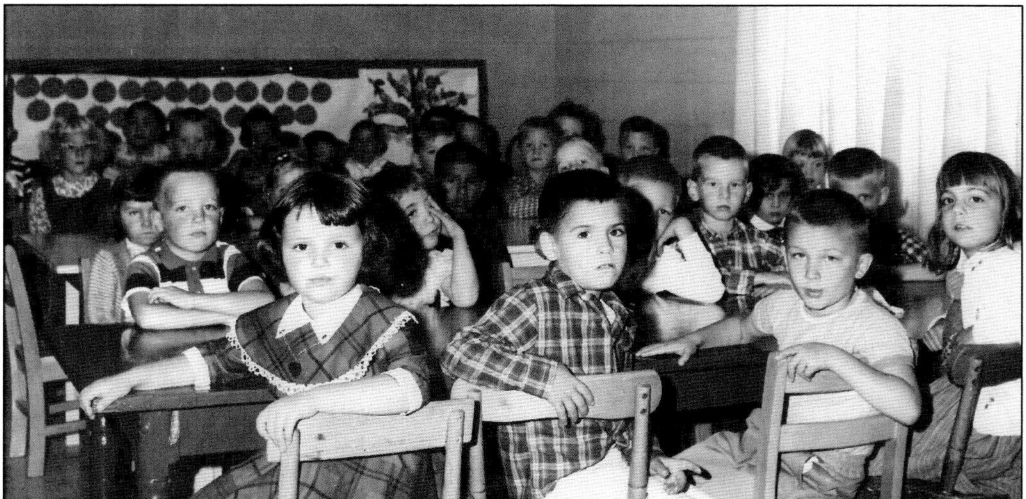

MOUNTAIN VIEW, 1966. These young students watch nervously as the photographer takes their picture. Stan Oda, Rex Calloway, and Mary Wolf Neilson are among the students in Mrs. Keatley's classroom at Mountain View Elementary, located on the north side of Quincy. (Courtesy of the *Quincy Valley Post-Register*.)

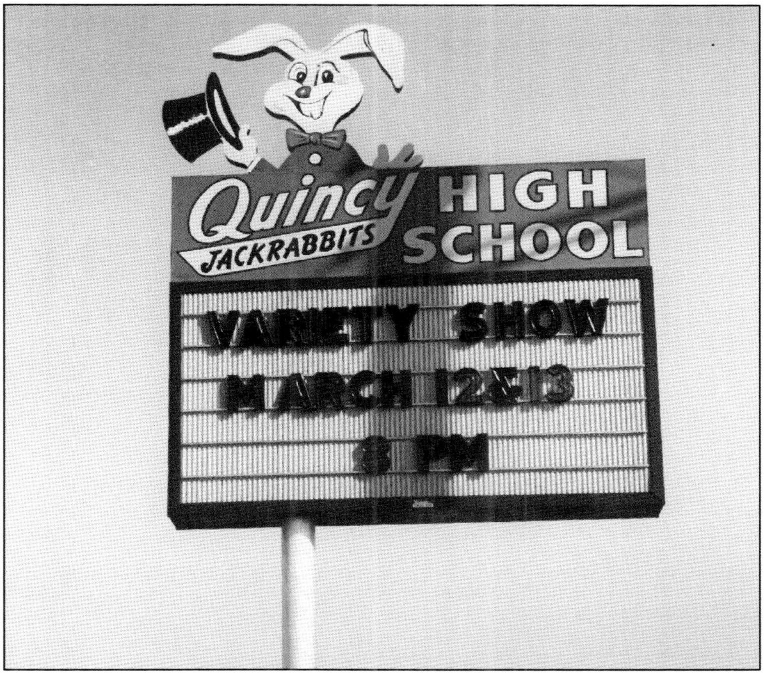

Quincy Jacks, 1965. Where else but in Quincy can a high school reader board be found sporting a jackrabbit in a top hat? Quincy High School adopted the jackrabbit as their mascot early on, admiring the tenacity and agility of the nemesis of the early farmer. (Courtesy of the *Quincy Valley Post-Register.*)

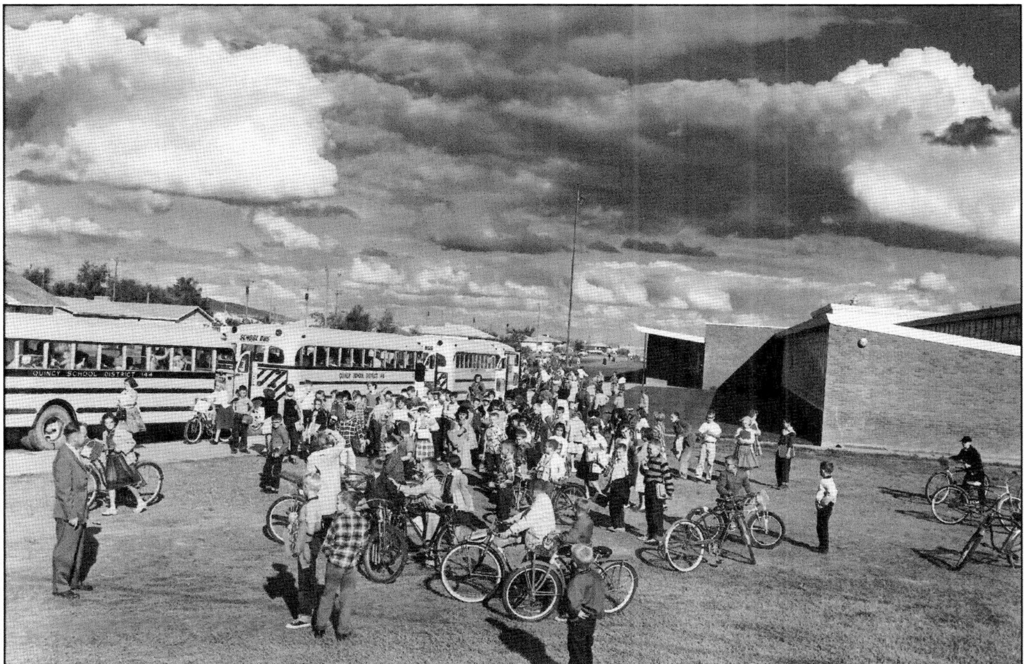

Buses and Bicycles, 1959. Pioneer Elementary School children anxiously await the signal to return home after a long day at school. The buses and the bicyclists seem lined up to race home after a day of learning and play. Principal James Culp can be seen standing in the left foreground. (Courtesy of the Quincy Valley Historical Society.)

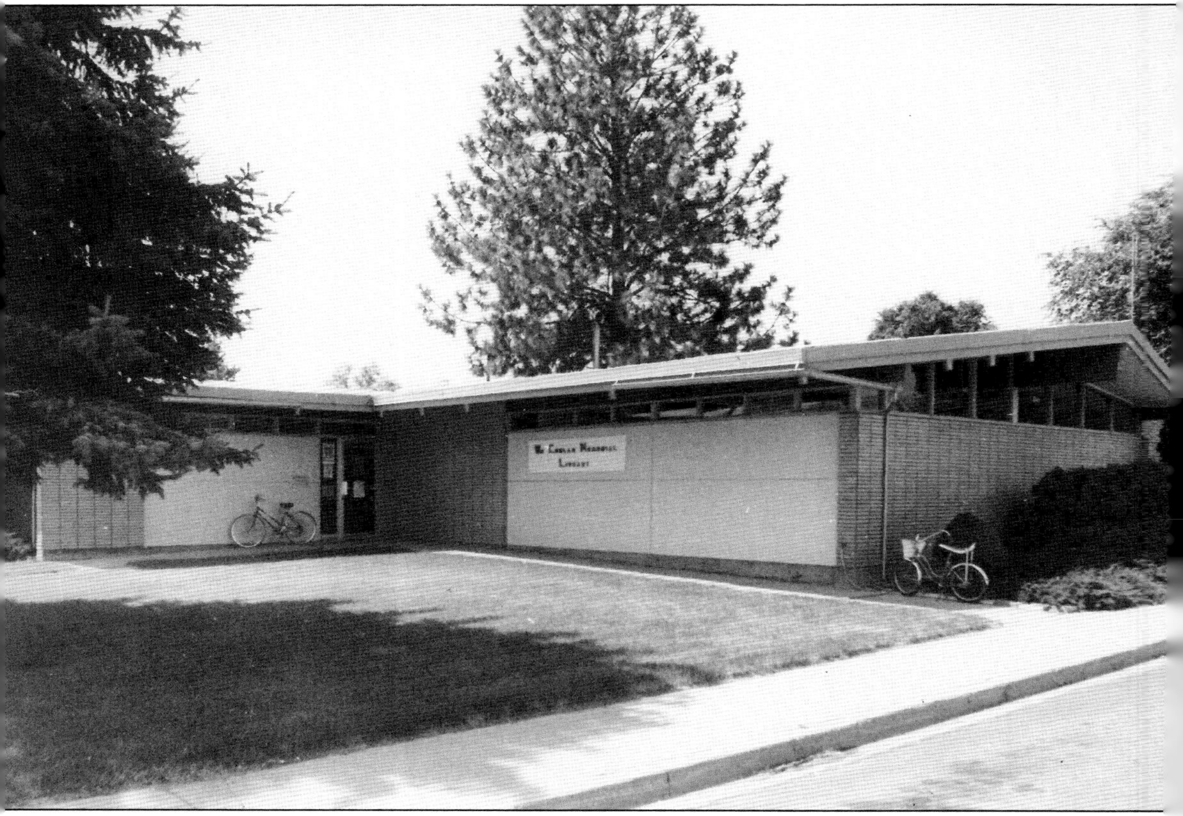

William M. Conlan Library. Arriving in 1902, the Conlan family homesteaded just south of Quincy, later moving into town as owner/operators of a small store and Shell service station when the first automobiles arrived in the area. When William passed away in 1955, he left a legacy of $13,333 to the City of Quincy for use in the construction of a building to be used exclusively as a library. Since the 1920s, the Women's Club had provided library space and volunteer staff in their building. William loved books and wanted to promote reading. The William M. Conlan Library was dedicated on December 18, 1960, with a large crowd in spite of icy roads. Conlan was the town's first school bus driver, built the first water tower near the old city hall, was the first official repairman of the schoolhouse flagpole, and was the founder of a boy's camp near Leavenworth. His favorite hobbies, carving wooden ship models and building ships in bottles, grew out of his adventures sailing around Cape Horn in South America. (Courtesy of the Quincy Valley Historical Society.)

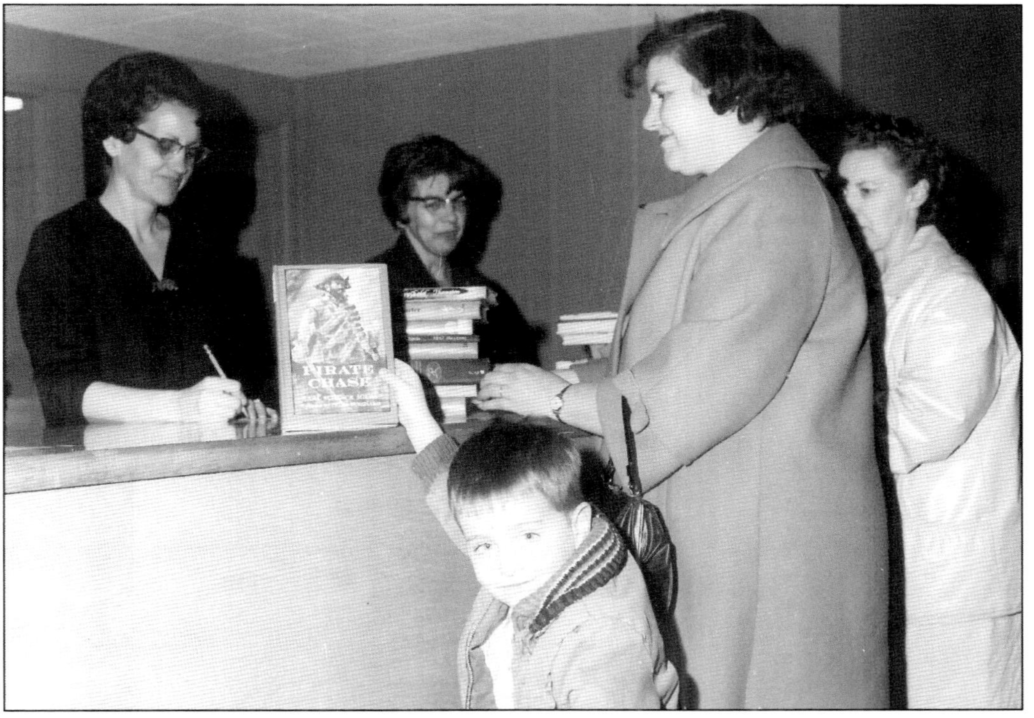

Quincy Library, 1966. Librarian Rowena Christensen, in the back, helps patrons check out books in the Quincy Public Library housed in the William M. Conlan building. The young boy in front is checking out an adventure story. The public library continues to be a center of the community, moving into a new and larger building in 2011 to meet the demand. (Courtesy of the *Quincy Valley Post-Register.*)

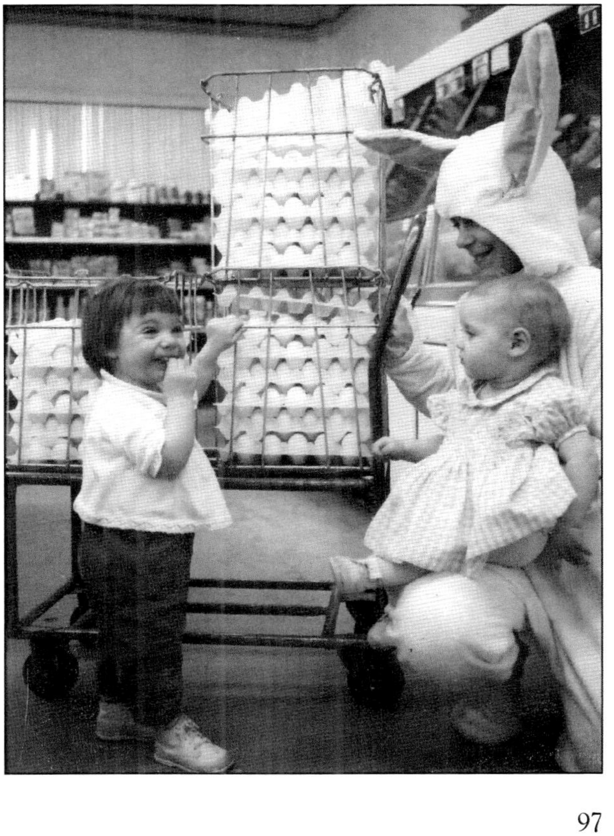

Easter Bunny, 1967. In a family-oriented farming community, it was inevitable that jackrabbit's cousin, Peter Rabbit, would pay a visit to the children of Quincy each Easter. Here Peter stops by a local store and chats with two youngsters next to a display of farm-fresh eggs ready to be taken home and dyed for the traditional Easter egg hunt. (Courtesy of the *Quincy Valley Post-Register.*)

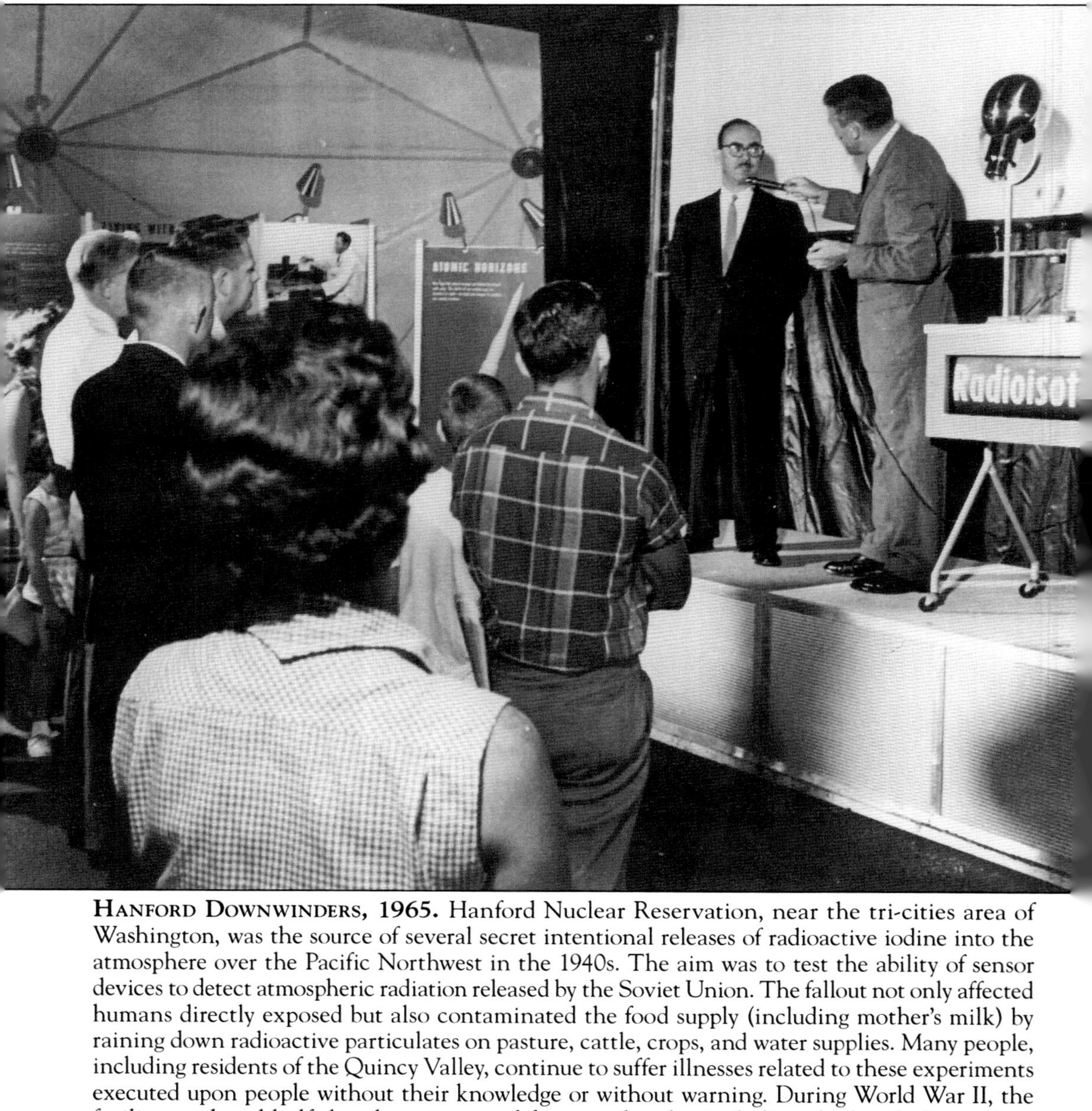

HANFORD DOWNWINDERS, 1965. Hanford Nuclear Reservation, near the tri-cities area of Washington, was the source of several secret intentional releases of radioactive iodine into the atmosphere over the Pacific Northwest in the 1940s. The aim was to test the ability of sensor devices to detect atmospheric radiation released by the Soviet Union. The fallout not only affected humans directly exposed but also contaminated the food supply (including mother's milk) by raining down radioactive particulates on pasture, cattle, crops, and water supplies. Many people, including residents of the Quincy Valley, continue to suffer illnesses related to these experiments executed upon people without their knowledge or without warning. During World War II, the facility produced half the plutonium used for atom bombs, including the bomb dropped on Nagasaki, Japan. This picture shows a scientist demonstrating the use of a Geiger counter to detect radiation. (Courtesy of the *Quincy Valley Post-Register*.)

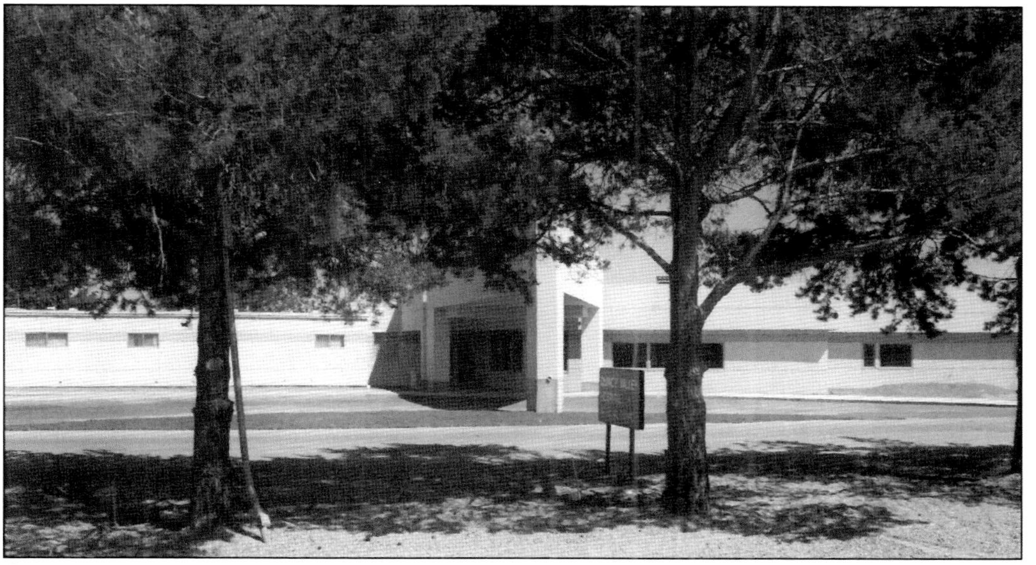

Quincy Valley Medical Center, 1990. The new Quincy Valley Medical Center, as seen above, opened its doors for business on June 23, 1990, holding the first of several annual health fairs. Below, an unidentified visitor chats with Evelyn Pappe Tuttle (second from left) of Dr. Phillip W. Seaberg's office. Pat Krom (standing) and Ann Knutson (right), both of Dr. Jay W. Magnuson's office, also staffed the combined dental care booth at the event. The fair was designed to educate valley residents about good health care practices, encourage them to get regular checkups, and create an awareness of the importance of preventive care. (Both images courtesy of the Quincy Valley Chamber of Commerce.)

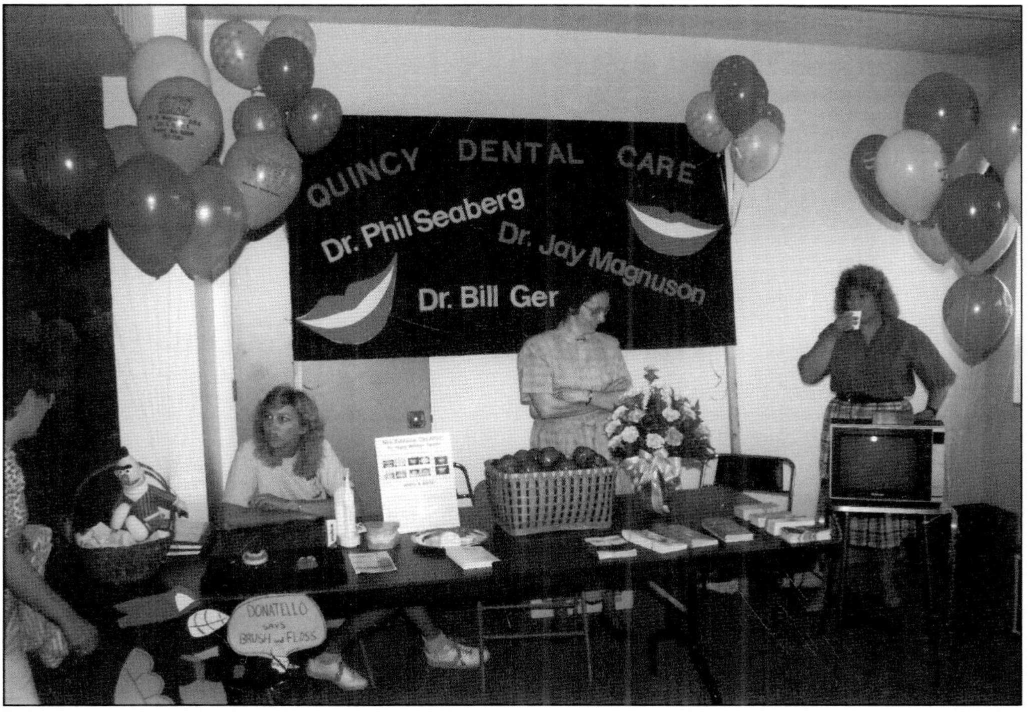

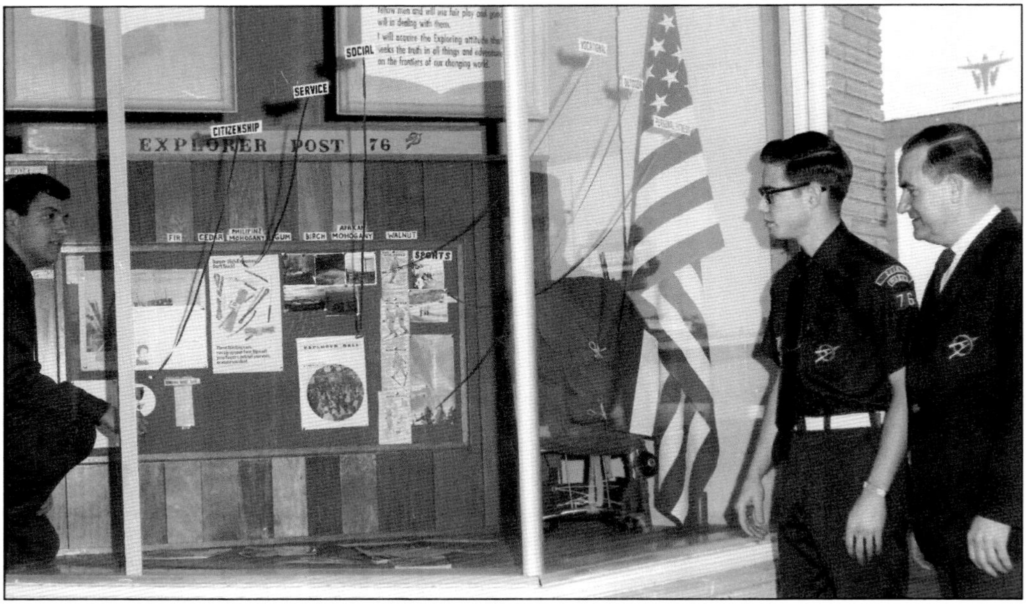

Quincy Boy Scouts. In the image above, Chuck Steele and Eldon Hope (right) observe while Phil Bell arranges the downtown display of LDS Explorer Post 76 during Boy Scout week in 1967. A year later, Quincy Troop 101 was selected to perform color guard duties during the dedication of the new observatory building at Dry Falls near Sun Lakes State Park. Troop members seen below are, from left to right, Paul Taylor, Bob Golmen, Fred Naigle, James Taylor, Ray Valdez, Bill Naigle, Steve Naigle, and Jan Cooper. Boy Scout Eagle projects have benefited the community in many ways, including a census of the local cemetery, installing a sprinkler system at the Reiman-Simmons House Museum, and installing signs along roads so passersby may identify the crops growing in the fields. (Both images courtesy of the Quincy Valley Post-Register.)

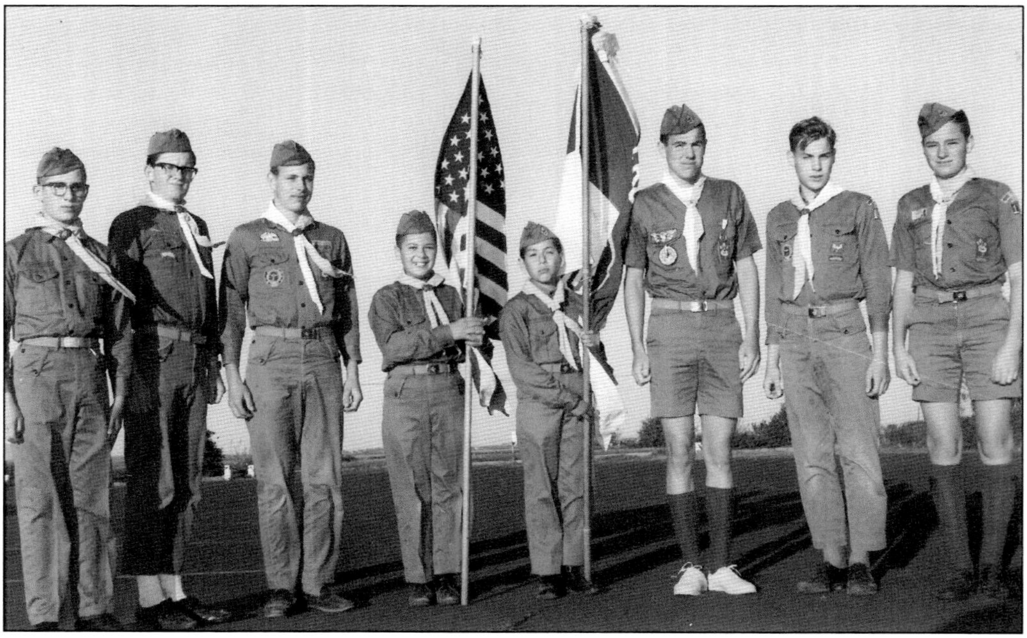

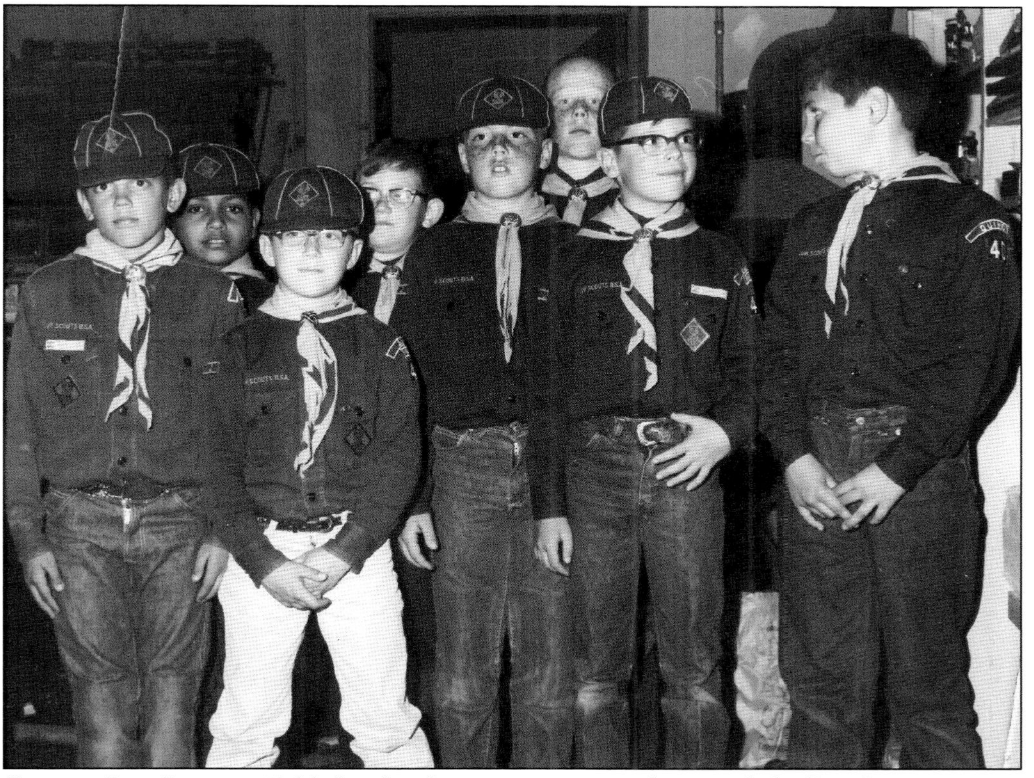

Quincy Cub Scouts, 1966. Leaders have to start somewhere, and the Boy Scout program begins training its future leaders in the Cub Scouts. This picture shows the boys of Den 2, Pack 40, including a future Boy Scout leader. James Thayer, the tallest boy in the back row, continues the tradition by serving many years as a leader in local LDS Troop 76. (Courtesy of the *Quincy Valley Post-Register*.)

Ephrata Baseball Team, 1965. Every small community has its neighboring rival. In the Quincy Valley, there is no doubt that nearby Ephrata has been the local nemesis for at least two generations. Green jacks and orange tigers are destined to compete for primacy on the field since the first baseball games between the two towns began in the early 1900s. (Courtesy of the *Quincy Valley Post-Register*.)

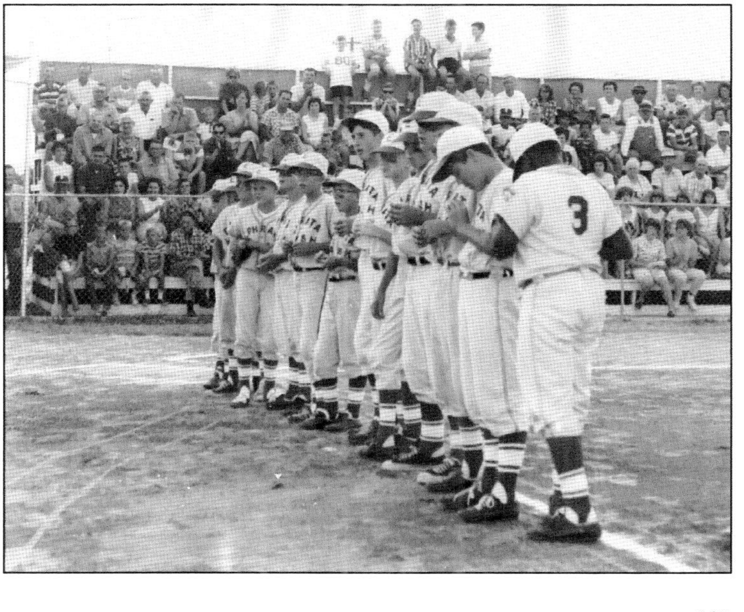

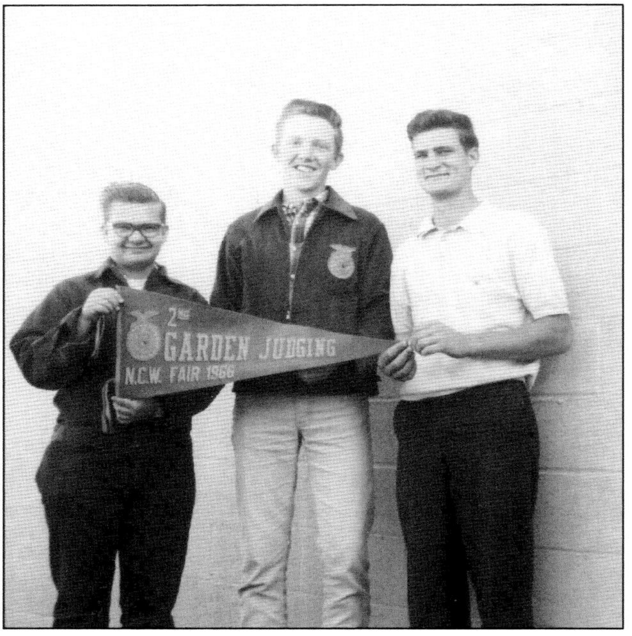

FUTURE FARMERS, 1966. Future Farmers of America is an organization designed to promote farming and leadership in the agricultural community. Frank Goodwin (left), Tom Gregg (center), and Wallace Bushman placed second in garden judging during the North Central Washington Fair held each summer in Douglas County. (Courtesy of the *Quincy Valley Post-Register.*)

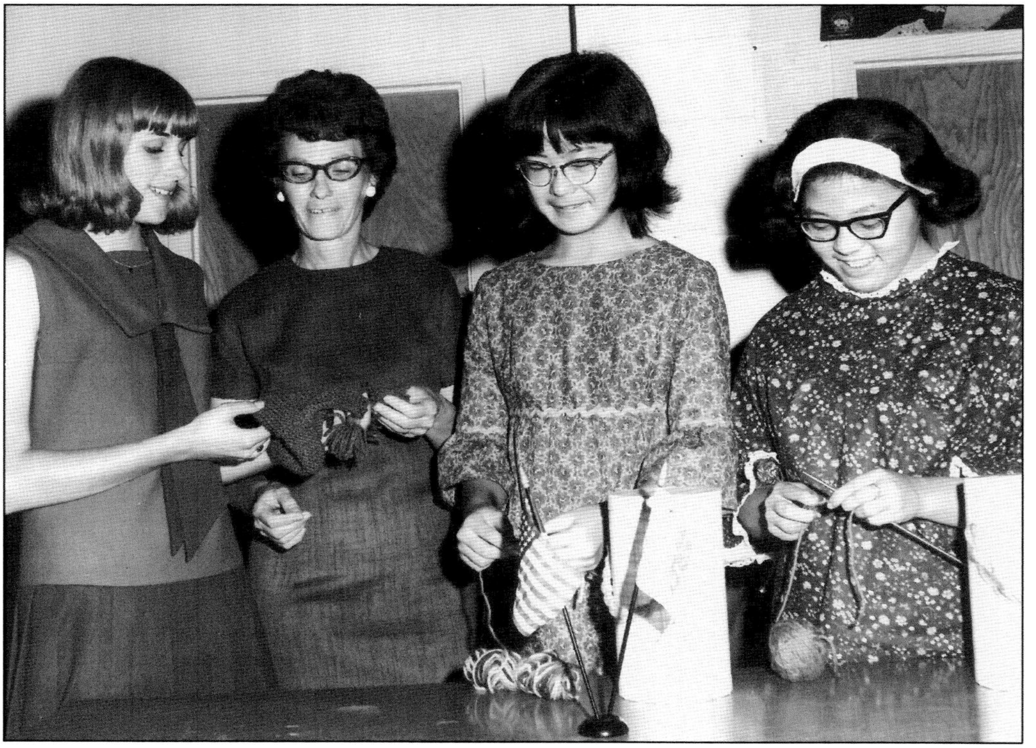

4-H KNITTERS, 1966. One of the mottoes of 4-H is to learn by doing. In this picture, Lonabel Kissell, the former owner of Kissell's Variety Store, teaches three 4-H girls how to knit. From left to right are an unidentified girl, Lonabel Kissell, Jan Kikuchi, and Connie Higashiyama. Lonabel currently owns the local ceramic shop. (Courtesy of the *Quincy Valley Post-Register.*)

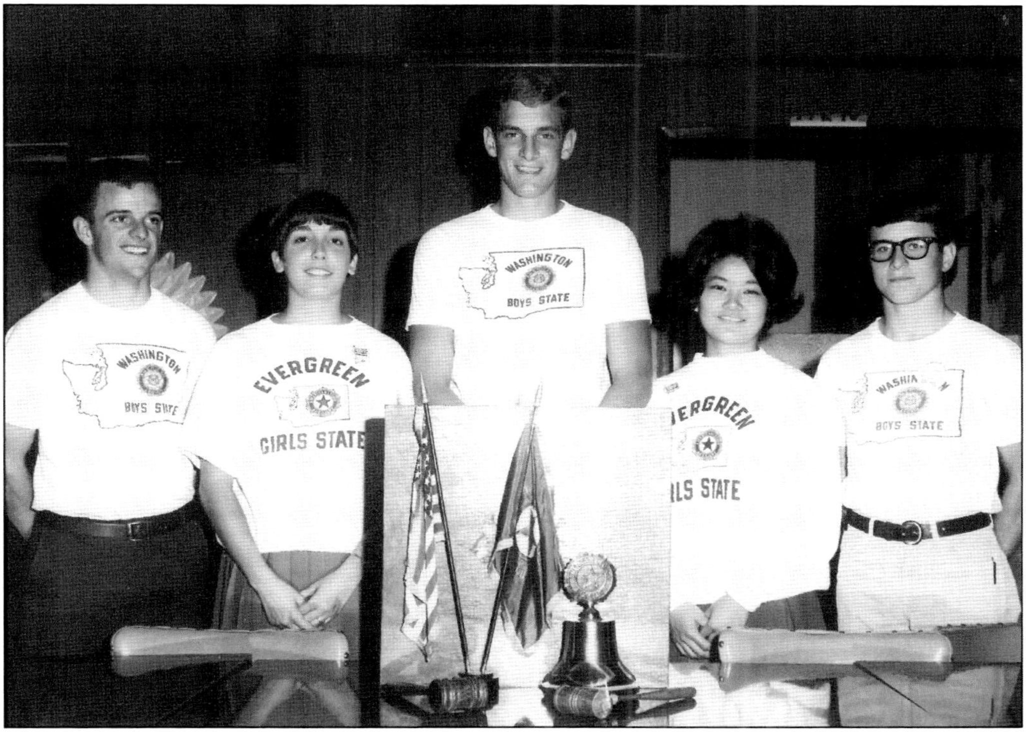

EVERGREEN BOYS AND GIRLS STATE, 1966. Quincy's youth were also interested in political and civic leadership. Interested high school students are sponsored by the local American Legion Post to provide training in those areas. The 1966 attendees were, from left to right, an unidentified young man, Terri Forge, Greg Forge, Sherri Jo Konishi, and another unidentified young man. (Courtesy of the *Quincy Valley Post-Register.*)

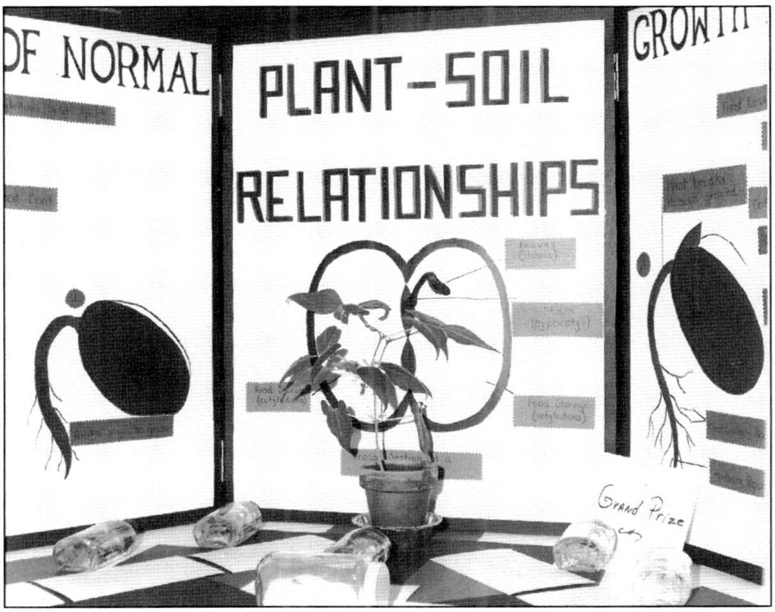

SCIENCE FAIR, 1965. Understanding the science of plant and soil relationships is an important component of any successful farming operation. Raising a healthy, abundant crop requires a basic understanding of the science behind it. Quincy students won the grand prize for their ability to demonstrate these concepts. (Courtesy of the *Quincy Valley Post-Register.*)

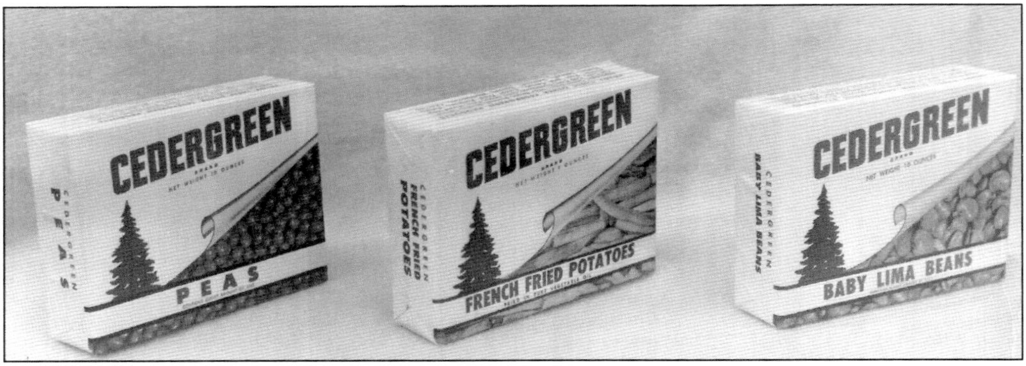

Cedergreen Frozen Vegetables, 1967. The Cedergreen brothers packed frozen vegetables at their plant in Winchester using locally grown produce. In 1942, the Cedergreen family was instrumental in preventing the internment of several Japanese American families on the West Coast by offering them farming jobs in the Quincy Valley. Many were already growers for the company. (Courtesy of the *Quincy Valley Post-Register.*)

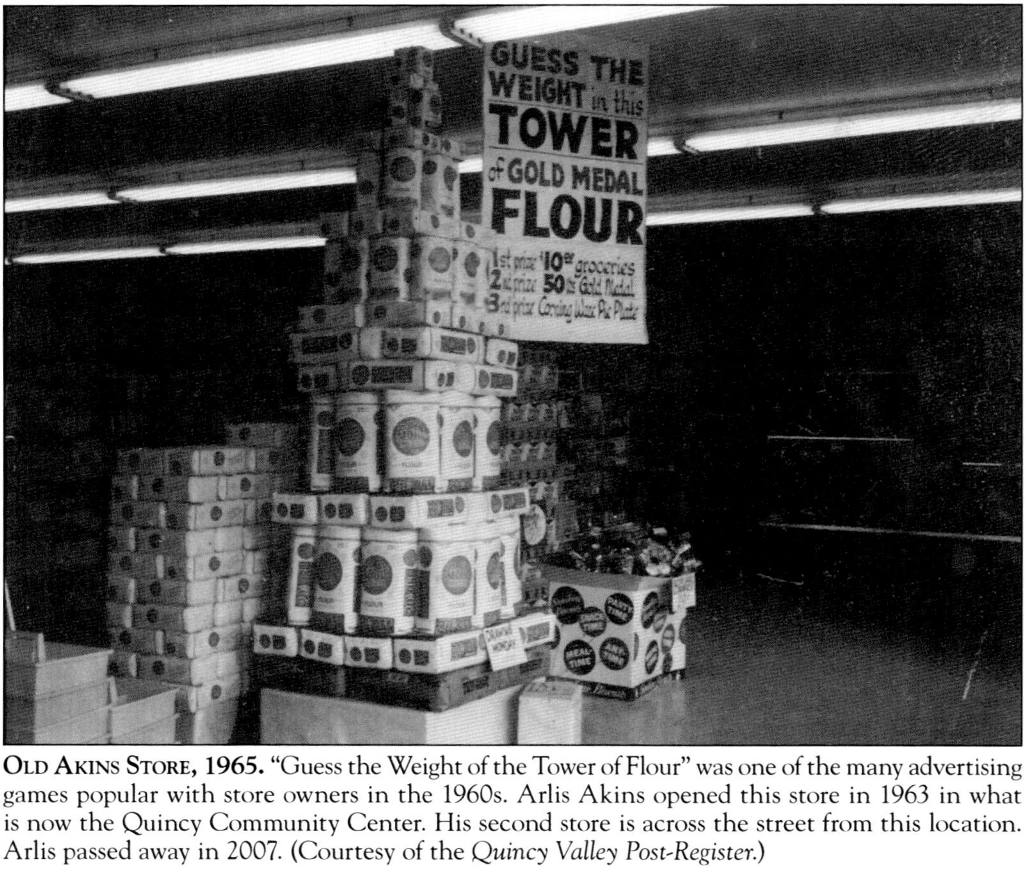

Old Akins Store, 1965. "Guess the Weight of the Tower of Flour" was one of the many advertising games popular with store owners in the 1960s. Arlis Akins opened this store in 1963 in what is now the Quincy Community Center. His second store is across the street from this location. Arlis passed away in 2007. (Courtesy of the *Quincy Valley Post-Register.*)

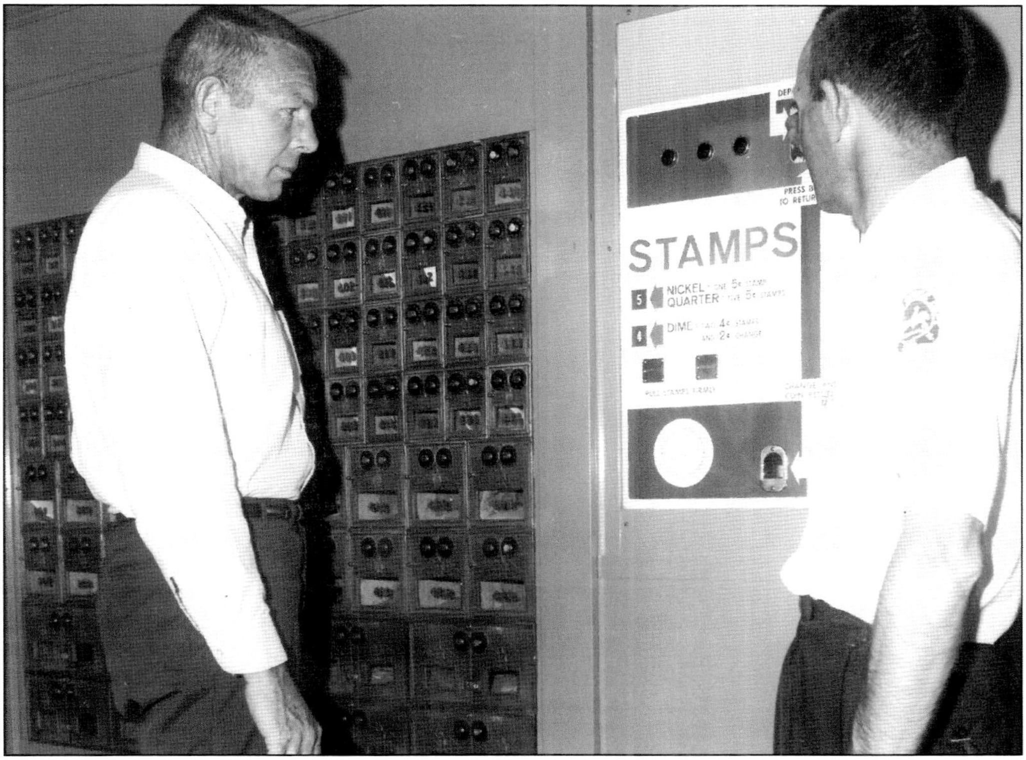

QUINCY POST OFFICE, 1965. Quincy postmaster Ralph Nickels shows off the new stamp machine. The first stamp in Quincy was purchased in 1902 by Conrad Weber, or so he always claimed. In the early days, mail arrived by train and was tossed out in large canvas bags. Outgoing mailbags were hung on a pole west of town, the trainmen snaring them as the train rushed by. (Courtesy of the *Quincy Valley Post-Register*.)

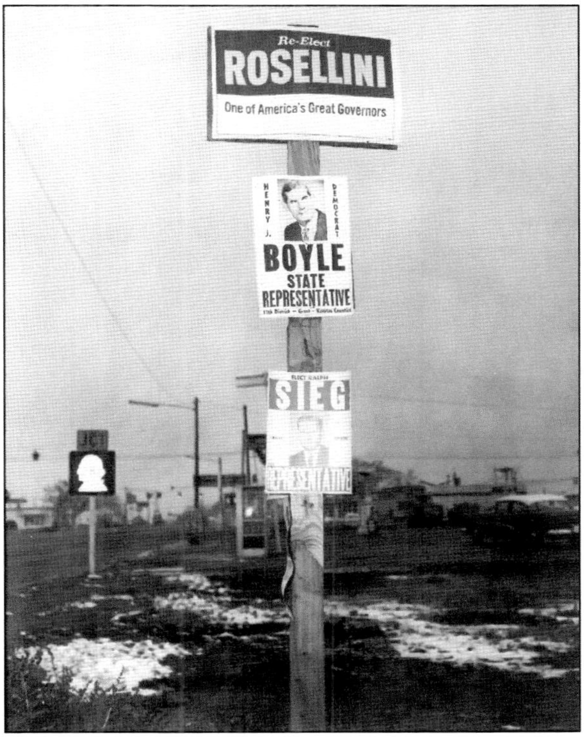

POLITICS, QUINCY STYLE. Campaign signs on posts are a sign that election season has arrived. Politicians have often come to the Quincy Valley, from Pres. Theodore Roosevelt in 1904 to Gov. Albert Rossellini on July 4, 1957, when the town of George was dedicated. Gov. Christine Gregoire visited on June 21, 2010, to celebrate the expansion of the Microsoft data server farm. (Courtesy of the *Quincy Valley Post-Register*.)

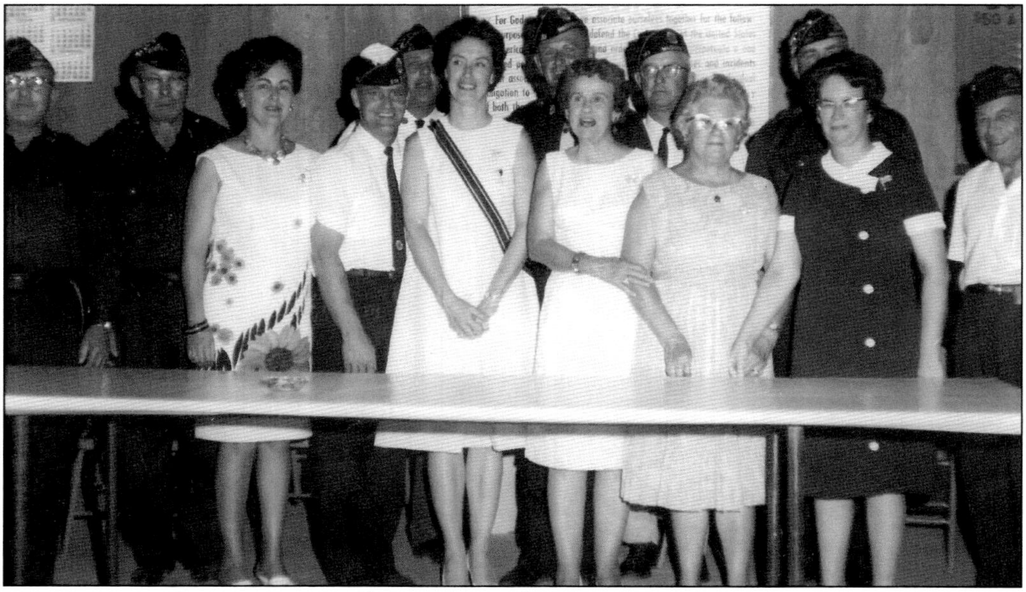

The American Legion, 1967. The Lambert-Schulz Post No. 183 and the Ladies Auxiliary of the American Legion are an important part of life in the Quincy Valley. They provide a place for veterans to socialize, provide information, sponsor youth programs and essay contests, as well as providing color guards for holidays, funerals, and other special events. This picture shows the newly installed officers for the year 1967. (Courtesy of the *Quincy Valley Post-Register*.)

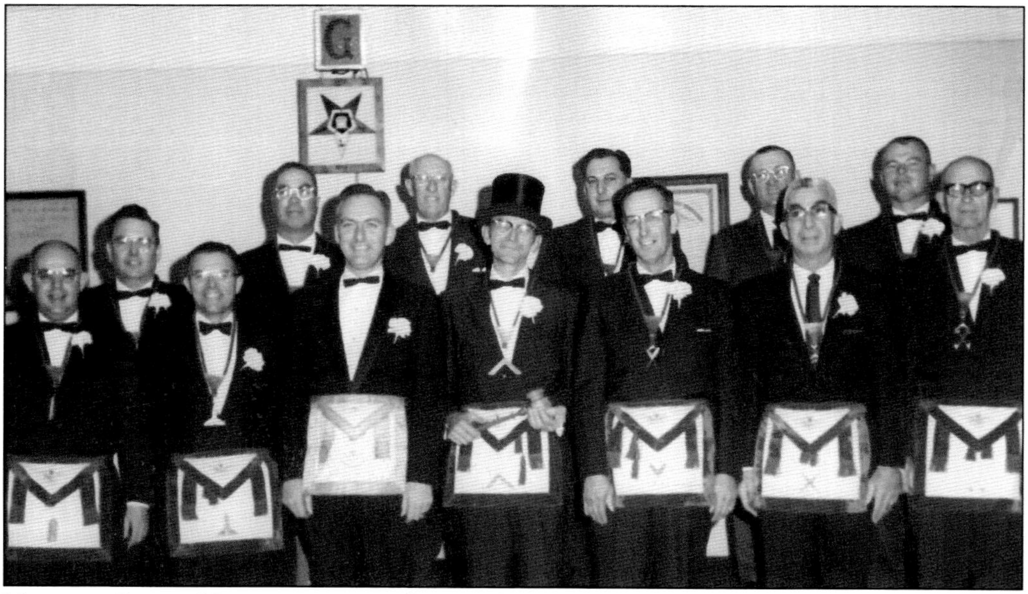

Masonic Lodge No. 161, 1967. Chartered in 1907, Masonic Lodge No. 161 is the oldest continuing service organization in the Quincy Valley, along with its women's auxiliary, the Order of the Eastern Star. From left to right are (first row) Keith Adams, James Curdy, Robert Graham, Karl Weber, J. B. Anderson, W. E. Jones, and D. T. Martin; (second row) Wayne Tetherow, Milo Ahrens, Jess B. Miller, Orville Dubee, W. R. Cordell, and Wilson Lough. (Courtesy of the *Quincy Valley Post-Register*.)

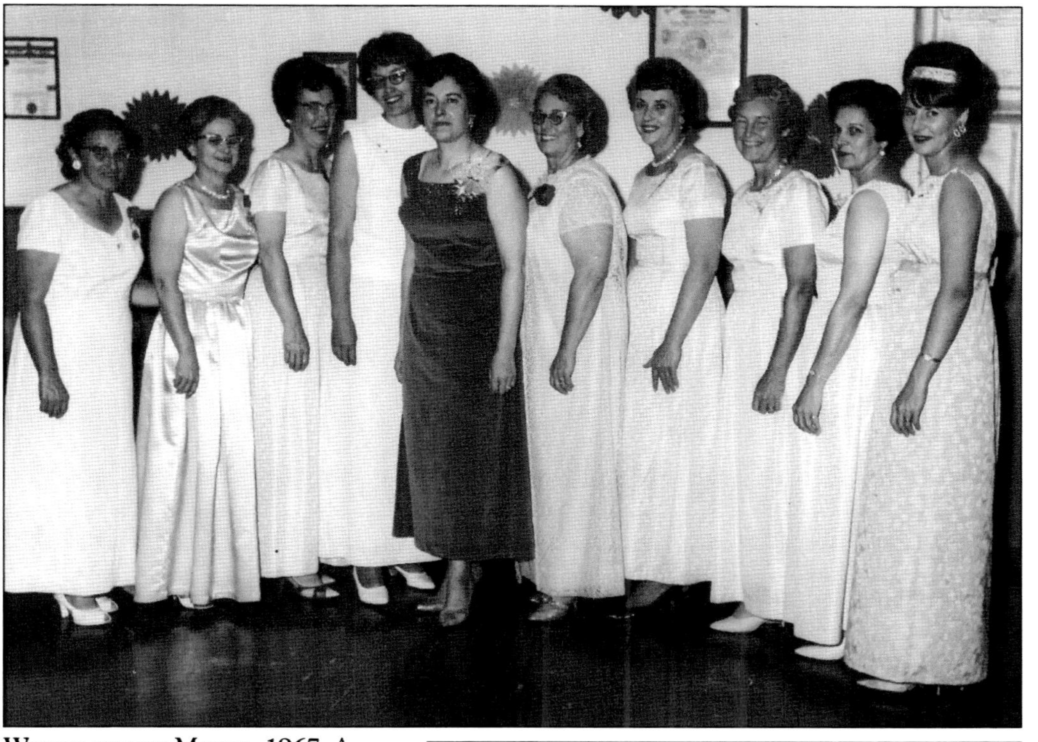

WOMEN OF THE MOOSE, 1967. A family-oriented community service auxiliary to the Moose Lodge, the Women of the Moose was founded nationally in 1913. From left to right are Florence Close, Edna Fish, Ann Schmidt, Marvelyn Hewitt, Betty Simpson, Elma Gardner, Nelda Grant, Eva Davis, Esther Hoffner, and Melba Wells. (John C. Eckerson photograph; courtesy of the *Quincy Valley Post-Register*.)

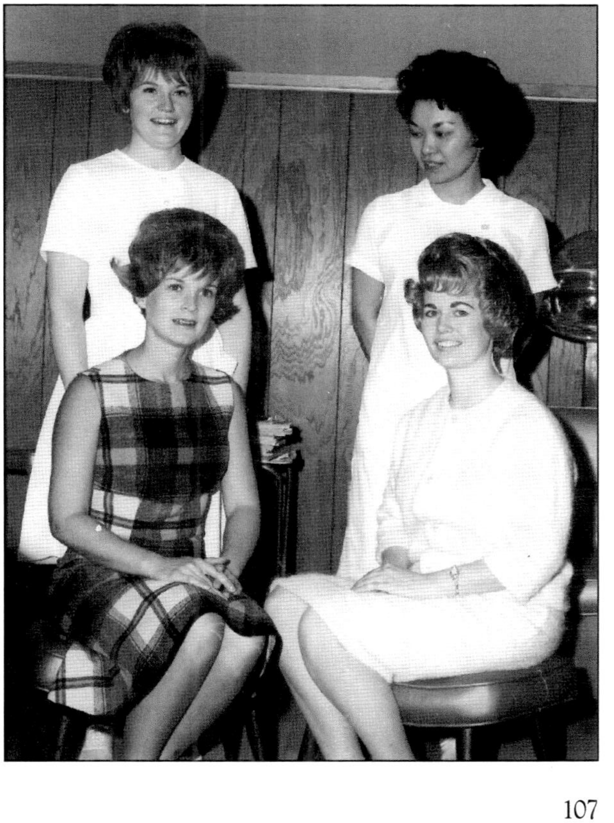

KIM'S BEAUTY SHOP, 1966. Kemie Oda and her stylists made sure the women of the Quincy Valley sported the latest hairstyles for several years. Sitting are Roberta Grigg (left) and LaRae Hope Webley; standing are Sally Patton (left) and Kemie Oda. Sally Patton continued with her own shop when Kim's closed. (Courtesy of the *Quincy Valley Post-Register*.)

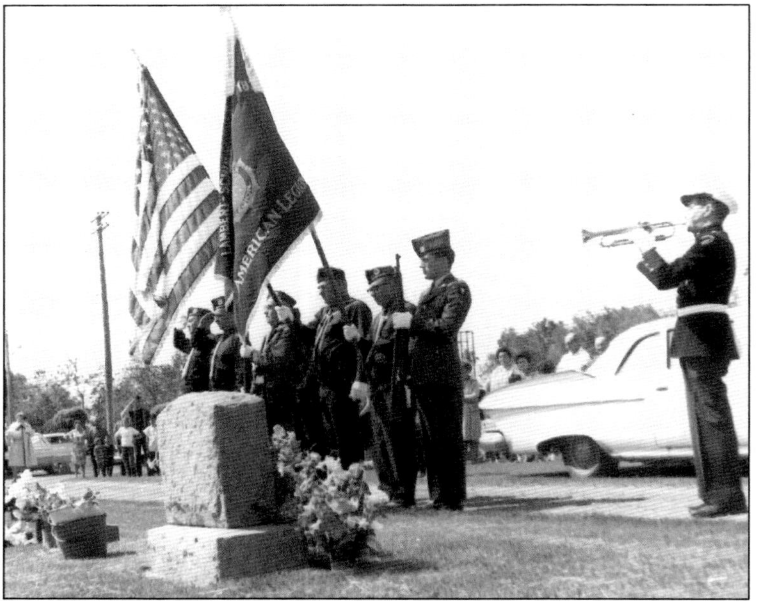

Memorial Day, 1967. Military ceremonies on Memorial Day are a continuing tradition in the Quincy Valley. Community members of all ages meet at the cemetery at sunrise every year to post over 100 flags—each one named for a veteran buried there. Pictured here is a traditional ceremony to honor all veterans, living and dead, performed by the Lambert-Schulz American Legion Post No. 183. (Courtesy of the *Quincy Valley Post-Register.*)

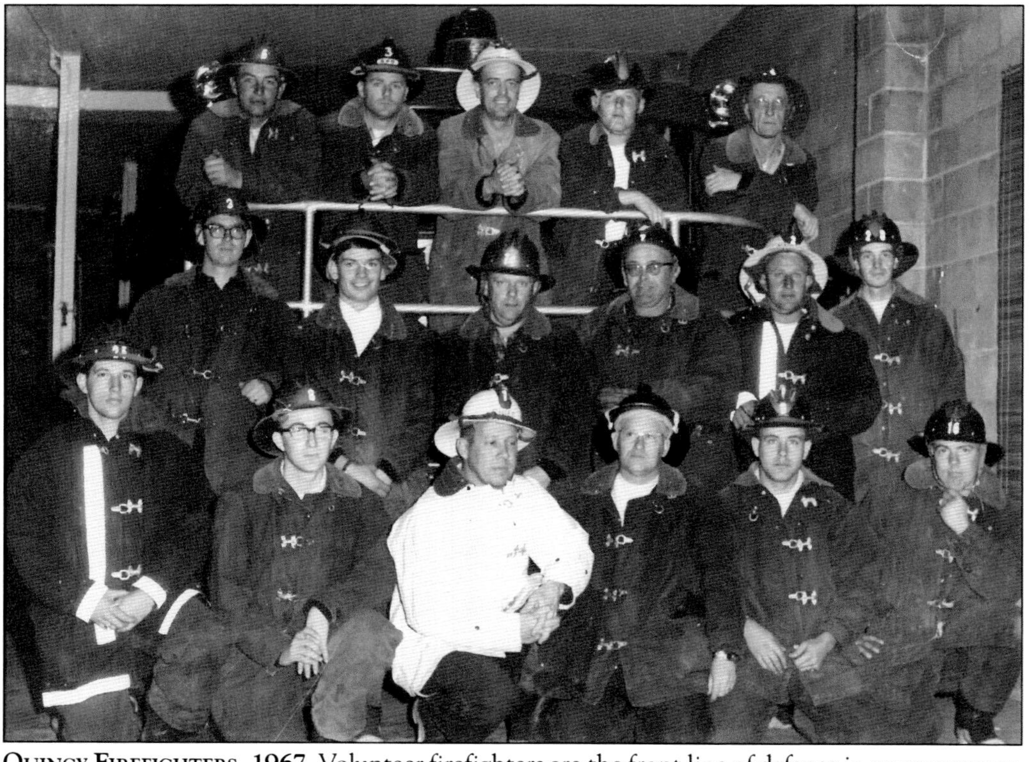

Quincy Firefighters, 1967. Volunteer firefighters are the front line of defense in an emergency. They are the original Homeland Security force. From left to right are (first row) Ron Burns, Bill Woodward, Don Simmons, Jim Burns, John Young, and C. F. Smith; (second row) Jerry Fairfield, Bill Doerr, Jim McClure, Bob Besel, Dick Zimbelman, and Cleve Schuchman; (third row) Don Weil, Tom Hess, Les Fortier, Dean Andrews, and Joe Keller. (Courtesy of the *Quincy Valley Post-Register.*)

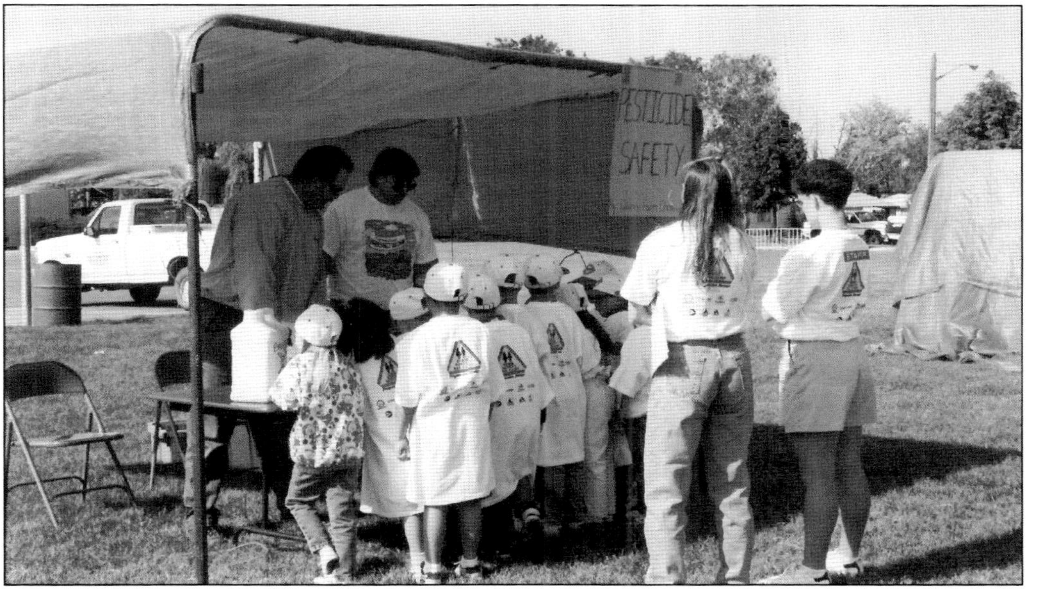

Farm Safety Day Camp, 1998. This first annual event was attended by 200 Quincy Valley children, who were divided into 11 groups named for various farming industry companies, such as John Deere or Stemilt. Classes were taught safety techniques around the house and farm. Here one group learns about pesticide safety. (Courtesy of the Quincy Valley Chamber of Commerce.)

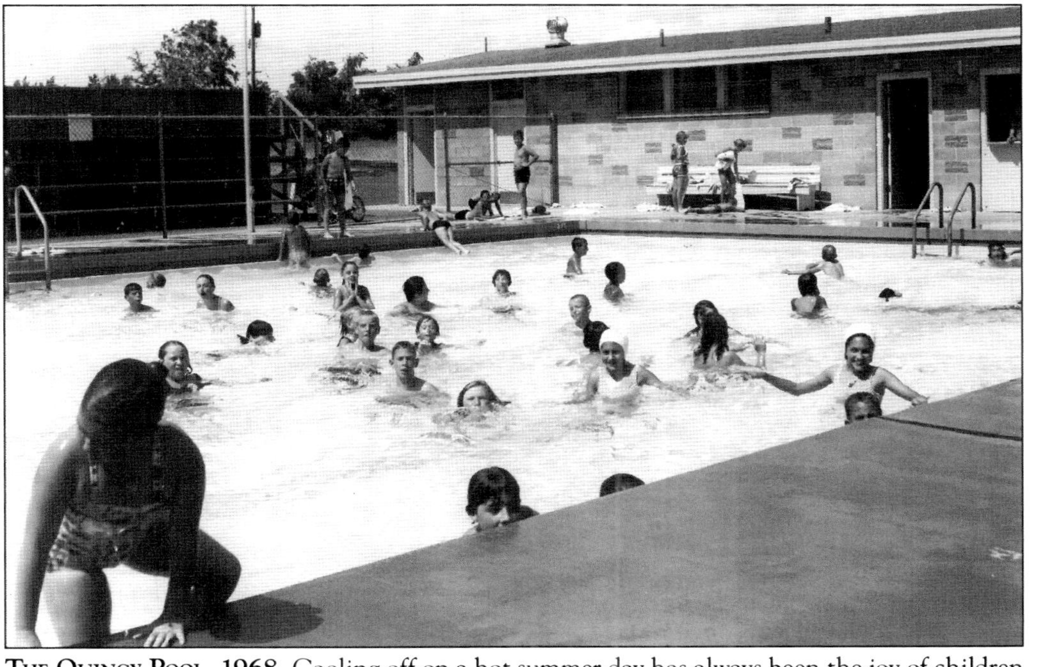

The Quincy Pool, 1968. Cooling off on a hot summer day has always been the joy of children and adults. In the early days, people would have to go down to the river. Later irrigation canals were too dangerous. A swimming pool was the perfect answer. The pool pictured here remains in use, but with new features added, it has become an aquatic center. (Courtesy of the *Quincy Valley Post-Register.*)

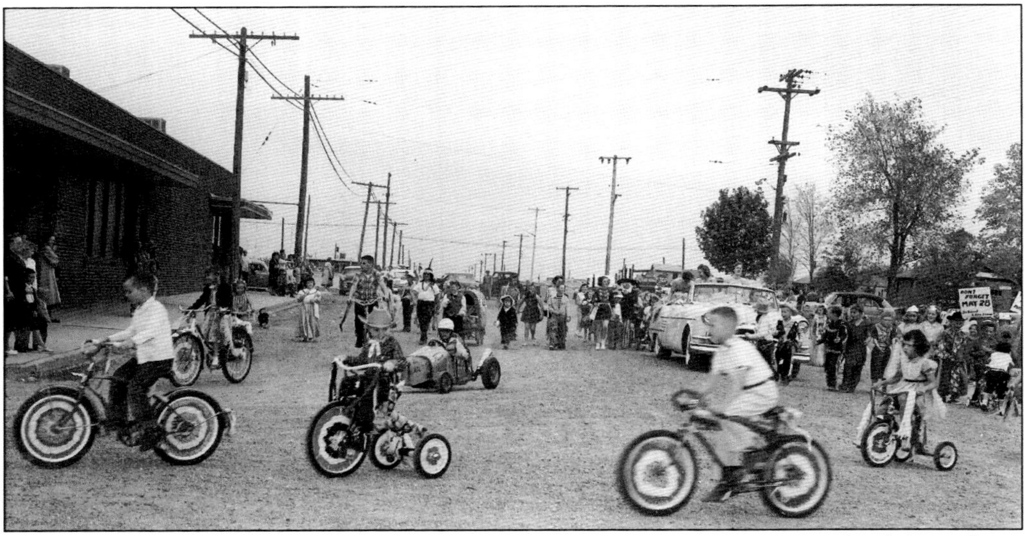

Hot Wheels 1950s-Style. The littlest road warriors parade their fancy street rods while cowboys, Indians, and pioneers bring up the rear, showing off their costumes in a typical Quincy Valley parade. The Turf restaurant can be seen on the left, while The Creamery is in the background. The roads were still unpaved at this time. (Courtesy of the Quincy Valley Historical Society.)

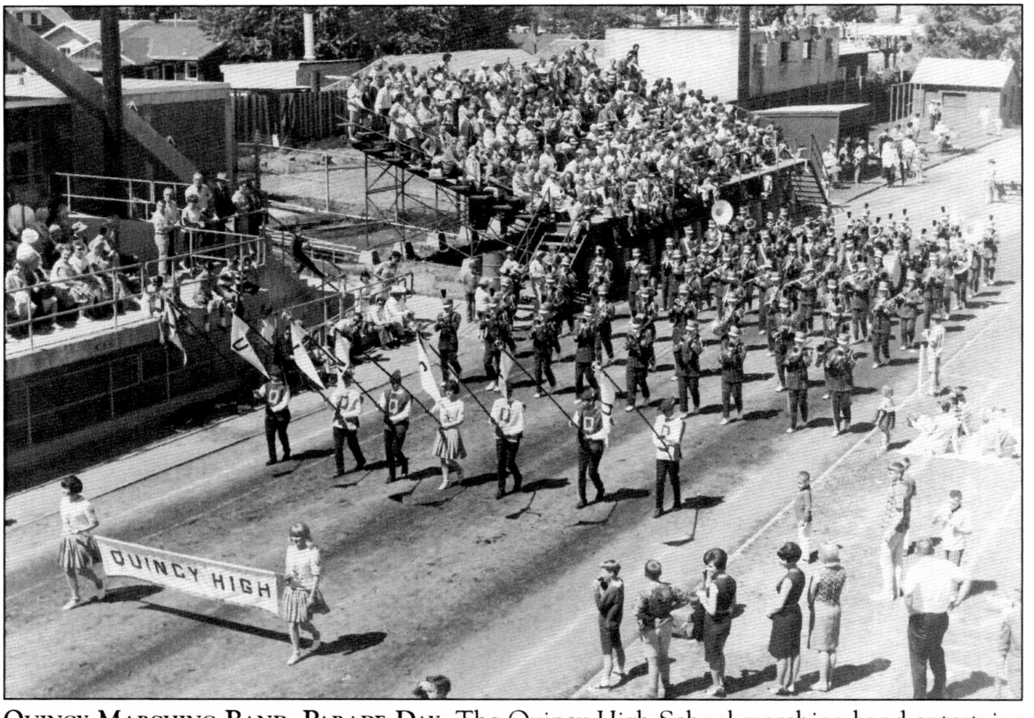

Quincy Marching Band, Parade Day. The Quincy High School marching band entertains listeners during the annual Apple Blossom parade in nearby Wenatchee. The first parade was held in 1919. Apple Blossom is the oldest major festival in Washington, pausing only for three years during World War II. Quincy often participated with floats and bands. (Courtesy of the *Quincy Valley Post-Register.*)

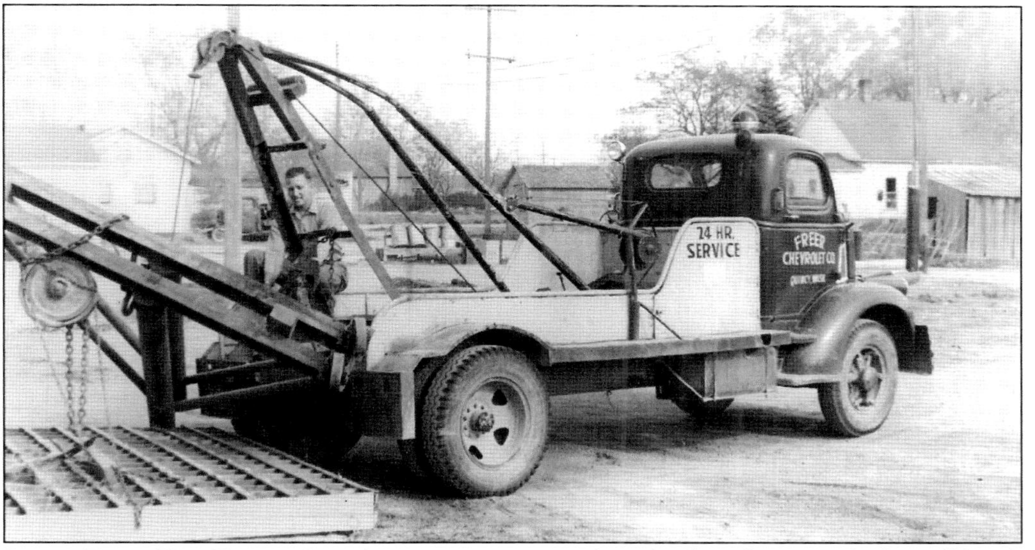

Steele Freer Tow Truck. One thing is more certain than death and taxes: vehicles will break down. Steele Freer's heavy-duty tow truck rescued many a stranded traveler or farmer. His son, Chris Freer, carries on the Freer car sales tradition in Quincy. (Courtesy of the Quincy Valley Historical Society.)

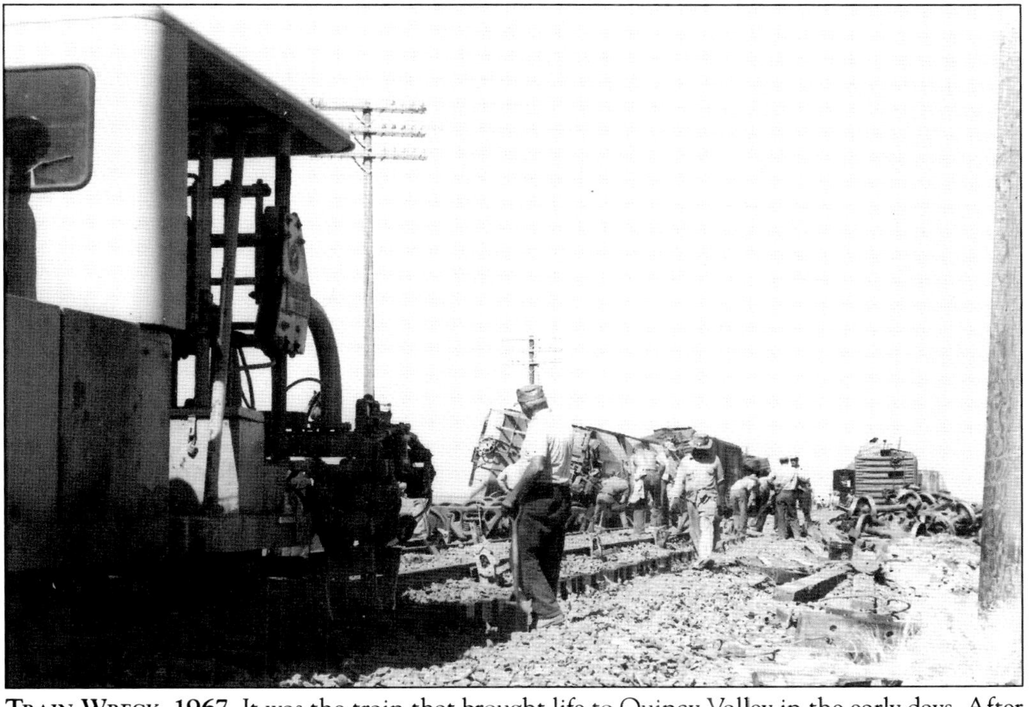

Train Wreck, 1967. It was the train that brought life to Quincy Valley in the early days. After irrigation, trains took Quincy's produce to the world. Today with the creation of the intermodal terminal, trains transport goods to and from the ports in Seattle on a daily basis. One will occasionally leave the track, but it is quickly removed, and commerce continues. (Courtesy of the *Quincy Valley Post-Register.*)

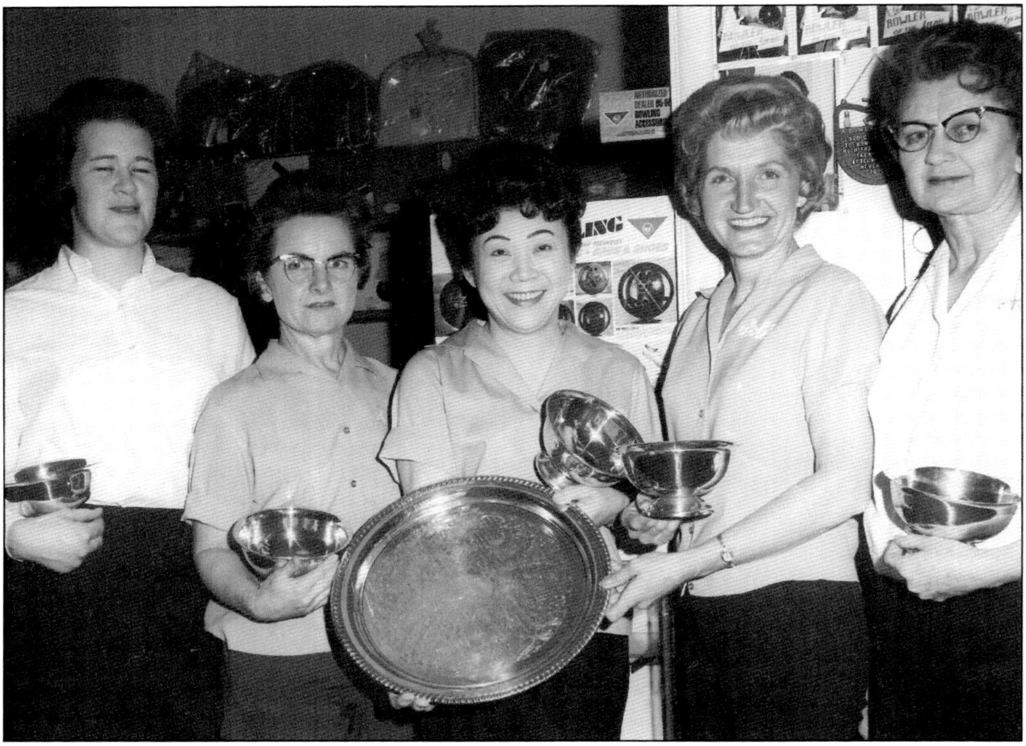

WOMEN BOWLERS, 1967. Clarence and Louise Kyle opened the Basin Bowl in 1956, Quincy's first recreational business. It became a popular sport and social activity. One of the winning teams is pictured here. From left to right are Barbara Dodge, Metha Koeneman, Frances Yoshino, Goldie North, and Ann Banko. (Courtesy of the *Quincy Valley Post-Register.*)

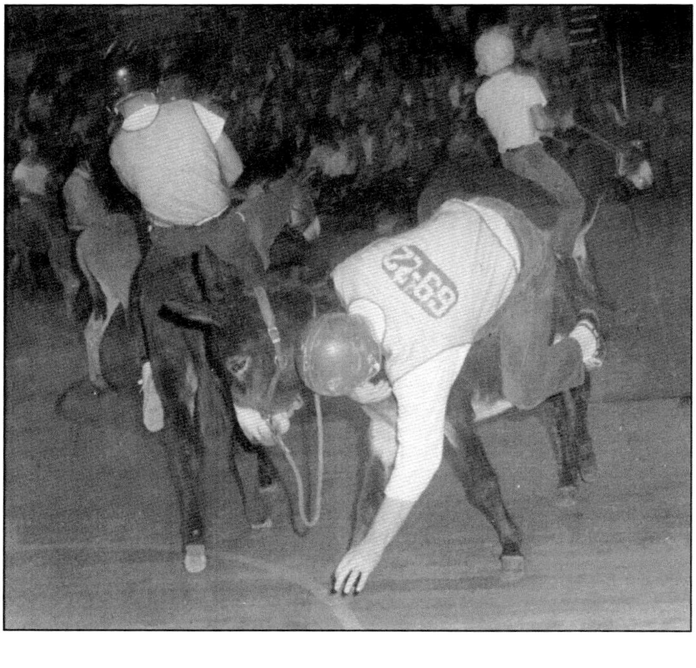

DONKEY BASKETBALL, 1969. Trained donkeys and untrained riders compete against each other in an unruly game of basketball. These were popular fund-raising events, filled with much laughter at the antics on the court. Here one rider hopes to save himself from a fall. (Courtesy of the *Quincy Valley Post-Register.*)

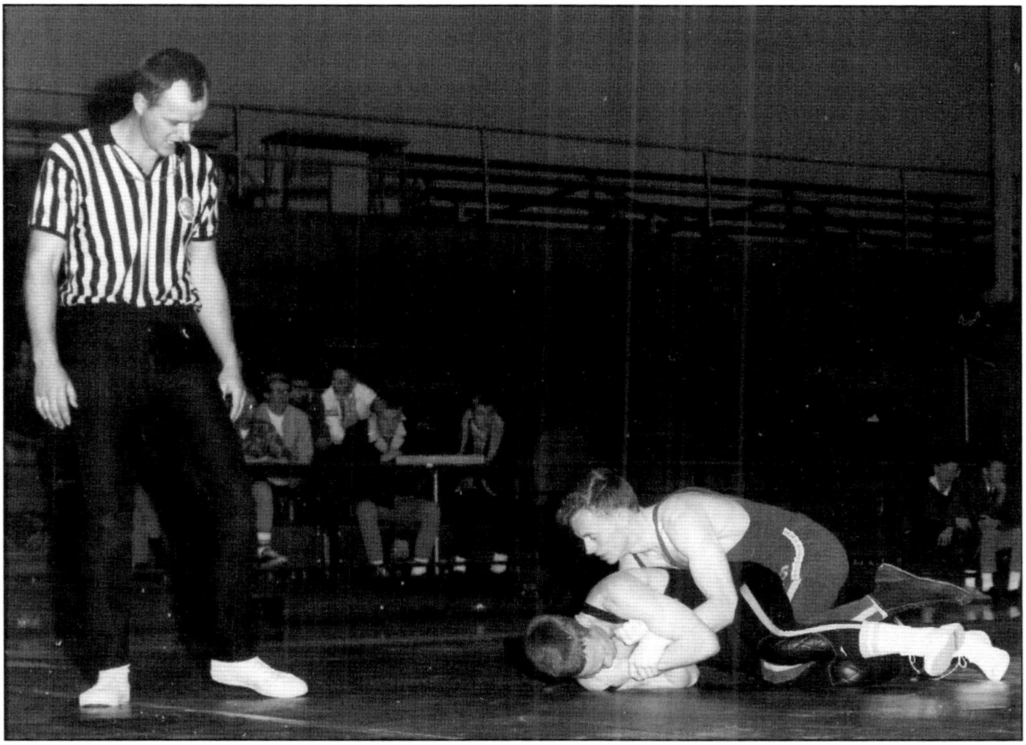

QUINCY WRESTLING MATCH, 1966. Wrestling has long been a staple of Quincy High School sports. It requires commitment and hours of hard training to be successful. The six sons of Bruce and Mary Ann Webley (descendants of early settlers) and the Ibarra family are only the most recent examples of this dedication. (Courtesy of the *Quincy Valley Post-Register.*)

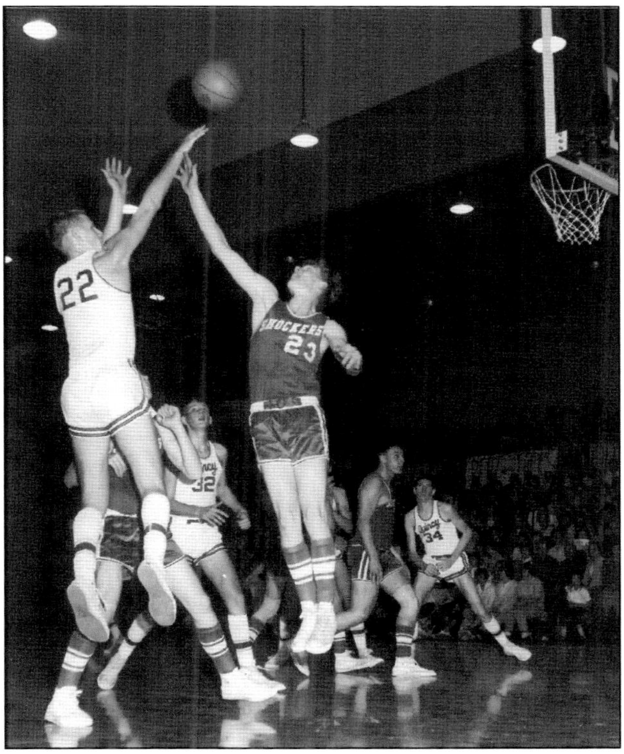

QUINCY BASKETBALL, 1966. Basketball teams for both boys and girls were formed as early as 1910. Each year since 2003, Quincy halts traffic on its downtown streets and puts up hoops for the Annual Dru Gimlin 3-on-3 Tournament fund-raiser for the Dru Gimlin Foundation. Dru was a popular and talented player killed in a tragic car accident. (Courtesy of the *Quincy Valley Post-Register.*)

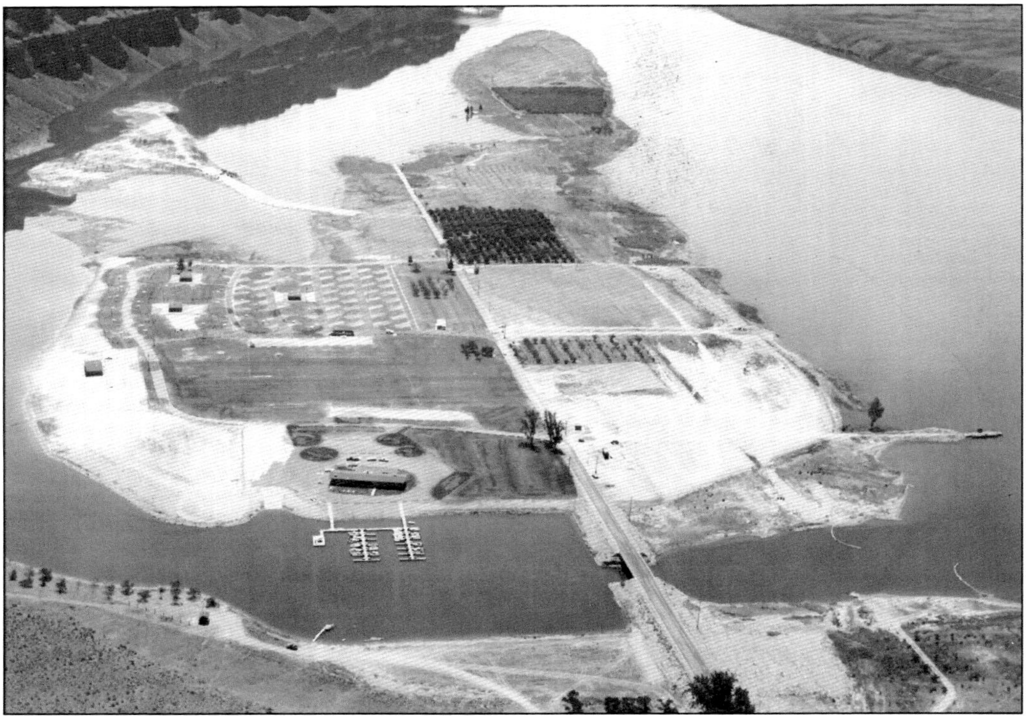

CRESCENT BAR, 1967. Crescent Bar was flooded by the filling of the Wanapum Dam in 1963. Landowners were bought out, and the Public Utility District of Grant County decided to create a park and rent the land left dry. A recreational area with a golf course, picnic and boating areas, campsites, trailer facilities, and restrooms was created. The picture above shows Crescent Bar at this stage. Speed boat races were among the activities available to visitors, and the whole town would turn out for the day. Boy Scouts and the Lions Club are assisting with the races in the picture below. (Above, courtesy of the Quincy Valley Historical Society; below, courtesy of the *Quincy Valley Post-Register.*)

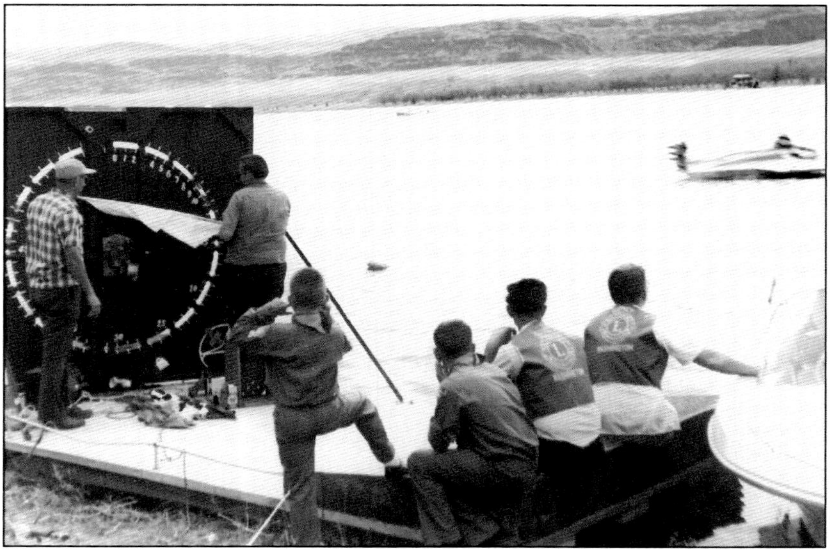

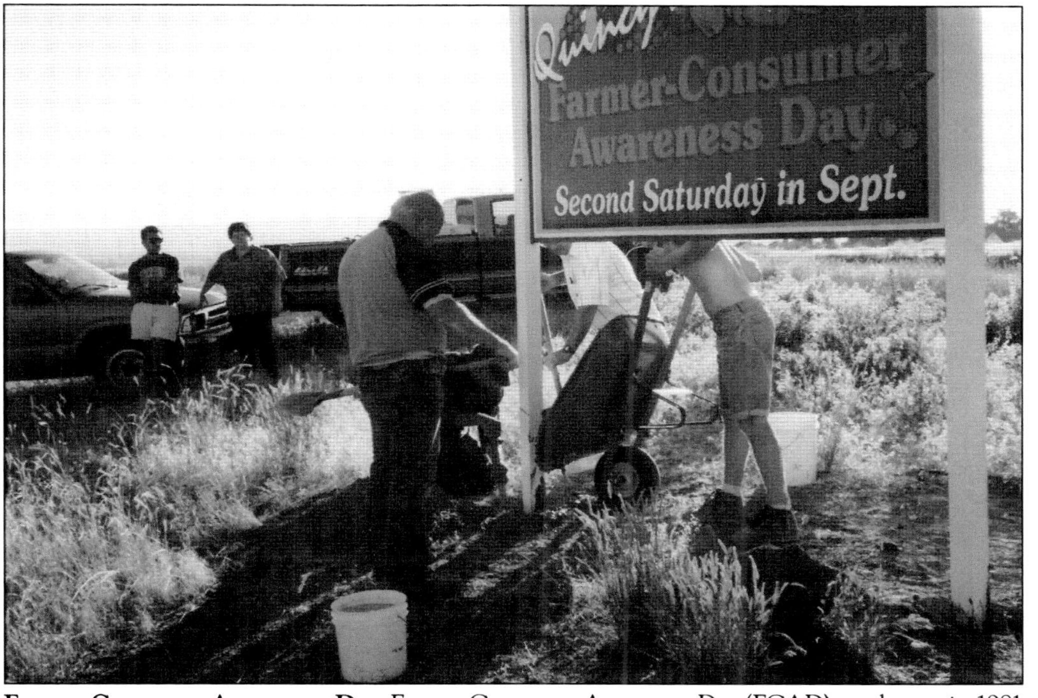

Farmer Consumer Awareness Day. Farmer Consumer Awareness Day (FCAD) was begun in 1981 by local farmer Dennis Higashiyama, who became frustrated while listening to radio personality Paul Harvey talk about a woman who complained to her grocer about the high cost of food. The grocer explained about paying wages, costs, and, of course, the farmer. Her reply was to get rid of the farmer because everyone knew that food comes from Safeway. Dennis Higashiyama decided to do something about it. An annual event for over 25 years, FCAD provides a fun and educational experience for everyone who wants to know where food comes from. As shown below, school buses take visitors on tours of local farms, orchards, and wineries, as well as pointing out local geology. (Both images courtesy of the Quincy Valley Chamber of Commerce.)

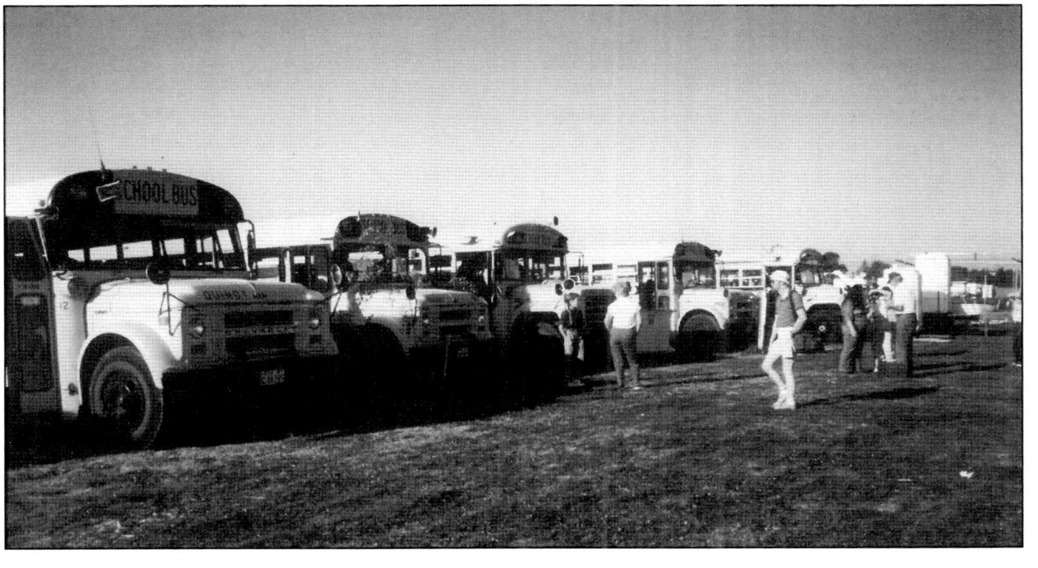

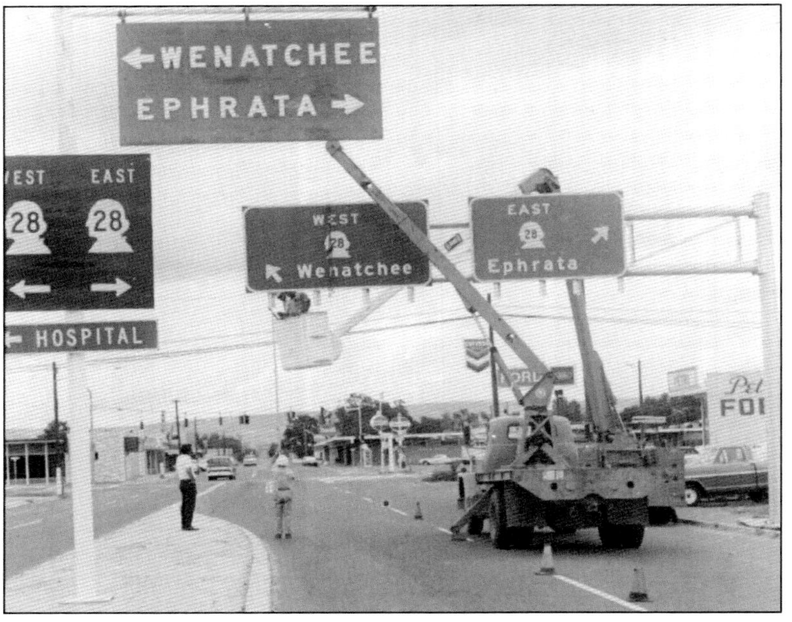

FINDING ONE'S WAY. These road signs were placed at the main intersection in Quincy. The town's children have long been taught their cardinal directions by a simple phrase, "East is Ephrata, and West is Wenatchee." It seems to work. There is no record of anyone getting lost in downtown Quincy. (Courtesy of the *Quincy Valley Post-Register.*)

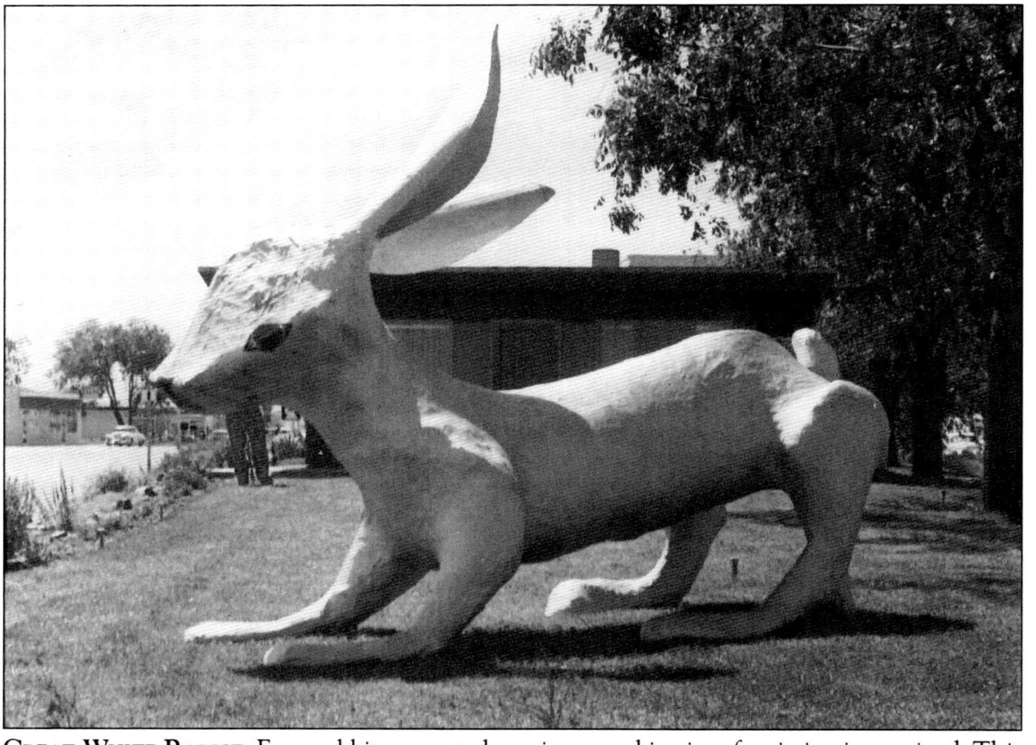

GREAT WHITE RABBIT. Even rabbits seem to have increased in size after irrigation arrived. This impressive specimen was discovered on the lawn of the chamber of commerce building one day. Lydia Westover believes that her husband, Quinn Westover, created this for one of his parade floats. Perhaps it was unable to read road signs and never made it to the Apple Blossom parade in Wenatchee. (Courtesy of Kaye Baumgartner.)

Seven

Wired for the 21st Century

The history of the Quincy Valley is not complete. Its motto is "Opportunities Unlimited," and with the organization of the intermodal terminal, the establishment of the area as a center for data server farms, the changing face of agriculture with new crops (like blueberries), and the growing wine industry, its future is bright.

Faith is still an important component in the lives of the people. A cursory glance at the telephone book shows 17 different denominations in a community of about 6,000 residents, many offering services in English and Spanish.

Family continues to be important. Education is still a priority. Public school, home education, and the new private Quincy Valley School are available. A new library is expected soon. Parks have been updated, and a new sports complex funded by the Paul Lauzier Foundation has been opened. Paul Lauzier was an early settler of Grant County.

Farming and related industries remain the mainstay of the economy. Microsoft, Yahoo, Intuit, and Sabey have introduced a new type of farm, the data server farm. Huge facilities housing hundreds of computer servers now grow out of the sagebrush desert on the north side of town.

The future of Quincy is best symbolized by the way Yahoo takes care of its weed problem. In keeping with the current trend of minimizing its environmental impact, the company has turned to a time-honored chemical-free method to reduce weeds around its buildings: a small herd of goats is brought in several times a year to eat the weeds and provide a little natural fertilizer at the same time. In this one scene, agriculture and technology blend harmoniously, a blending of past and present to create a vibrant future for the Quincy Valley.

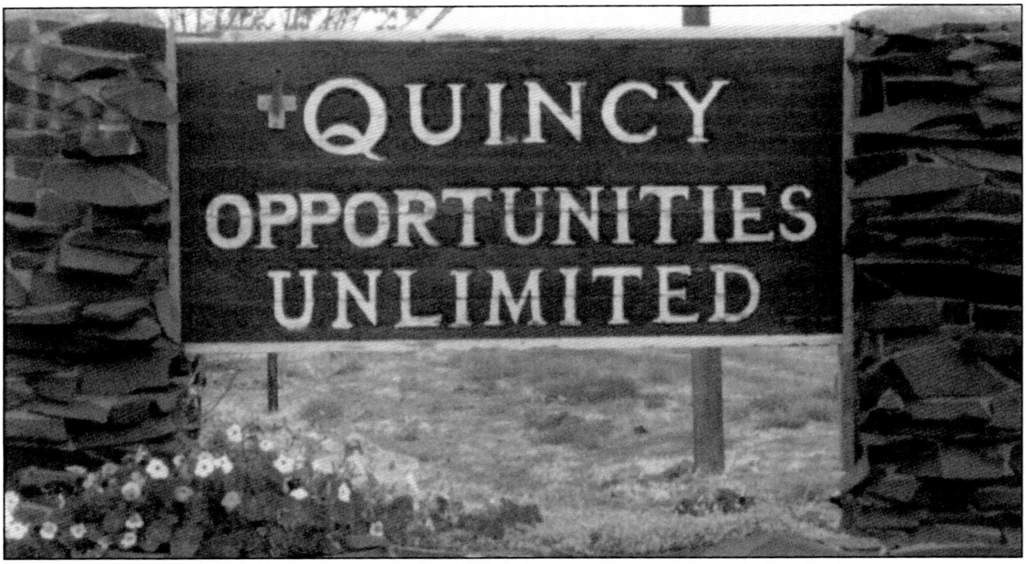

OPPORTUNITIES UNLIMITED. Farms, orchards, industries, businesses, technology firms, wineries, outdoor concerts, cultural events, golfing, resorts, rock climbing, hunting, fishing, horseback riding, camping, bicycling, boating, and swimming all make the Quincy Valley a destination for modern settlers and vacationers. Early settlers may have dreamed of turning a sagebrush desert into productive cropland, but they never could have imagined the abundance of the Quincy Valley. (Courtesy of the Quincy Valley Chamber of Commerce.)

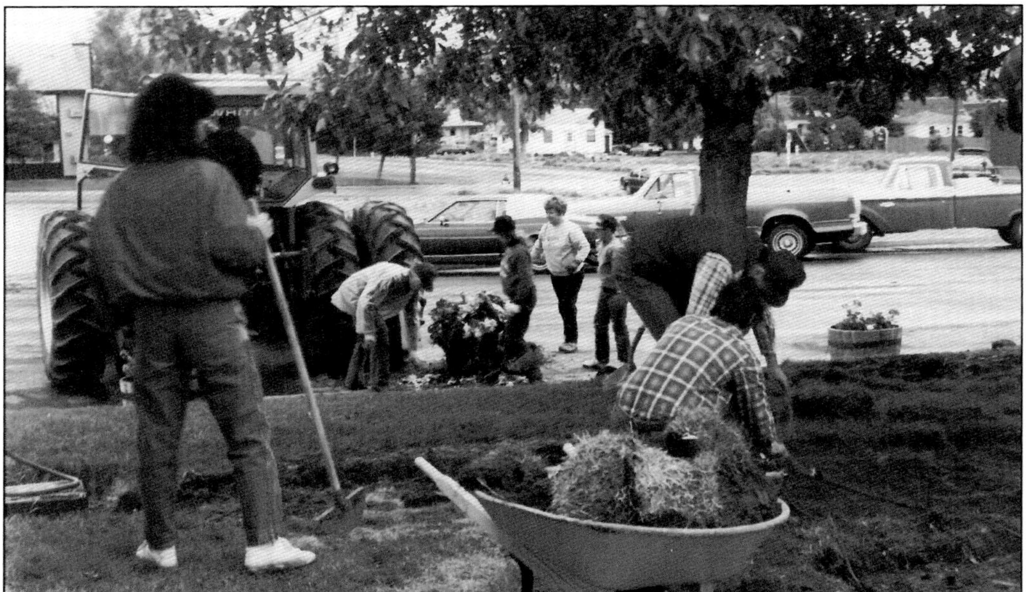

QUINCY BEAUTIFICATION PROJECT. Pictured here are volunteers from the Quincy Valley Chamber of Commerce working to beautify one of the main roads through Quincy. Many volunteers have planted cannas, tulips, and other flowers in an effort to make Quincy a beautiful place to live. Norma Culp, who spearheaded this project for several years, received the 2004 Jefferson Award for her efforts. (Courtesy of Quincy Valley Chamber of Commerce.)

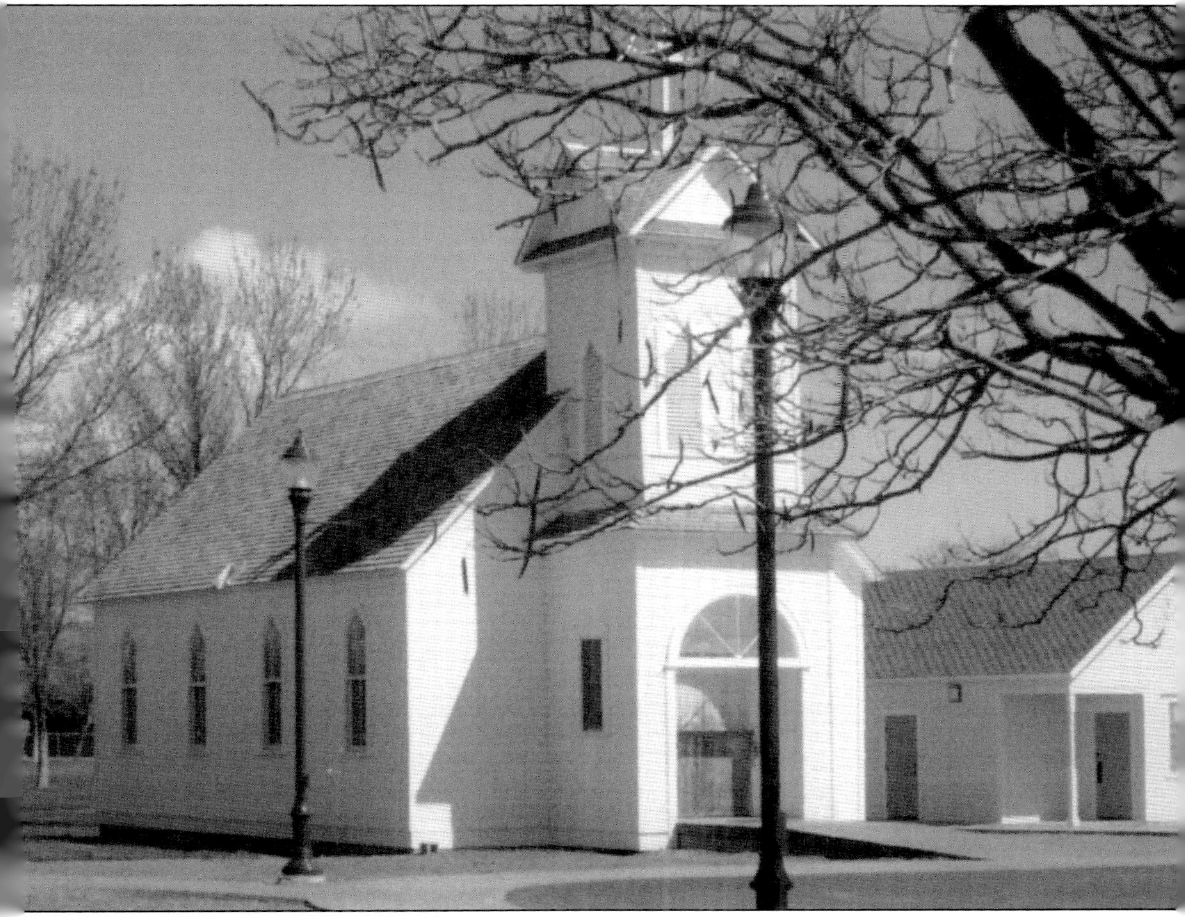

QUINCY PIONEER CHURCH. Built in 1904, the Quincy Pioneer Church was originally a community church shared by Lutherans and other Christian congregations. Its first pastor was the Lutheran reverend Christian Mack. Eventually it was renamed the St. Paul German Lutheran Church and used for worship until the congregation moved into a new building in 1951. The original building became home to other denominations, such as the Assembly of God, the Friends Church, and the Pentecostal Church. St. Paul Lutheran Church bought back the building in 2006 and gifted it to the Quincy Valley Historical Society. It was moved to the site of the Reiman-Simmons House later that year. It has been restored and will be dedicated soon. The Quincy Valley Historical Society will begin hosting its annual Old-Fashioned Christmas in the building. The church has already presided over its first wedding and will be the scene of many more social and cultural events in the future. The expression of religious faith continues to be an important part of life in the Quincy Valley. (Courtesy of the Quincy Valley Historical Society.)

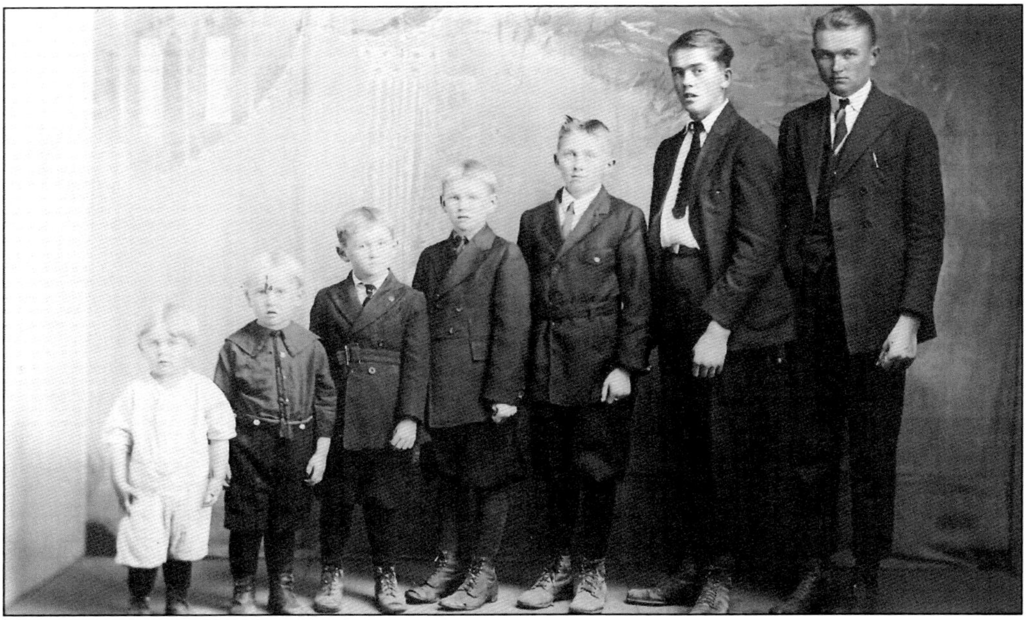

The Children of Quincy. The most valuable crop raised in the Quincy Valley has always been its children. Reared in families with a strong work ethic and religious faith, this crop grows strong, intelligent, and eager to make its mark on the world. Above is a picture of seven brothers dressed in their Sunday best for a formal picture about 1910. Below are the happy faces of children enjoying fun in the sun. The children of the Quincy Valley have always been its future. They live and work on all continents and serve in all branches of the military, yet their souls are anchored to the little corner of the world that nurtured them, the Quincy Valley. (Above, courtesy of the Quincy Valley Historical Society; below, courtesy of the Quincy Valley Chamber of Commerce.)

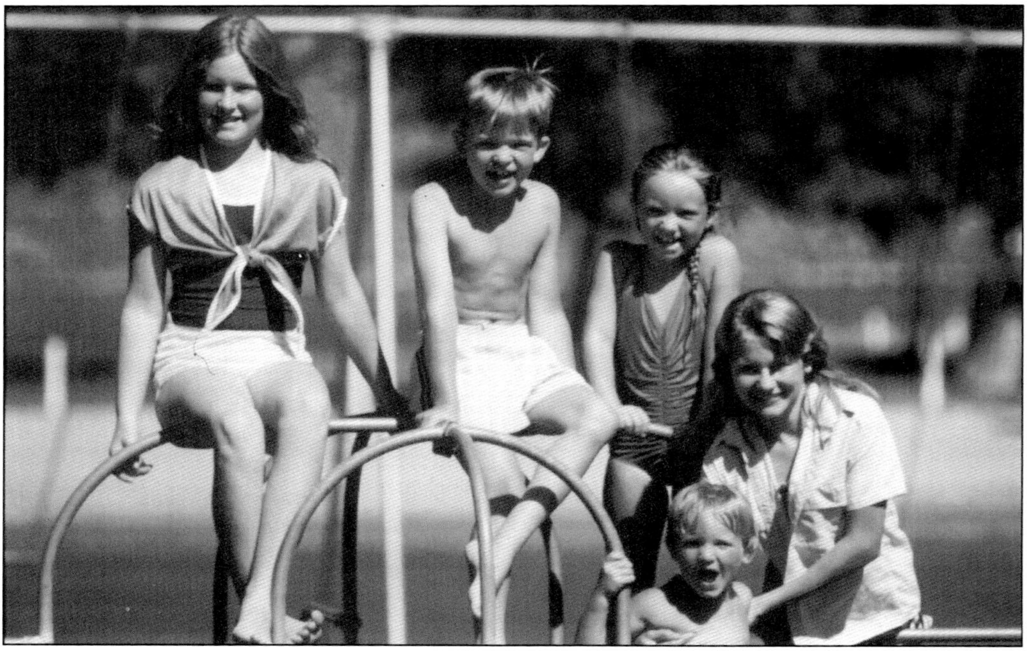

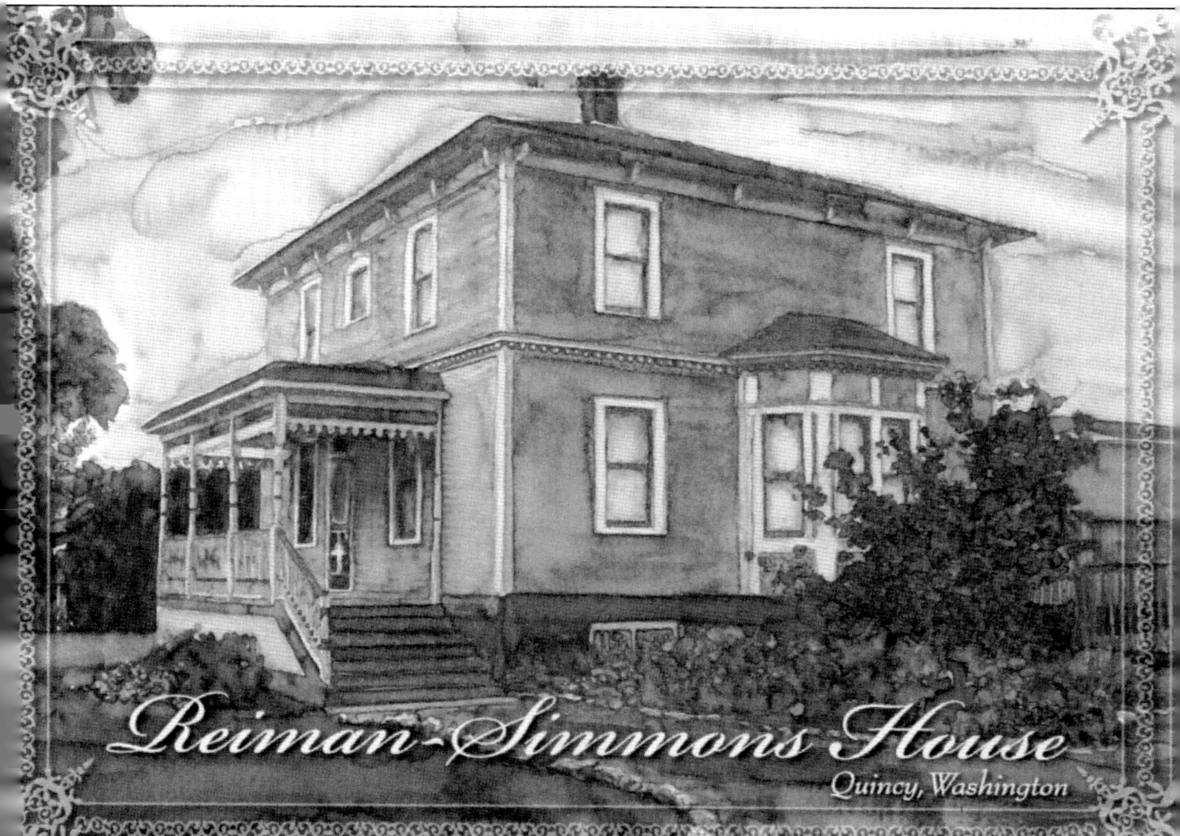

REIMAN-SIMMONS HOUSE. The Quincy Valley Historical Society has lovingly overseen the restoration of this 1904 farmhouse. It was awarded the 2008 Outstanding Achievement in Stewardship Award by the Washington State Department of Historical Preservation. The Reiman-Simmons House is listed on the Washington Historic Register and the National Register of Historic Places. It functions as an educational community center, with annual events including Time Travelers, a living history field trip for elementary students; Harvest Fest each October, a day for the whole family to experience living history; WineFest, an annual event to celebrate the glorious grape and raise funds for educational projects of the society; ladies' teas; weddings; receptions; and other social events. It also hosts traveling exhibits on various subjects of interest to the Quincy Valley community. (Kerry Siderius painting; courtesy of Quincy Valley Historical Society.)

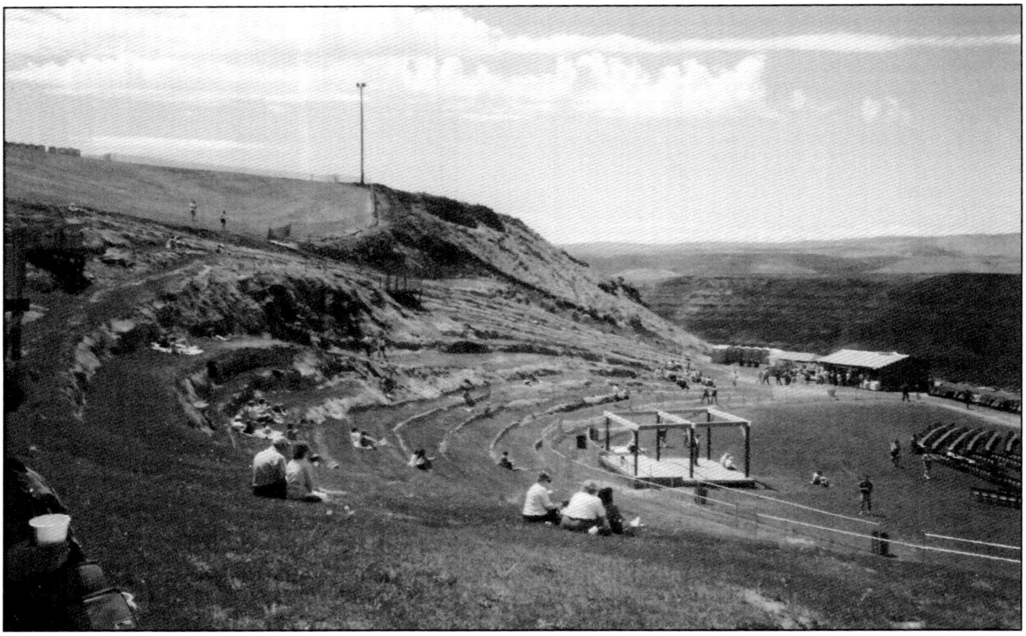

GORGE AMPHITHEATER, 1994. The Gorge Amphitheater began in 1985 as the Champs de Brionne Music Theater adjacent to the Champs de Brionne Winery near George, Washington. Today the winery is known as Cave B, featuring the Cave B Inn at Sagecliffe, and Tendrils restaurant, which raises most of its in-season produce on the Cave B property. The Gorge became a rock 'n' roll venue in 1988 when Bob Dylan played there. Major groups and music tours—such as Sasquatch, Creation Fest, and Vans Warped Tour—regularly play the Gorge. Quincy's own Christian Music Hall of Famer, Bryan Duncan, has returned home to play Creation Fest with his Sweet Comfort Band. Above, the amphitheater seats 25,000 in outdoor lawn terraces. Below, the Moody Blues rock the basalt cliffs. (Courtesy of the Quincy Valley Chamber of Commerce.)

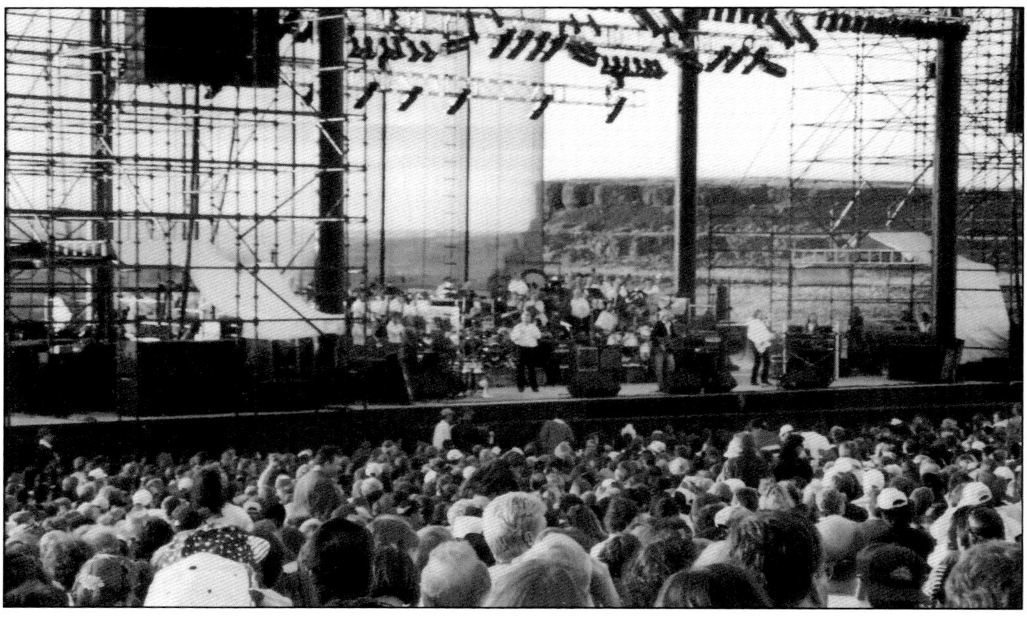

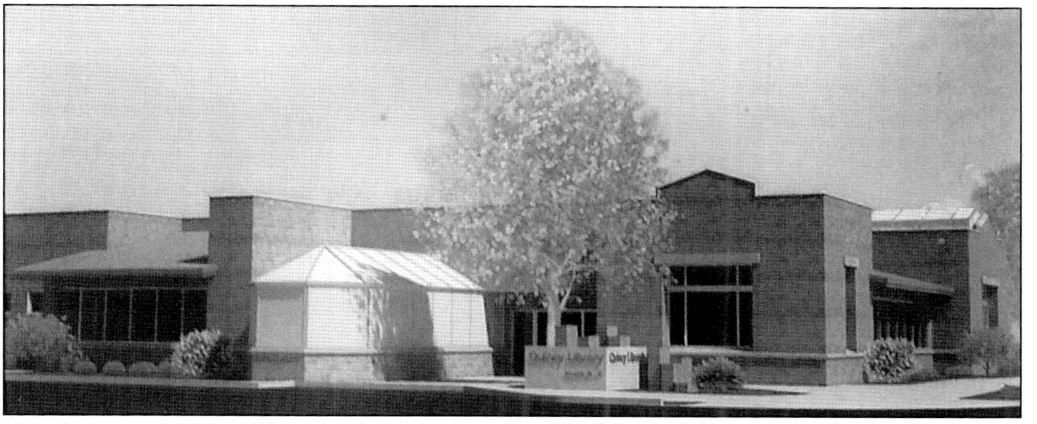

New Quincy Library. The new Quincy Library is scheduled to be completed soon. The Quincy Public Library is one of the mainstays of the community, providing a place for reading, research, and indoor recreation with book clubs, story times, meeting space, and computer access. A total of 344 children participated in the 2009 summer reading program "Be Creative at Your Library," logging 4,549 hours of reading. (Courtesy of Schiree Ybarra.)

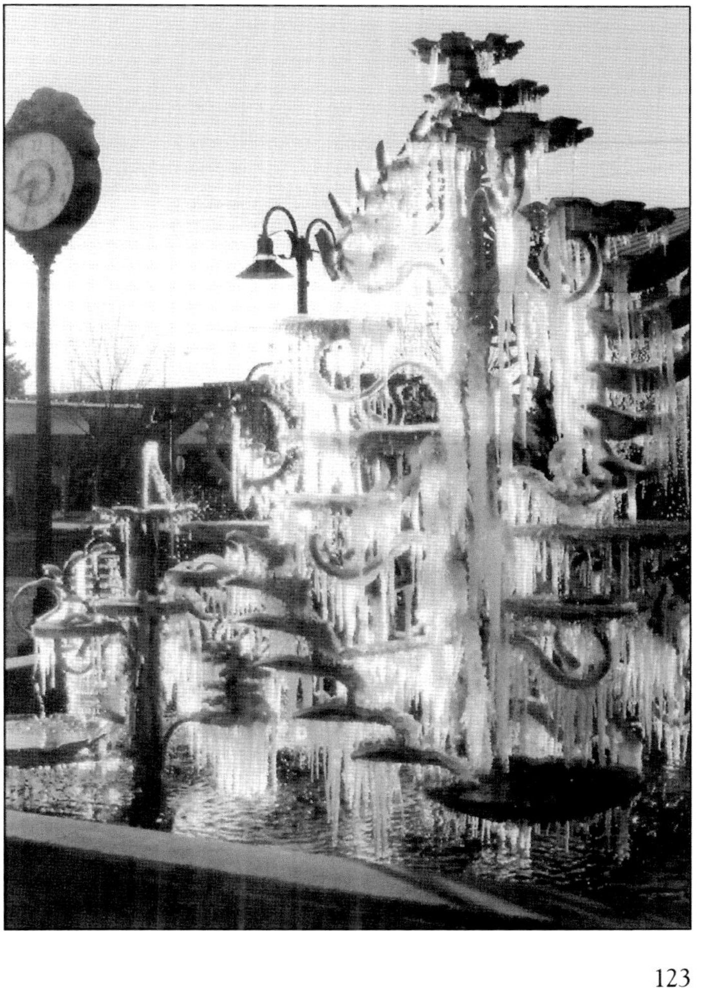

Rotary Park Fountain. This fountain was handcrafted by father-and-son team Scott and Chris Lybbert, with the help of Bob Konen and Kooy Irrigation. Representing the harmony between farming, town life, and water, each piece was originally part of farm equipment that was artistically welded together, centrally placed in the town plaza, and brought to life with the water that has nourished a vibrant community for over 100 years. (Courtesy of Scott Lybbert.)

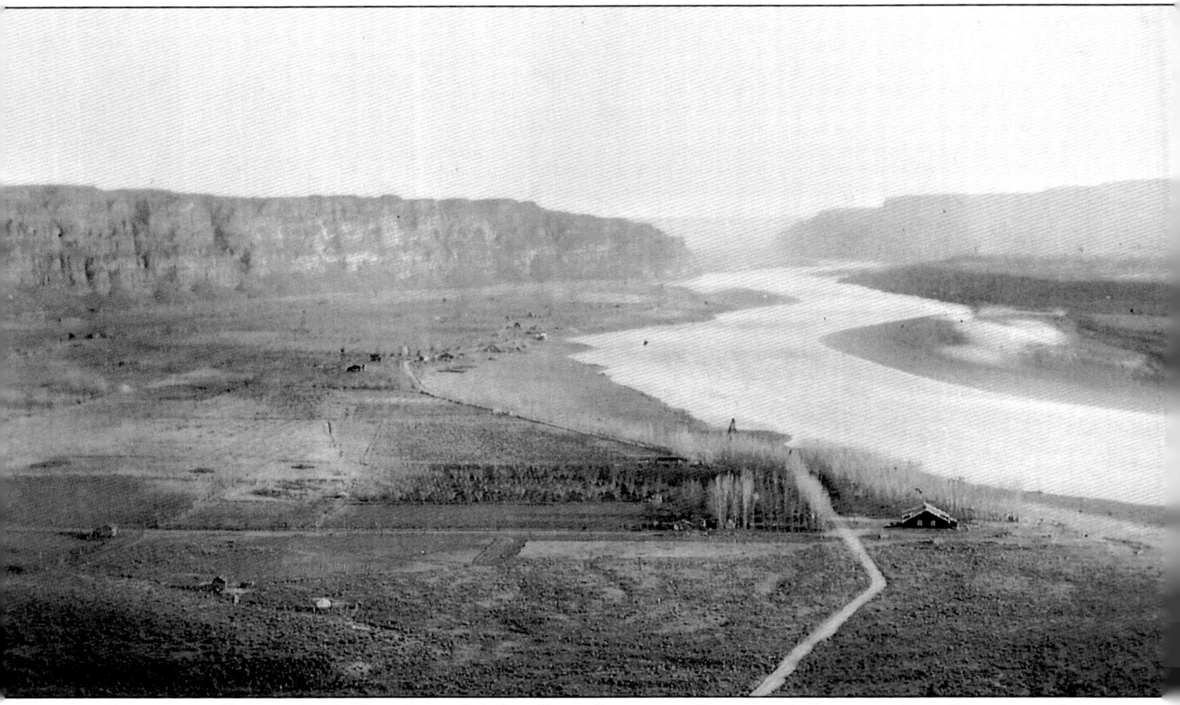

CRESCENT BAR, 1918. Frank and John Struchtmeyer first seeded ground at Crescent Bar in 1903. It soon became a very productive land dotted with orchards, fields, and farmhouses and had its own fruit label. In 1963, Crescent Bar farms were purchased by the Grant County Public Utility District when the completion of the Wanapum Dam flooded the low-lying land along the Columbia River. It became a recreational area with a golf course, trailers, and, recently, an abundant crop of condominiums for visitors seeking a respite from wet weather on the West Coast. Leases are due to expire soon, and local residents hope to once again freely enjoy the benefits of long summer days and family gatherings along the river, as they did for so many generations in the past. (Courtesy of Fran Miller.)

White Heron Cellars in Trinidad. Wineries are a growing industry in the Quincy Valley, from Cave B, to Milbrandt Vineyards at Ancient Lakes, to Jones of Washington. People are awakening to the flavorful delights of domestic wine. Events at the wineries enhance the cultural offerings of the area, including the annual WineFest at the Reiman-Simmons House. At right, the vineyards of White Heron Cellars overlook the Columbia River. Crescent Bar can be seen on the left, while the Gorge Amphitheater hides in the cliffs above the last bend in the river towards the south. On a clear summer's night, the rhythm of concerts at the Gorge Ampitheater can be heard on the hill where this vineyard is planted. White Heron Cellars is owned by Cameron and Phyllis Fries, who began wine-making in 1986. (Both images courtesy of White Heron Cellars.)

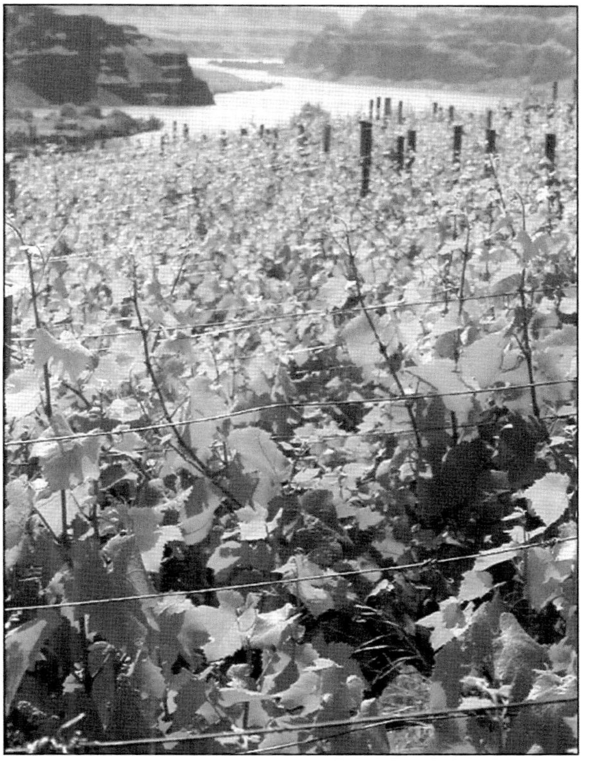

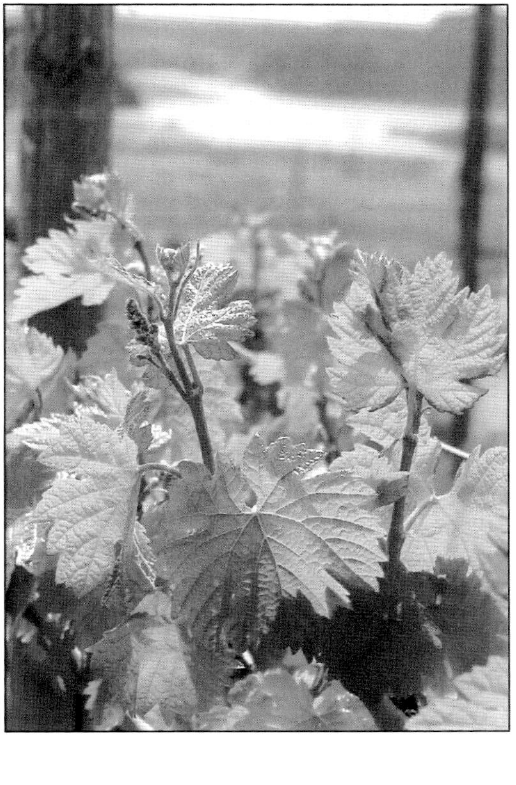

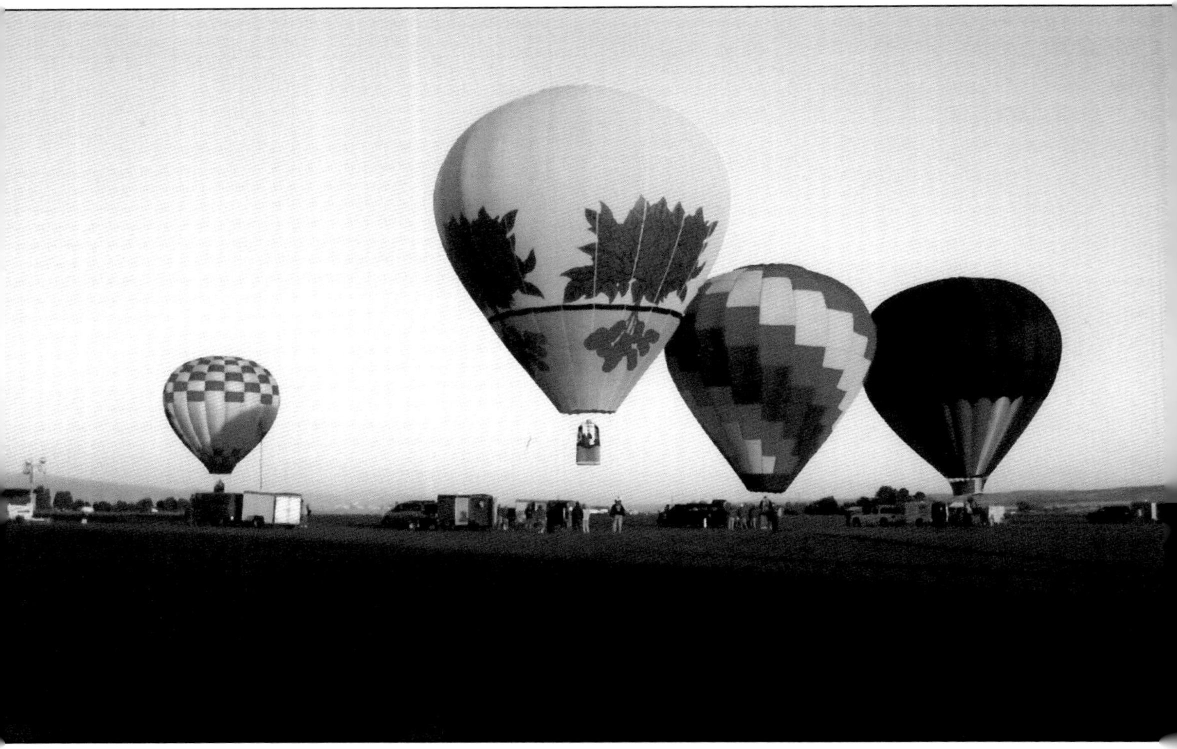

Hot Air Balloons, 2009. The economic future of the Quincy Valley is symbolized by these hot air balloons rising to soar in the skies during the first annual Quincy Valley Balloon and Wine Festival, which was hosted by Parties On The Green at the Twin Firs Turf Farm owned by Kent and Kim Bacon. While Quincy continues to be an agricultural center with its food production plants and intermodal transportation terminal, its ideal location and inexpensive hydropower have brought major Internet companies to the area. Microsoft, Yahoo, Intuit, and Sabey have all constructed, or will soon complete, large data centers. The Quincy Valley not only feeds the hungry people of the world, it also feeds people hungry for information. As the hot air balloons rise in the warm desert air, the Quincy Valley is also rising to meet the soaring needs of the 21st century. (Courtesy of Kim Bacon and Parties On The Green.)

BIBLIOGRAPHY

Centennial Book Committee. *Growing in Grace: St. Paul Lutheran Church*. 2007.
Morris, Faye. *The Birth of a Town*.
———. *They Claimed a Desert*. Fairfield, WA: Ye Galleon Press, 1976.
Murray, Matthew L. "Census of the Quincy Cemetery." (Eagle Scout project, 2000.)
Pilliar, Gar. "Boomtown in the Desert." (Compilation of *Quincy Hill* newspaper articles, 2006.)
———. "Narrative Statement of Significance." National Register Application, Quincy Valley Historical Society, 2008.
Seedorf, Martin F. "Runways and Reclamation, The Influence of the Federal Government on Moses Lake." *Columbia Magazine* vol. 8, issue 2 (1994).
Smith, Herb. "History of Crescent Bar and Trinidad." (History and compilation of news articles, 1994.)
www.ancestry.com
www.bestapples.com
www.ccrh.org/comm/moses/community2.html
www.ccrh.org/center/posters/amer/history.htm
www.nwcouncil.org/history/grandcouleehistory.asp
www.usbr.gov/pn/project/columbia_details.html
www.vancouver.wsu.edu/crbeha/ma/ma.htm